CW00943098

About the Author

Roger Bloor is a retired Consultant Psychiatrist and Senior Lecturer with a passion for history and poetry. He has a MA in Poetry Writing from Newcastle University. He was shortlisted for the Arnold Bennett Book Prize 2018 and 2019 and was the winner of the 2019 Poetry London Clore Prize. He has authored and co-authored many chapters in medical textbooks and published widely in academic journals. He researched the material for this biography over many years and travelled extensively in the UK and America to track down the true story of Dr John Pocock Holmes.

'The Sad Vicissitudes of Life' a
Biography of Dr John Pocock
Holmes (1784–1858)

To Alannah

Best Wishes

Roger N Khon

8th December 2023

Roger Bloor

'The Sad Vicissitudes of Life' a Biography of Dr John Pocock Holmes (1784–1858)

Olympia Publishers

London

www.olympiapublishers.com
OLYMPIA PAPERBACK EDITION

Copyright © Roger Bloor 2023

The right of Roger Bloor to be identified as author of
this work has been asserted in accordance with sections 77 and 78 of the
Copyright, Designs and Patents Act 1988.

All Rights Reserved

No reproduction, copy or transmission of this publication
may be made without written permission.
No paragraph of this publication may be reproduced,
copied or transmitted save with the written permission of the publisher,
or in accordance with the provisions
of the Copyright Act 1956 (as amended).

Any person who commits any unauthorised act in relation to
this publication may be liable to criminal
prosecution and civil claims for damage.

A CIP catalogue record for this title is
available from the British Library.

ISBN: 978-1-80074-560-5

First Published in 2023

Olympia Publishers
Tallis House
2 Tallis Street
London
EC4Y 0AB

Printed in Great Britain

Dedication

For Jon, Graeme and Isobel.

Acknowledgements

Thank you to the staff of the National Archives in Kew, the Willard Library in Evansville Indiana, the South Union Shaker Village in Auburn Kentucky, the Oak Hill Cemetery in Evansville, the Archives of Manitoba, and the Special Collections Library of the University of Keele for all their assistance. Many thanks to my family and friends who have supported me whilst I was writing this book and finally to Sara Levy who patiently worked her way through the initial manuscript with her unerring eye for detail and accuracy.

Preface

In writing this account of the life of John Pocock Holmes, I have used a number of original sources including my transcripts of Holmes' original handwritten journals and quote from these extensively. In the interests of historical accuracy and consistency, I have quoted verbatim from the sources, with the result that some descriptions and terms such as those used to describe the people of the native American nations are anachronistic and in a modern context would be unacceptable.

The term 'Indian' used widely in the journal entries was used as a generic term and refers to people from a variety of aboriginal groups in the area including the Cree, Chipewyan, Blackfoot, Beaver, Assiniboine and Ojibwa nations. Where it has not been possible to decide on the nations being referred to, then the term 'Indian' has been used in the text. The term 'mixed blood' was used to refer to marriages between local women and company employees. Children from 'mixed blood' marriages were referred to as 'half-breed,' a term that was common in the records in the 1800s. In addition, the terms *métis* (mixed) and *brulé* (burnt) originally used by the French Canadians also occur.

I have used nomenclature for place names that is consistent with the period. The current use of 'Hudson Bay' and 'Hudson Bay Company' is therefore given in the possessive form in maps and text. I have provided a glossary for any terms which may not be familiar to the reader or where the modern usage differs from that of the period.

Table of Contents

Chapter 1

The End of the Story?

'A painful lesson of the sad vicissitudes of life.'

On Saturday, April 11th, 1858, the steamboat 'Union', plying along the Green River, docked at the busy river port of Evansville, Indiana and amongst its passengers was a destitute man who by his appearance was above the age of eighty. Helpless, and with one eye totally destroyed by disease, the other inflamed, he was all but sightless. He was paralysed in one leg, confused and delirious. He appeared to have no friends or companions with him and was unloaded and placed on the deck of Mr O'Riley's wharf boat on the banks of the Ohio River. He remained there unattended and without help from Saturday evening to Sunday afternoon when one Dr Allan C Hallock, a local pharmacist and owner of the local insurance agency, visited him and arranged for him to be cared for in the shack of a *'black nurse'* known as *'Aunt Hannah'*. The old man died on the evening of Thursday April 15th, 1858, a stranger without friends or support apart from that offered by Dr Hallock and Aunt Hannah.

After his death, papers in his possession revealed that the old man was, in fact, Dr John Pocock Holmes, a Member of the Royal College of Surgeons of London and that he had previously been a surgeon with the Hudson Bay Company. Following that, he became a successful and well-known doctor with a practice in Fish Street, Doctor's Commons, London and had enjoyed connections with some of the highest members of the profession and society in England.

O'Riley Wharf Boat. *Source: Willard Library, Evansville*

The report in the Evansville Journal of the death of Dr John Pocock Holmes in such sad circumstances was soon copied in numerous newspapers across America, and then the story crossed the Atlantic to Greenock in Scotland, the destination of the American sugar trade boats, being the shortest route across the Atlantic. From Glasgow, the news travelled rapidly across the country back to London, from where Dr Holmes had left for America some sixteen years earlier. The report of his death from the Evansville Journal was published in many newspapers and in The Lancet, one of the foremost medical journals of the time. What was it about the story of his death that attracted such great interest?

The article in the Evansville Journal of April 19th, 1858, summed up the key factors which made the story so intriguing.

'He was evidently a man of correct habits and great intelligence. By what misfortunes he who had enjoyed high professional reputation and had been the associate and friend of eminent men, was left homeless and poor and dies at last alone in the shanty of a poor negro nurse, is unknown. It is a painful lesson of the sad vicissitudes of life.'

Chapter 2

A Rural Clergy Family

'The roads in this part of the county in winter are intolerably bad for the journeying of curates in the performance of their religious duties'

In the summer of 1783 Ann Holmes, wife of the curate of South Leverton, a small rural village in Nottinghamshire, struggled on in the third month of her pregnancy during the hottest July for two hundred years. This was her third child and the heat was made more unbearable by the heavy sulphurous fogs which hung in the air for weeks accompanied by unnatural thunder storms and oppressive humidity.

The villagers would recall for many years the remarkable event that August, when they witnessed the sight of the Great Meteor which passed over the country from North to South, illuminating the sky with an eerie glow, as it travelled to the east of South Leverton. The meteor, called by some the Flying Dragon or Draco Volans, trailed multiple balls of fire in its wake, and the noise as it passed through clouds was likened to a hot iron being put into water. This was nothing compared to the very sudden and violent explosion which it produced, preceded by a terrible rumbling, which lasted for more than a minute. In the village, some of a superstitious nature would talk of emanations from the decomposing bodies in the churchyard igniting and setting off fireballs, others talked of babies' souls coming down from heaven, while there were those who claimed that the meteor presaged the birth of a son. Ann, as the wife of the curate, would be expected to discourage such primitive superstitions, but after having two girls, a boy would be welcome.

A meteor shower in the night sky. *Source: Mezzotint after H. Robinson, 1783. Wellcome Collection*

The winter, when it came, was harder than expected and the Nottinghamshire countryside, with its unsurfaced tracks and roads, was as usual almost impassable in places. Ann must have worried throughout the winter each time her husband, the local curate, left for his religious duties, how she would manage if the baby came early and he was delayed in his return. Her husband had to travel from church to church in the area and could be away for the whole day.

In the midst of the unnaturally cold winter which heralded the New Year of 1784, Ann went into labour. In isolated communities such as South Leverton, the only assistance would be from one of the women in the village who acted as midwives. So Ann and John's third child, christened John Pocock Holmes, was born on January 9th, 1784. John senior entered the details of the birth in the parish record book of St Mary's All Saints in the village, as he had with his two previous children.

John Holmes, labouring as a curate with absentee vicars, and now with three children to clothe and feed, must have rejoiced in the scathing attack published as a footnote to Thoroton's History of Nottinghamshire published in 1796.

'Oh, ye appointed pastors of the flock of Christ; ye fortunes favourites who live at ease, and 'fare sumptuously every day' from the bounty of good and pious men, now no more: Ye who were chosen as comforters to the people of God, have pity on your less fortunate brethren, who are devoted to go from place to place thro' rough and rugged passages, buffeted by storms and tempests, in seasons the most inclement. While ye are housed and sheltered from the severities of the winter, carpeted below and canopied above, with wines sparkling and delicious fruits sweetly smiling on your tables, these men of sorrow struggle for a poor pittance, disgraceful to their profession, insufficient for their wants, and above all, perhaps obliged to render the service of the Almighty contemptible by the irregularity of its performance. Let reason, let religion which teaches us sublimely the duties of man to his neighbour, fill ye with compassion, that ye may retire from this life with a blessing from him who teaches justice and loves mercy.'

The Reverend John Holmes' career commenced at the age of twenty-two when he was ordained as a deacon on June 9th, 1771, at Brodsworth, a small village north of Doncaster.

The minimum age for appointment as a deacon was, in theory, twenty-three and the posts were intended as a transitional stage in progression to becoming a priest. John was eventually ordained on July 11th, 1773, when he was twenty-four. The ceremony took place at the Archiepiscopal Palace at Bishopthorpe near York, after which he was nominated to 'the cure of Bubwith', a village fourteen miles south of York, with a stipend of around £30 a year. Whilst the regulations for ordination prescribed a degree as being required, there was discretion on the part of a bishop to waive this. In the case of John Holmes, the bishop Robert Drummond appointed him, although he did not possess a degree, judging that he possessed sufficient learning to qualify for ordination. He was appointed as a curate at South Leverton in August 1777 with a stipend of £40 per annum, and three years later at the age of thirty-one, he married Ann (Anna) Modd on September 26th, 1780, at Tuxford in Nottinghamshire.

Marriage to a curate such as John meant that Ann, then aged thirty-three, was facing a married life with someone who had a meagre income and probably not enough to employ any servants. As a curate, John had no security or pension and no guarantee that he would become a vicar, even if the current incumbent died or resigned. She was, however, marrying 'a gentleman' in the eyes of society, although John's role as an employee of the vicar, and his poor income, would have led to some of the wealthier families in the parish regarding him as somewhat lower in station than his profession indicated. With an absentee vicar, the bulk of the parish duties fell to John, but this was compensated for in part as the vicarage was available for the family to live in. If the vicar had been resident then John would have had to secure accommodation at his own expense within the parish.

The vicar of South Leverton, the Reverend Samuel Simon Lawry, had been appointed as vicar in 1779, but three years later had also taken up an appointment in Bedfordshire nearly one hundred miles away, where he was Rector of Blunham. This was a very valuable living with an income of £400 a year, a sum which would allow a comfortable existence, enough to employ a cook, a housemaid, a boy and maintain a genteel lifestyle. The living was under the gift of a Lady Lucas with seventy acres of glebe land and free living in the Rectory, which was also very valuable and under the patronage of the Earl of Hardwicke. South Leverton had a history of absent incumbents, and John Cleaver, who replaced Simon Lawry on his death in 1806, is recorded as having read a service once in 1807 but was never seen in the Parish again. These absences meant that the local curates such as John could supplement their income by travelling to deliver services in the area, but also meant a considerable amount of time on the road. To support a family and still maintain a moderately prosperous life, John would need to earn £100 a year, an amount that would allow the family to engage a young maid servant, paid at a very low wage, and afford a ticket to a circulating library.

Curate of the parish. *Source: 'The Curate's Lot'*

John and Ann's first child, Catherine, had been born in the summer of 1781 and christened at the church in the village. In the summer of 1782, the second daughter of the family had been born and was christened Elizabeth Birkett Holmes, the ceremony being performed in the village church. Her second name of Birkett is likely to have been a family name of either the Holmes or Modd families. There were in Georgian and Victorian times some fashions for how children were given Christian names, particularly sons, with the first son sometimes being named after the paternal grandfather, the second after the maternal grandfather and the third after the father. With daughters a similar system was in use with the first daughter being named after the maternal grandmother, the second after the paternal grandmother, the third after the mother and the fourth daughter after the oldest maternal aunt. The use of surnames as second names had a revival in the Victorian era and whilst the use of a family surname was popular, occasionally the surname used may have resulted from a bequest, which involved the addition of the benefactor's name to the recipient, or sometimes the name of a close friend or famous person or hero of the times was used.

It was a year after Elizabeth's birth, during that cold winter of 1784, that John and Ann's first son was born, followed a year later by a second son, George Modd Holmes, his middle name being a reminder of Ann's family name. On October 19th, 1786, Ann gave birth to a third daughter named Sarah, who died at the age of two and was buried on January 31st, 1788, at South Leverton. The greatest risk period for the death of children around the age of two was in the first three months of a year, particularly in years when the weather was exceptionally cold. Epidemics of scarlet fever and measles were common during this period and in cities, up to one in five children died before their second birthday. Rural communities tended to have lower death rates but in a rural village at this period, one in three of the deaths would be expected to be in those aged two or below. Almost a year to the day of Sarah's death, Ann gave birth to another son, Charles, who was born on January 3rd, 1789. Charles was destined to follow his father's calling and become a priest in the Anglican Church. After the death of Sarah, another tragedy was to hit the family when in 1791 Catherine, the eldest child, died at the age of ten. The loss of Catherine only three years after the death of Sarah left the family with Elizabeth, John, George and the two-year-old Charles.

The family's home in this small Nottinghamshire village was within close reach of the church and the free grammar school in Church Road, endowed by John Sampson in 1691 to give education to boys from the village. Girls were specifically excluded from attending. The endowment included an instruction that the board of trustees must include a minister of religion residing within the parish of South Leverton, who was to receive the annual rental of £20 a year from the school. The master of the school was to be a graduate, or otherwise an orthodox minister, who, in addition to the basic skills of reading and writing, was to teach English, Latin, and Greek. John Holmes senior did not have a degree, but as an ordained priest would have been able to take up the post as the master at the school, particularly as the vicar was an 'absentee' and the £20 a year would have been welcome to add to his £70 stipend as a curate.

The family income increased in May 1797 when John Holmes senior also took on the curacy of Littleborough, a village some five miles north of South Leverton, with a stipend of £40 per annum and the use of the Vicarage House or £15 in lieu of it. This appointment was a perpetual curacy, which meant that although the priest who held the vicar's appointment still took the income from the parish, he was legally obliged to provide an adequate salary for his curate. More importantly, having been licensed by the bishop as a perpetual curate, John could only be removed from the post by the bishop rather than being at the mercy of the vicar, who could otherwise have removed him from the curate's post on a whim. For all practical purposes, a perpetual curate was the same as a vicar and was entitled to a pension on retirement. The definition of what was an 'adequate salary' could, however, be given a wide interpretation by the incumbent.

John Pocock Holmes and his brothers George and Charles would have been entitled to attend the Sampson's School and receive a free education. Elizabeth, however, would be excluded, as girls were not admitted to the school until the middle of the nineteenth century. The provision of a good education was unusual for such a small village with a parish of fewer than sixty families and a population of three hundred and fifty-four, situated as it was at the centre of a rural economy. The village was located some five miles east of the bustling market town of Retford and was noted for its views across the countryside to Lincoln Cathedral, some twenty miles to the east. The rural North Clay division of Northamptonshire was a farming community mostly untouched by the noise and pollution of industry such as coal mining, brewing, silk manufacture, hosiery and lace-making that were common in the county. Within the village, the majority of the neighbours were farmers with a few tradesmen such as a blacksmith, wheelwright, tailor, shoemaker, shopkeeper and public house landlord providing the essential materials and support for the farming community.

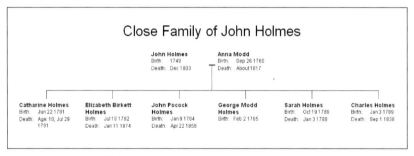

Holmes family tree. *Source: The Author*

The life of the family of a curate was not an easy one. Descriptions of married curates in this period describe their living conditions as often being worse than a labourer or servant. Curates could be seen '*with his shoes out of toes and his stockings out of heels, wandering about in an old russet coat or a tattered gown*'. In his history of Nottinghamshire, Thoroton describes South Leverton in some detail, '*The church is dedicated to All Saints, has an agreeable appearance; but nothing extraordinarily attracting within or without. The roads in this part of the county, in wintertime, are intolerably bad for the journeying of poor curates in the performance of their religious duties, particularly if what I have learned in this part of the county be true, 'that a certain curate in the neighbourhood has only £12 per ann. for his duty at one church, that he is praying & preaching about 40 times in the year, besides extra duty.' He in consequence of this poor pittance, serves five Churches on a Sunday! perhaps, for which, he is no better paid*'.

The Holmes family of South Leverton are well documented in the parish records at the Salterwell Diocesan record office and elsewhere. The Reverend John Holmes died in December 1803 at the age of fifty-four when John Pocock Holmes was nineteen years old. His sister Elizabeth was by now twenty-one but still unmarried, George was eighteen and the youngest, Charles, only fourteen. The family income would be considerably reduced, as the income from their father's clerical positions would cease on his death. The probate of the Reverend Holmes' Will, dated July 6th, 1804, records his details as John Holmes, late of South Leverton in the County of Nottingham in the Diocese of York, and the administrator of his Will is his wife Ann Holmes, of South Leverton.

Ann was to survive for a further fifteen years, dying in 1818 aged seventy-one and was buried at South Leverton on June 18th, 1818. A year after Ann's death her daughter, Elizabeth, married the Reverend J. Mickle on June 28th, 1819, at the church in South Leverton. John Mickle was nine years younger than Elizabeth, who was thirty-seven when they married. He was first the curate and then in 1834 became the vicar at South Leverton when he moved into the vicarage with Elizabeth. In 1851 the census records them still at the vicarage, together with their servant, Mary Pilgrim, and a fourteen-year-old groom, Thomas Belverstone. In addition to the living at South Leverton that was worth £152 a year, John Mickle also held the incumbency at Apesthorpe which was worth an additional £100 a year. Tragically, Mickle shot himself in the head with a horse pistol on October 27th, 1866, leaving Elizabeth, referred to in the reports as Betsey, a widow. The jury at the inquest found that '*the deceased destroyed himself whilst insane*'. The newspapers reported that '*The ruling passion of the deceased through life seemed to be the accumulation of money*'. Elizabeth continued to live in South Leverton after her husband's death and in 1871 was living with her niece, Elizabeth Birkett Fletcher, at 70 Village Street, South Leverton and was by this time 'blind from old age'. She died in 1874 at the age of ninety-one and her gravestone in the churchyard at South Leverton bears the inscription, '*Elizabeth Birkett Mickle — Widow of The Rev John Mickle — Died 11 January 1874*'. Elizabeth left all her estate, valued at under £800, to her niece, Elizabeth Birkett Fletcher, who, with her husband Henry Fletcher, the postmaster of North Muskham, had looked after her in her old age. Elizabeth Fletcher was recorded as the only next of kin.

The youngest son of the Holmes family, Charles, had followed his father into the Church of England, becoming the rector of St. Mary's Church, Kirkby in Lincolnshire in 1833 and dying of 'apoplexy' in 1838. The records indicate that he had an MA degree, which would have been obtained at either Oxford or Cambridge University. It would appear that Charles was unmarried and upon his death, all his effects were sold off at auction and included:

'*All the valuable Household Furniture, Glass, Linen, China, Library of books, Nag Mare (quiet in harness) new gig and Harness, a well-bred Pointer Bitch and puppy, single barrel gun, Implements of husbandry, several stacks of tares, oats, well-got hay, seeds, and straw to be taken off the premises, and about one acre and a half of potatoes, and other effects.*'

John Pocock Holmes was to keep in touch with his sister Elizabeth over the years, but his career and travels would take him away from his native Nottinghamshire as he sought to build a life for himself. Whilst his sister and brother remained close to their place of birth, John was set on a path that would see him travel many thousands of miles away to a life which his employers would acknowledge required '*enduring fatigue and hardship*'.

Chapter 3

The Making of a Surgeon

'Every candidate for ſerving a medical apprenticeship ſhould be about ſixteen years of age; and ſome advantage may be expected from his having an inclination for the profeſſion.'

Little is recorded concerning Holmes' early life after his father's death in 1803 when Holmes was nineteen. He needed to support himself as the estate of his father was left to the widowed Ann, who would need to support his sister Elizabeth, who was unmarried, and his brothers, who were only eighteen and fourteen years of age.

Holmes underwent training as a surgeon, and his profession was recorded as 'surgeon' when he obtained employment with the Hudson's Bay Company in 1805. The education of surgeons in this period was largely unregulated and in the main consisted of an apprentice system with a period of attendance at a surgical training course. By 1800, it was necessary to pass an examination to obtain membership of The Royal College of Surgeons. The College was created that year from the receipt of a Royal Charter awarded to the former Barber-Surgeons Company of London. An apprenticeship for a surgeon could start at the age of thirteen and last for seven years. The training was practical and would also involve learning the trade aspects of the profession, such as keeping the books and formulating and preparing the common medicines used by surgeon apothecaries.

Later in life, Holmes began to use the qualification MD in some of his writings. An MD qualification could have been obtained from a number of universities including Edinburgh, Glasgow and Medical Schools in France. His use of 'Mr' in his communications rather than 'Dr', and his description of himself as a 'surgeon-accoucheur' rather than a physician, coupled with his subsequent membership of the Royal College of Surgeons, would indicate that his training was by apprenticeship and attendance at lectures and demonstrations rather than via a university. He did, however, talk to acquaintances about having worked in hospitals in Paris, and this was one method of acquiring training and exposure to clinical teaching that some eighteenth and nineteenth-century students chose as a preferred method. This was instead of, or in addition to attending hospitals in London or one of the two other centres of teaching at Edinburgh and Glasgow Medical Schools.

To be accepted as a surgeon in 1805, Holmes would have needed to have completed an apprenticeship and have experience as an assistant to enable him to provide suitable references and certificates. Such an apprenticeship would usually have started at the age of around fourteen. The decision by a family to start a son as an apprentice to an apothecary or a surgeon was not an easy one; there would be the expense of the apprenticeship and the prospect of training that might last up to seven years. Setting up a successful surgical practice in the early 1800s was not easy for a young surgeon, although those who were well-connected and had excellent social contacts were able to benefit from patronage, which could compensate for any lack of skill. Advice to young surgeons at this time was to look at alternative sources of employment such as the Army, the East India Company, the

Hudson's Bay Company, or to take a post as a ship's surgeon. Hospital appointments were the subject of fierce competition and candidates had little chance of being appointed on the basis of talent alone. Appointment was unlikely unless they were *'connected with the staff by family or other ties, or had a large command of capital'*. In addition, some of the major centres were virtually closed shops, with Surgeons and Assistant Surgeons forming *'a snug family party'*. Apprentices to some Hospital Surgeons might have expected to be appointed only after the payment of large premiums made on the understanding that this would secure them a post after qualification.

As the young Holmes had neither strong family connections nor access to the required capital, he looked away from hospital posts towards alternative sources of both income and experience. The Hudson's Bay Company employed surgeons both as ship's surgeons and as surgeons for their posts across the Hudson Bay Territory. A position with the company promised a good income and the prospect of a pension on return to England. So it was that in 1805, Holmes took up a contract with the Hudson's Bay Company in the post of a surgeon and prepared to make the journey across the Atlantic to a new life in the wild and inhospitable regions of the company's vast territory.

Chapter 4

Surgeon Trader

'Pro pelle cutem' — 'We seek the skin for the sake of the fur'.

The Hudson's Bay Company was formed by a Royal Charter, awarded in 1670 by King Charles to his cousin Prince Rupert and seventeen nobles and gentlemen. The charter gave the company, described as, 'The Governor and Company of Merchants-Adventurers trading into Hudson's Bay', the sole right to trade in the Hudson Straits and the land on the coasts of the straits. The purpose of the company was to purchase furs from the indigenous hunters in exchange for arms, ammunition, clothes and other commodities.

The history of the company is well documented, by reason of the detailed trading records and personal accounts contained in reports to the company by its employees. Daily journals of the events in trading posts, combined with collections of letters such as those of Colin Robertson, throw a detailed light on the lives of the traders and also their competitors, as well as the indigenous population. By compiling these various sources, it is possible to trace the progress of John Pocock Holmes over the period of 1805 to 1821, when the company employed him either as a surgeon or a trader. The edited collection of Colin Robertson's letters contains an appendix with biographical notes of a number of the individuals mentioned in his correspondence, including a section on John Pocock Holmes. From this short biography and the biographical notes of the Hudson's Bay Company, it is possible to chart the outline of his time with the company in a chronological list. The various posts which he was stationed at were located on the west of Hudson Bay in Manitoba and are contained within a radius of five hundred miles from Churchill Factory, which was situated on the bay at ninety-five degrees of longitude and between fifty-five- and sixty-degrees latitude.

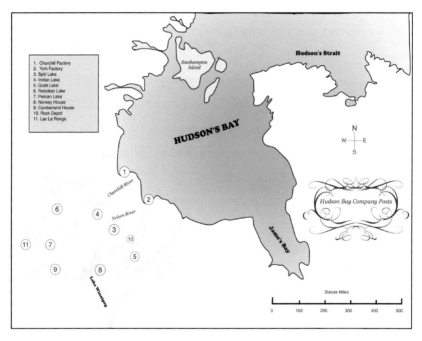

Map of Hudson's Bay. *Source: The Author*

122

CR

I *John Pocock Holmes* of *London, Surgeon* Aged
24 Years ————————————— do hereby Covenant and Agree
to and with the Governor and Company of Adventurers of *ENGLAND*, Trading into HUDSON's-BAY,
and their Successors, to serve them for the Term of *Three* ——— Years, to commence from the ~~Time~~

the date hereof unless sooner Recalled, after the Rate of Two day Forty Pounds pr Annum, and if I intend to return after the Expiration of this Contract, to give One, or if Inland Two Years Notice to the Chief of the Factory, but if no such Notice be given, then to Stay One Year longer if required after such Notice shall have been given at the same Wages, & under the like Terms, Agreements, Provisions, & Penalties, & Forfeitures as is mentioned in this Agreement.

And to Ship myself upon the first Vessel or Ship that the Committee of the said Company shall Order me to embark in, that shall go, or is bound for HUDSON's-BAY; where I oblige myself to stay according to the aforesaid limited Time, and to do, and perform such Labour and Work, and obey such Commands as the Governor in HUDSON's-BAY, or chief Factor there, shall impose upon me. During my being in the said Company's Service, I will, with the utmost Hazard and Peril of my Life, in my Station, with Courage and Fidelity, maintain and defend the said Company's Factory and Factories, Territories, Rights, Privileges, Goods and Properties, against all Enemies whatsoever, either Foreign or of our own Country: and to the utmost of my Power, will cause the same to be maintained and defended by all others, according to the Duty of my Service: And I will in all Things submit myself to the Commands and Discipline of the Governor or Commander in Chief for the said Company, and all other my superior Officers, by his Directions. And during my Abode there, I will not directly or indirectly Trade to and from any Place within the Limits of this Company's Charter, for my own particular Account, or for any other Person or Persons, save only for the said Company, in any Furs, Skins, or other Commodities whatsoever, with the *Indians*, or with any Nation inhabiting or trading in or about HUDSON's-BAY. And that whatsoever Commodities I shall Trade for there, or get into my Possession, shall be only in Trust, and for the sole Use and Benefit of the said Governor and Company and their Successors. Any Person that shall drive any private Trade, I will endeavour to hinder, their Names I will detect, the Commodities so Traded for I will discover, as much as in me lies, to the Governor in the Bay, and the Committee of the said Company for the Time being. And in Case I the said *John Pocock Holmes* ——— shall make any Breach or Default of, or in Performance of all, or any of the aforesaid Covenants, Agreements, or Things, Then I and my Executors and Administrators will not only forfeit and lose all Wages, Salary, and Monies, as by Virtue of this Contract, or otherwise, shall be due to me, or them, from the said Governor and Company, or their Successors, which I do hereby enable them to detain to their own Use and Benefit; But also I and my Executors and Administrators will, for every such Breach or Default, also forfeit and pay to the said Governor and Company the Sum of *Eighty Pounds* ——— of lawful Money of *ENGLAND*, over and above all Damages that may arise, or happen to them, by Reason, or Means of such Breach or Default. In Witness whereof I have hereunto set my Hand and Seal this *Fifteenth* Day of *May* ——— in the Year of Our Lord God 17 *1805*

Sealed and Delivered in
the Presence of Us;

Arth.r Ball
Edward Roberts
John Pocock Holmes

Holmes' Contract. *Source: Hudson's Bay Archives.*

33

Beneath the bare chronological outline of his career lies a considerable amount of detail, revealing a fifteen-year period when he alternated between roles of surgeon and trader, married, had three children and lived up to the description of a 'surgeon-adventurer'. The skills and knowledge he gained during these years were to play a part in his subsequent career and personal life and to influence his standing and position both in society and his profession in later life.

It was on May 17th, 1805, that Holmes attended the head offices of the Hudson's Bay Company to enter into a contract of employment as a surgeon to the company. His contract was initially for three years and he would be paid at a rate of £40 per year. He was obliged to give a minimum of one year's notice if he wished to return to England before the end of the contract, two years if he was employed at an inland station rather than at one of the main factories on the coast. If no notice was given before the end of the contract, then the company had the right to extend his contract for a further year. The detail of the contract set out the penalties for breaching any of the rules and regulations concerning private trading. These included the loss of all wages, salaries, and monies as well as an additional forfeit of two years' wages, which in Holmes' case amounted to £80.

So at the age of twenty-one, and only nineteen days after signing his contract, Holmes sailed to take up his post as a surgeon to the Hudson's Bay Company. The voyage from England to York Factory on Hudson's Bay was hazardous at the best of times, but more particularly so in 1805, which saw the escalation of hostilities between France and England, as Napoleon prepared his invasion plans. The only English merchant ships allowed to sail across the Atlantic alone were those of the Hudson's Bay Company and the East India Company, and they were heavily armed. All other merchant ships had to sail in a convoy protected by British warships. These convoys could amount to over a hundred and seventy ships and often stretched for six miles, taking five weeks to cross the Atlantic in good conditions and up to fourteen if the weather was adverse. A Hudson's Bay Company ship such as the Prince of Wales or the York, both of which completed the round trip from England to Hudson's Bay in 1805, would take up to ten weeks or more to complete the outward voyage.

Holmes' journey started in London by taking a passenger boat from the London Docks to the port of Gravesend, from where all the Hudson's Bay Company ships departed. The Committee of the Hudson's Bay Company traditionally held a celebratory meal on the eve of the annual supply ships' departure. The arrival of the committee's ship was greeted with great excitement and ceremony as the ships fired welcome salutes of blank cartridges. The dinner was *'as good and substantial as a lavish expenditure of cash could make it'*, the officers of the ships were the invited guests of the committee, and this would include Holmes as a surgeon, and therefore one of the Company officer class.

It was on May 29th, 1805, that the Hudson's Bay ships, moored at Gravesend some twenty miles from London, fired their guns to signal their departure, and took on pilots to navigate them along the Gravesend Reach and past the Nore sandbank at the estuary of the Thames. The pilots remained on board to navigate along the twelve-mile stretch of water along the Kent coast and close to the notorious Goodwin Sands. The journey from Gravesend to the sheltered areas at Hope Bay could, with favourable winds, take only twenty-four hours, but other travellers reported waiting there two days on the Prince of Wales before the wind and tide allowed the journey to be completed.

Hudson Bay Company Ships

Once the wind and tide were satisfactory, the HBC ships sailed northward towards the coastal port of Yarmouth. This part of the journey was very much weather dependent and could take up to a week of sailing before the estuary was left behind and safe anchorage made at Yarmouth. The Gravesend pilots disembarked at Yarmouth, and the ships then set off on their journey north along the east coast of Britain heading for the Orkney Islands. This 'northabout' route offered a safer passage and easier navigation than the western route through the English Channel, especially in this time of war with France and the risk of attack from French war boats. The voyage from Yarmouth to the Orkneys would typically take two weeks, and the ships would then sail through Scarpa Flow and anchor off the town of Stromness. Once they reached Stromness, the ships fired seven guns to notify the citizens of Stromness that they had arrived. This was a signal for the inhabitants of the town that boats would be coming ashore to reprovision and buy supplies, and in some cases to take on board Orkneymen recruited to work for the Company. After a short stay, the ships, now provisioned and with local pilots aboard, would set sail to reach the open sea. The last part of their navigation out of port led them past the 'Old Man of Hoy', a four-hundred-and-fifty-foot-high landmark rock pillar where pilots from the Orkneys would be dropped off on the island of Hoy. The ships were then faced with the task of navigating across the Atlantic to the Hudson Straits. The journey so far from Gravesend to Hoy would have lasted up to a month, and the crew now had to tackle a further four-week voyage to their destination, York Factory.

As the ships left the shelter of the coast and embarked on the Atlantic, this was for many passengers their first experience of the fury of the sea, and less than a hundred miles out the experience of a strong headwind gave many their first experience of seasickness. One passenger commented: *'it threw me into such a state of languor, that I felt as though I could have willingly yielded to have been cast overboard, and it was nearly a week before I was relieved from this painful sensation and nausea, peculiar to seasickness.'* The long voyage consisted of alternating experiences of a monotonous view of a featureless ocean and periods of rough weather with high seas punctuated by the occasional appearance of whales or dolphins and glimpses of the Northern Lights.

The ships set course for the Hudson Straits and relied on

the experience of the ship's master, for the Admiralty charts of the area were notoriously inaccurate, and the compasses would show significant changes in accuracy as the voyage proceeded. The increased changes in the variation of the compass were thought by some officers to be due to the presence of a 'magnetic mountain' which disturbed the compass. As the ships came into the same longitude as Greenland, a drop in temperature signified the presence of ice. This was a danger as they got closer to the Hudson Straits, where there were always large masses of ice drifting out of the straits and along the coast of Labrador. It is in this region that icebergs could be encountered, and navigating through the iceberg regions, particularly in fog, was a hazardous procedure with the risk of the ships being dashed upon them. Those who had not witnessed the vast field of ice and icebergs which floated past the ships were amazed at the size of the ice mountains, reaching up from one to two hundred feet above the water. They were described as resembling vast mountains with deep valleys between them and lofty cliffs above, all passing in silent grandeur, except when falls of ice produced a noise like distant thunder.

Having spent weeks in the open ocean, the prospect of entering the Hudson Straits and nearing the journey's end was appealing. However, the reality of the vast *'gloomy nature: the black craggy mountains on shore'* and *'the aspect of the countless icebergs on all sides'* tempered the enthusiasm of those who were new to the region. The voyage through the Hudson Straits towards York Factory was arduous, with shifting packs of ice hemming in the ships and massive icebergs drifting close by. The HBC ships were well equipped for journeying in these conditions, with strengthened hulls and a good supply of ice axes and grappling lines for dealing with the solid ice which often hemmed them in. Despite the hazards of navigating the Hudson Straits, the sailors had many years of experience and few ships were lost. The crew was, however, always mindful of the risks of navigating through ice fields. Captain Scoresby of the company ship the Eddystone commented: *'It may be easily imagined that the strongest ship can no more withstand the shock of the contact of two fields, than a sheet of paper can stop a musket ball'*.

As the ships emerged from the ice fields, there was the welcome sight of land and a safe anchorage at York Flats. The arrival of the annual supply ships was a cause for celebration for the residents of York Factory with the prospect of new supplies, packages of letters and news from home. For some of the passengers, however, York Factory was not their final destination, and those who were to be stationed at other Company locations faced further long and hazardous journeys across land and water to their stations. Holmes was to spend his first year stationed at Churchill Factory; this necessitated either an overland journey of a hundred and fifty miles or a sea journey along the frozen coast of the Bay which was not considered navigable until at least the third week of July.

Chapter 5

Learning the Trade

'Like all other servants, surgeons signed formal contracts which required them to submit to the Factor and perform any tasks requested in addition to their specific medical duties'.

For the next stage of his journey, Holmes transferred to the Hudson's Bay Company ship King George, which sailed from York Factory to Churchill once the bay was clear of ice, arriving on August 16th, 1805. Having unloaded the passengers and cargo, the ship made ready and set sail back to York Factory on August 25th.

The arrival of Holmes as a surgeon at Churchill Factory would be very welcome, as a month earlier there had been two incidents where the assistance of a surgeon had been needed, and the lack of one at the factory had been a serious issue. In the first incident, a local hunter had sustained a serious stab wound in the shoulder during a fight, and in the second, a gunshot wound had caused a severe injury. The Churchill Factory Journal entry records the event and the effects of the lack of a surgeon:

'...a great accident, one of them in firing at some geese out of a canoe had the misfortune to hit the man who sat before him and shot his left hand to attoms, now at a great loss what to do as amputation is absolutely requisite and having no Surgeon no one here can do it and the Packet News tell me that the Surgeon at YF is gone inland to attend one of their officers who is sick. Shall endeavour to keep it

from mortification until the Ships arrival when I hope he will be able to get proper assistance, the Indian who was stabbed is in a fair way of recovery.'

Whilst Churchill Factory was an important base for shipping goods inland and back to England, there were only fifteen people permanently based there. These included the newly arrived chief William Auld, his deputy William Topping, Holmes as surgeon and a number of skilled tradesmen such as the Craft-master, Carpenter, Boat Builder, House-wright, Blacksmith, Cooper, Steward, Tailor, and Sawyer as well as three labourers. The Officers at Churchill, which included Holmes, were mainly occupied in going out on shooting expeditions for partridges, which were particularly plentiful in the area. William Auld makes little mention of any sickness or injuries occurring at Churchill Factory that would have required Holmes' skills as a surgeon. He does, however, note that the man who suffered the gunshot wound to his hand survived and also records an injury to himself in May 1806 when he tripped *'trying to avoid a drunken Indian and had the misfortune to snap the sinew of my leg'* and was confined to his room. The details of any illnesses or treatments of patients would have been recorded separately by Holmes, as the surgeons kept their own records to maintain confidentiality for their patients.

In 1806, whilst at Churchill Factory, Holmes followed the practice of many company employees in taking a wife from the local population. Holmes took as his wife a local woman called Ke-che-cow-e-com-coot, alias Wee-misti-goos, also known as Elizabeth or Betsy. She was one of the daughters of Matthew Cocking, who had served with the company from 1765 to 1782, and returning to London, had settled in York where he died in

1799. Matthew Cocking married three local women in succession during his time with the Hudson's Bay Company but did not take any of his family with him to England. He did, however, make provision for the three wives and their daughters, ensuring that they had an annuity, which was sent to the company to be paid into an account for them to use to buy goods at the company stores. This would have meant that Betsy and her sisters were able to enjoy a more comfortable lifestyle than they may have expected.

Ke-che-cow-e-com-coot (Betsy) was born in 1775 and was only seven when Matthew Cocking returned to England. She remained with her mother and sister until she married Chief Factor Thomas Stayner in 1797 at the age of twenty-two. That year Stayner returned to England for the winter and whilst there married Sarah Elizabeth Bayliss in London on January 5th, 1798. During his stay in England, he visited with Betsy's father, Matthew Cocking, who had lost contact with his native family since he left Hudson Bay fifteen years previously. Cocking, in his Will of 1797, had stated that he presumed they were all dead.

Stayner returned to Hudson Bay in the early part of 1798, and following the visit, Matthew Cocking added a second codicil to his Will. He stated that his native wife Le-lo-es-com was dead and that their daughter Betsy was living as a 'companion' of Matthew Stayner, and ensured that his daughters had a continued annuity of £6 a year each. Betsy and her sister traded the annuity for supplies such as blankets, kettles and twine although the Council of York asked that part of the annuity was given as; *'Ginger Bread, Nuts, etc. as they have no other means of obtaining these little luxuries, with which the paternal fondness of a father formally provided'*. Betsy had three children by Thomas

Stayner, who was during this time Chief Factor at Churchill Factory. Stayner retired to England in 1801, leaving on the company ship King George, taking with him his two daughters, Ann and Sarah, but leaving Betsy at Churchill Factory with the third daughter. Betsy remained at Churchill Factory where she met Holmes and followed the custom of many of the local women in remarrying once her husband had left the country. It was common practice for women who were described as 'mixed-blood' to remarry when their husbands returned to England, and it was not uncommon for women to have two or more husbands during their life. This would ensure that she retained her status as the wife of an Officer and also give some assurance that she would be able to support her children even if the annuity from her father or her previous husband ceased.

The practice of a 'country marriage' to either a local woman or a 'mixed-blood' woman had been accepted and was widespread by employees of both the North West Company and the Hudson's Bay. The Companies' views on the practice varied over time, the advantages of close links with the indigenous people being seen to be good for trade by building close family links with them, but this was balanced by concerns over the cost to the Company of supporting the families of these marriages. Marriages to 'mixed-blood' daughters of the senior Company Officers were seen by some to have advantages over marriage to native women, bringing with the union a family connection to an influential Company Officer, who might be able to assist in promoting the career of a young junior employee. The country marriages or 'a la facon du pays', to mixed-blood women were not carried out with the usual ceremony or legal requirements of marriage in England, and there would often be no exchange of vows or documentation to recognise the marriage. The Hudson's Bay Company did not officially support marriages to local women but recognised it had no power to stop them from occurring. The Company had, by the time of Holmes' marriage, reluctantly accepted that the families of employees might be provisioned at the Company's expense but made it very clear that such a responsibility ceased at the death or retirement of the employee.

Having spent a season at Churchill Factory learning how the company operated and acquiring the skills needed to survive in the challenging conditions of an inland trading post, Holmes was ready to be sent out to experience the life of a fur trader. He was stationed for the next season at Nelson House with Mr George Charles, an experienced trader who had been with the Hudson's Bay Company since he joined as an apprentice in 1785. Mr Charles had served at a number of inland trading posts over the years and was well thought of by the company. George Charles had arrived at Churchill Factory on June 20th, 1806, bringing down the furs he had traded during the season. Mr Auld noted his arrival with pleasure, but expressed his sorrow in observing that Mr Charles was 'in very bad health'. Despite his ill health, Mr Charles set off back to Nelson House on July 1st with three boats and sixteen men, accompanied by Holmes and Betsy.

Nelson House on the Churchill River was in competition with the North West Company, and George Charles had a lot of experience in dealing with his opposition. In 1803, he had been involved in arresting Louis Duplein, a North West trader, who had taken by force thirty beaver skins from another trader. Charles had invited Duplein over to his house for breakfast and when he confessed to the theft, put him in irons and sent him back to Churchill Factory to await trial. Towards the end of the season at Nelson House, Mr Charles became unwell, with what was described as 'Palsy and Putrid Fever'. Putrid fever was a term used for typhus, a disease transmitted by the human body louse, and particularly prevalent in prisons and onboard ships, leading to other names such as 'jail fever' or 'ship fever'. There was at the time no effective treatment for typhus, and it would be treated by bleeding and measures to reduce the patient's temperature, but up to sixty per cent of cases resulted in death. As the Post Surgeon, Holmes would have been responsible for treating Mr Charles but would have known that the disease was in all probability likely to prove fatal. In addition to his concern over his patient, Holmes had the added worry that his wife Betsy, who was now pregnant, would be at risk of contracting the disease.

On February 12th, 1807, Holmes and Betsy had their first child, a son, George. Betsy and George avoided contracting typhus, but Holmes reported that Mr Charles died from the disease on March 11th, 1807. Betsy and Holmes remained at Nelson House with George until the end of the season when they moved further inland to another post at Reindeer River.

Holmes spent the season of 1807 to 1808 at Reindeer Lake. This was one of the many Hudson's Bay Company Posts that were opposed by the North West Company, and reports of the behaviour of the Canadians towards the Hudson's Bay Company men at Reindeer Lake were recorded in the journal for 1806 — 1809. It was reported that the men had to 'stomach affronts varying from actual imprisonment, robbery of Indians, brutal ill-treatment and assaults in their own houses, to allegations that their whiskey was bad and to swearing and blaspheming without either manners or discretion'. William Auld, when he visited Reindeer Lake House, was not impressed with the place and felt that the poor state of the house compared with the North West Company House would not encourage the local hunters to trade with the Hudson's Bay traders, describing it as:

'The most miserable hovel that imagination can conceive. Surely such abominably disgraceful styes must affect the Natives. Dirty as they are, they must make shocking comparisons to our disadvantage. Such temporary shelter, infinitely below what an Ourang-Outang would have contented himself with, can only bespeak the glimmering dying lights of an expiring Commerce, not the residences of Britons, not the Settlements of the Adventurers of England'.

Holmes was employed as a surgeon during his time at Reindeer Lake, the Master of the House being Joseph Spence. Spence was a very experienced trader and had been at Reindeer Lake for the previous six years. The North West Company had established a station near Reindeer Lake, commanded by John Duncan Campbell, who was one of the partners of the company. Campbell waged a war of intimidation and robbery towards Spence and his men, and there were regular confrontations between the two factions.

Holmes' skills as a surgeon proved valuable to Spence when one of the local hunters was beaten so hard by one of Campbell's men that his rib was broken. Holmes treated the man, who was so grateful that he promised to leave the North West Traders as soon as he could and start to trade with Spence. When the man returned later in the summer, he attempted to join Spence but was prevented from doing so by threats of death from one of the North West traders who Spence described as 'A Great

Bruiser', known by the locals as 'The Devil'.

When Spence temporarily left Reindeer Lake in June 1808 on a journey to Churchill Factory, he left Holmes in charge for a period of two months. On his return journey, Spence stopped at Duck Lake to consult with Mr Jamison about where to send Holmes for the winter. It was decided that Spence would take a spare canoe with him back to Reindeer Lake and then send Holmes to Egg Lake at the mouth of Deer River, where it was expected that some Southern Indians would overwinter. Spence arrived back at Reindeer Lake on August 27th, and he immediately resumed charge of the post and two days later sent Holmes with three men in the canoe to winter at Egg Lake. They were supplied with some food and a few articles to set themselves up until they could get a further supply from Nelson House. Holmes managed to set up trade with the local hunters and by October had built up his supplies of goods to the point where he sent two men and a local boy to Nelson House with a quantity of pounded meat and fat and a request for goods that he needed in exchange. The men arrived at Nelson House on October 2nd. Mr Jamison was anxious and the men were able to return within a few days… 'Nelson House Journal 1808–1809', Hudson's Bay Company" to leave Nelson House on a journey to Weir Lake, so the goods requested were packed overnight, and the men were able to return within a few days.

Holmes was now well settled in at Egg Lake for the winter and some three months later, in February 1808, sent one of his men, James Moore, with a letter for Spence to inform him that he had heard no news from the people at the Lower Rat River since the fall. Spence sent Moore back to Egg Lake to seek out any news from England and Churchill Factory. Shortly after

Moore's departure, Spence's neighbour from the North West Company paid a visit and informed him that Holmes was '*feasting and lavishing away*' the property of the Hudson's Bay Company and was intending to leave the Hudson's Bay Company and go over to the North West Company. The relationship between Spence and the North Westers was very strained, and he had soon realised that they were determined to sabotage his trading at Deer Lake in any way they could. This ranged from killing and eating his dogs to making holes in his canoes below the water line so that they would sink when the men went out fishing. There would seem no reason to believe any information they gave him concerning Holmes, as they were known to have lied about many events.

Spence's contacts with Holmes were sporadic and usually by letter. Egg Lake was a staging point for messages to be sent to Churchill Factory, so Spence would send men down to Holmes with letters to be forwarded to the factory. In May, Spence sent two men in a canoe to Egg Lake to take letters from himself and Mr Charles to be forwarded to Churchill '*at the first opportunity*', as he was of the opinion that the ice on the Lake would prevent him leaving before the boat in the Rat River made the journey to the factory. When the two men returned from Egg Lake after ten days, they reported that they had left the letters but had not seen Holmes as he was away from the house with some Indians.

During his time as a surgeon at Reindeer Lake, Holmes was paid £40 a year, the amount being the same whether he was employed as a surgeon or as a trader. In his time there he incurred debts to the company of £4 17s for the purchase of twenty pounds of sugar, two and a half yards of cloth, twelve pounds of sugar loaf, one pound of tea, one pound of tobacco and two balls of twine. Against his wages, he drew bills of payment to the amount of £7 5s to his sister Miss Elizabeth B. Holmes. He was awarded bounty money of £2 15s, the fifteen shillings being a premium for trading three hundred made beaver skins.

After wintering at Egg Lake, Holmes was ordered to take charge of a trading post at Fish Weir Lake in Churchill District. For the season of 1808 to 1809, Fish Weir Lake is not listed as a Company station in the archives, but it is likely that this was a name for the Weir River station. The Weir River, which flows east into Nelson River, was also known as 'Old Fish-dam River', a translation of the Cree name Kesamachiskun, meaning 'dam of poles or twigs' for catching fish. The Nelson House journals of 1808 to 1809 make reference to Mr Jamison journeying to Weir Lake in October 1808.

The accounts book of Churchill Factory for 1809 records that Holmes was employed as an Inland Trader at a wage of £40 a year and that his contract was due to expire in 1810. He had fourteen shillings of debt to the company for the purchase of four pounds of sugar and ten pounds of moist sugar. He had also drawn £12 in bills of payment, this comprised £2 to William Lautit and a sum of £10 to Miss Elizabeth Holmes. Later payments show the recipient as Miss Elizabeth Birkett Holmes. These regular payments to his sister in England were to continue for several years, but there were no payments in the name of his mother. In addition to his pay, Holmes was awarded an Inland bounty of £2 and a premium based on the number of furs he had traded of £1 4s 6d.

There were six men stationed at Fish Weir Lake with Holmes, including William Tomison, Magnus Corrigal who was a tailor, and four labourers by the names of Elliot William, William

Sabiston, Thomas Stanyer and Henry Thompson. William Tomison had a long career with the company but had fallen out of favour and occupied some minor posts in his last years before retiring to England in 1810. He would not have been a good companion for Holmes, as he was known to have little interest in conversation with his fellow officers and had become an isolated and disliked figure. In terms of assisting with trading, he was not an asset to Holmes, as the Indians viewed him as a mean man who was reluctant to dispense brandy to them.

On January 17th, 1809, Holmes arrived at Nelson House with a local boy as they were in need of some articles. Holmes also required another man from Nelson House to come with them to Fish Weir as he and Jamison were having to send two of their own men to live with their traders to prevent the Canadians from stealing their furs. Holmes set off back to Weir Lake five days later with John Houston, a boy, four dogs and two sledges.

The season at Weir Lake was drawing to a close, and on the first day of June 1809, Holmes and Jamison sent four of their men down to Nelson House with a supply of pemmican, which was pounded dried meat mixed to a paste with melted fat. Holmes and Jamison had decided to wait on the track used to travel to the factory to await the arrival of William Auld, the Governor of the District, who was also going back to the factory. Auld was reported to have gone to Cumberland House from Reindeer Lake and was expected to return by the track. Some Indians and traders had gathered at the track to await the Governor, and one called Blue Coat was sent down to Nelson House to fetch a supply of brandy for them. Holmes' four men were sent to the new house at Nelson to work, as there was too much ice in the river to start sending the boats to the factory. Blue Coat was sent back to Holmes and Jamison with the requested supply of brandy.

By June 9th, there was no sign of the Governor arriving, so Holmes and Jamison travelled down to Nelson House, bringing with them the Indians, who had grown impatient waiting for the Governor and by now were all drunk on the brandy that had been supplied. It was not until June 13th that William Auld arrived at Nelson House ready to set off to the factory. Adam Snoddie had already sent two boats with ten men to the factory, as the delay in waiting for the Governor had depleted all their food supplies and the fishing at Nelson House was very poor. Holmes remained at Nelson House with Messrs. Tomlinson, Raymond, Snoddie, and Charles. William Auld was the Superintendent of the District who had arrived on June 13th while on his expedition from Reindeer House. Auld was also a surgeon, having studied medicine at Edinburgh for three years, but is believed not to have qualified for a degree. He was hired as a surgeon by the Hudson's Bay Company in 1790, but like many surgeons, his career with the HBC was more to do with the fur trade than surgery. In his journal he recorded:

'Mr Holmes I have appointed to proceed with three men to establish a post to the S.E. of the Frog Portage where the Indians mean to winter most year. He has goods sufficient until he will get more of a large complement of men in the Fall.'

Holmes was operating during this period in the capacity of an Inland Trader, and his journal kept from 1809 to 1810 records the details of the events that occurred at the post during the period. It documents the daily occurrences at what became known as Bedford House and his journey from Nelson House to establish the post. Holmes set out from Nelson House on June 19th, 1809, having had less than a week to prepare for the expedition. His expedition team consisted of three men and a local guide and they travelled with a group of Indians who were heading to Egg Lake to overwinter. The journey as far as Egg Lake took eighteen days and was undertaken in weather described as *'foul wind and rain'*. Egg Lake is at the confluence of the Reindeer and Churchill rivers and was some distance from the location that William Auld had specified in his orders to Holmes. When he arrived at Egg Lake, Holmes talked to his guides about the plans to continue further inland to set up a trading post.

'This day arrived at Egg Lake after a… of 16 days… of foul winds & rain

I informed the Indians of where I thought of going to settle they said I might please myself, but they would not go so far as the above mentioned place in Consequence of which I was obliged to stop here. I was not very anxious to go further myself for the whole of the Indians were left except 4, 3 of which were French Traders. In the evening 3 Indians & their familys arrived that accompanied us up brought over ½ Beaver skin only I gave them a little brandy & ammunition & Tobacco and sent them to hunt Moose.'

Frog Portage, which Auld had decided on as the best place for a new post, was a key overland route for carrying canoes and goods between the Churchill River and the Saskatchewan River. Unable to proceed further, Holmes decided to establish a new post on Egg Lake. While not as good a strategic position as Frog Portage, it was at a key point where the Reindeer and Churchill rivers joined. The post was one that the company was to find useful and was subsequently known as Bedford House. Holmes and his men were now faced with the task of constructing a permanent house to live in and to act as a trading post. Holmes had spent the winter of 1808 at Egg Lake but now needed to build a secure trading post to house the men and provide space for storage of the furs they would accumulate over the season. The structure of such houses was of wood, with mud used to fill in the gaps and provide some insulation, a stone chimney was built and the windows glazed with moose skin parchment. The construction, using freshly felled wood, could take many weeks during which their tents would be the only shelter. Once completed, the Egg Lake trading post soon attracted hunters wishing to trade furs, meat and other provisions and in August, Holmes had regular visits from hunters and their families. If the hunters had a quantity of skins or provisions, then they would discuss the trade and then disclose where the goods could be found. This often resulted in Holmes and his men making expeditions away from the house to collect furs. On some occasions, the hunters would bring their furs directly to the house. One such day was August 10th, 1809, when six canoes arrived bringing ten beaver skins, one black bear skin and two moose skins. Holmes recorded the trade in his journal: *'I gave them a little Brandy & ammunition in debt and sent them away in the evening.'*

The Company had a set of trading standards that placed a value on the traded furs expressed in terms of 'Made Beaver', often referred to as 'MB' in the post journals. An 'MB' was the most valued of the beaver furs, being the prime winter pelt of a beaver in good condition. Other poorer quality furs would be priced as a fraction of an MB and the trading standard equivalent in goods such as brandy, ammunition or provisions would be paid to the hunter. The Company also had a credit system whereby the hunter could be paid more than the value of the fur. This extra payment was termed a 'debt', and the hunter would be expected to bring in more furs or meat until the debt was repaid. The local hunters saw this as a matter of honour and would ensure that the debt was repaid. This system meant that the hunters were tied to the trader who held the debt and ensured that they were less likely to try and trade with the North West Company who were in competition with the Hudson's Bay Company.

In addition to trading for furs, the Egg Lake post was also to be used as a supply station for posts further away from Nelson House where the main supplies were held. This meant that Holmes needed to ensure that he had a surplus of supplies above those required to feed his men and dogs. On August 27th, two men arrived from Mr John Charles who had charge of the post on Deer Lake that was near the junction of Reindeer River with Churchill River. The men brought a request to supply *'40lbs of pounded beef meat and fat as well as two parchment moose skins for their windows'*. Holmes *'gave them many things that was requested and sent them away immediately'* to wait at the mouth of the Deer River, where a boat would be waiting for them to take them back to Deer Lake. On the very next day, a local hunter and two men arrived from Mr Fidler, who was waiting at the mouth of the Deer River and who also requested a supply of *'one hundred lbs of pemmican and two parchment moose skins'*. Holmes was able to supply these goods and sent them back with the men. Peter Fidler was a Hudson's Bay Company surveyor who mapped many of the routes in the Hudson's Bay Company area. The men were part of Fidler's 1809 expedition, exploring a route from Churchill River to Black Lake, searching for a good passage for the fur trappers to the country east of Athabasca Lake to avoid the long trek over the Methy Portage.

At the start of September, Holmes recorded that a trader from the North West Company had arrived at Egg Lake in opposition to him. He did not appear unduly concerned, as he wrote *'a Mr Chastelain, a Canadian trader, arrived as not got a single article to give an Indian'* and a week later Holmes was able to take trade away from the Canadian by settling a debt owed to John Charles. *'This Day an Indian arrived at the Canadian Tent he came over to my House & informed me he had 3 Beaver skins for me upon an Island about a mile from the house sent 1 of the men to fetch them immediately traded them for a debt belonging to Mr Charles.'*

Having supplied goods to Charles and Fidler, it was necessary for Holmes to replenish his supplies before the winter set in, and to arrange for Nelson House to send up the rest of the men he had been promised by Auld. On September 19th, he sent one of his men, William Coulter, with a local boy as a pilot to travel to Nelson House for a supply of men and goods. Over the next three weeks, Holmes traded steadily, but with the weather conditions worsening he began to worry about the supply of provisions he was expecting from Nelson House. He had a responsibility not only for the safety of his men but also for his wife Betsy and their young son, George, who was only two years old. Betsy was living at Egg Lake with Holmes, and her knowledge of the language would be an asset to her husband, as were her skills, such as splitting and drying moose skins.

'… the Man and Indian boy I sent down to Nelson House on the 19th of September not arrived as yet it being very cold snowing… weather I am afraid to trust any longer for the people from Nelson House. there being 2 Indians sent them to the Deer Lake for a few

things that I can not do well without having but 2 Men and cannot send them.'

However, a month to the day after their departure, the men who had travelled to Nelson House were sighted at the portages near Egg Lake. Holmes was clearly relieved, and his journal for October 19th reads:

'Thank God the people arrived from Nelson House in a big Canoe 4 Men all in good health excepting 2 whose feet are cut with stones & the cold being so severe caused them to swell very much indeed. I sent the 2 men & boy I had at the House to assist them over the 3 Portages.'

The trek from the portages to the house was challenging, and the men did not arrive back until late the next day. Two men had been sent up to join Holmes at Egg Lake and a third, William Osman, had been sent to go over to John Charles at Deer Lake. One of Holmes' men, Andrew Wilson, who had undertaken the journey to Nelson House, was suffering from frostbite and was not capable of working for some time, so the extra men were a timely addition to the employees at Egg Lake. The two Indians who Holmes had sent to Deer Lake on the 14th of the month with a request for supplies arrived back on October 24th bringing the things Holmes needed, accompanied by William Craigie, one of John Charles' men. The weather was now worsening rapidly, but Holmes made the decision to send Craigie and Osman back to Deer Lake before the conditions became too severe. The two men set off, taking some more supplies for Deer River and a packet of letters and a parcel for John Charles. Overnight the Egg Lake had frozen over, so the men had to walk to the portages where they had left their boats.

The weather conditions at Egg Lake deteriorated over the next few weeks and Holmes and his men set fishing nets under the ice to try and catch a supply of fresh food. The visits of the hunters with furs and provisions had reduced as the weather worsened, and by November 14th the situation with regard to food and supplies was becoming serious. With eight nets under the ice Holmes wrote: *'can scarcely get so much as will keep us alive'.* On November 19th an Indian arrived with thirteen beavers to repay his debt, but Holmes and his men were then to endure nearly two months of isolation in the snow and icebound conditions, with little prospect of obtaining enough fresh food to exist and a limited supply of dried food. Holmes recorded his fears in his journal on the last day of 1809:

'I have seen no Indians this month past, but I expect them every day and living is desperately bad we are 11 in Family besides dogs. 10 nets in the water and can scarcely catch 1 meal per day of all kinds of fish good and bad in consequence of which I have been obliged to give the men a little pounded meat & fat to help out. The Canadians are actually starving they have not a mouthful of Provisions we have only caught 212 white fish & 217 of all other kinds this month'.

The harsh winter had hit the local population hard as well, and on January 9th, 1810, two boys arrived at the house from the tent of one of Holmes' hunters, White Bird. They said that they were starving and their father was not able to walk because of hunger. Despite the precarious position of his own supplies, Holmes sent two men the next day to White Bird's tent with a little pemmican and a few fish that had been saved for the dogs. The men returned two days later and reported that White Bird was so starved he was not able to hunt for his family, he had however sent twenty-nine made beaver skins for trade. On the next day, White Bird's wife and son arrived to seek more help, and Holmes again sent them supplies of fish and, out of his limited supply of dried food, some flour and oatmeal. He gave his reason for helping that: *'he being such a good hunter I should be sorry to lose him'*. Over the next three weeks, Holmes continued to assist the family with supplies of fish and traded 20 lbs of ground beef and two lbs of grease for the beaver skins they brought over to Egg Lake. White Bird's wife informed him that if her husband got well enough to hunt, then they would not return to Egg Lake until the spring. Once recovered, White Bird travelled to Egg Lake on February 17th and traded nineteen beaver skins and 20 lbs of *'green meat'* (fresh meat) and left the next day. It was not until May 5th that Holmes heard from White Bird's wife that her husband had between thirty and forty skins, which Holmes could collect once spring arrived.

The harsh winter continued to cause problems for the Egg Lake Post, with very little fresh fish being caught. The Canadians in their house were in a worse state and started to follow Holmes' men on their expeditions in the hope of getting supplies. In April Holmes records:

'The Canadians followed my people but got nothing but a few scraps, they are starving no fish to be caught worth mentioning, If we had not got a good supply of meat… I do not know what we should have done.'

The winter finally ended its grip on Egg Lake on May 17th when Holmes was able to retrieve his nets from the lake as the ice broke up, and set up his nets out in open water. John Charles was able to make the journey down from Deer Lake, and together they agreed on their plans for the end of the season and the return to Nelson House. Holmes was concerned that White Bird still had a large supply of furs stored and the Canadians might *'plunder him'*, so he sent John Houston in a canoe to meet up with White Bird and arrange for the goods to be collected. Houston returned two days later and brought sixty-three made beavers and seven moose skins. On June 4th, 1810, the Canadians left their house and headed out. Holmes now felt confident he could leave Egg House and start off on the journey to Nelson House. He travelled to the mouth of the Deer River where his men were waiting, and on May 10th they joined up with two boats and twelve men whom they had arranged to join on the journey back to Nelson. The large canoes, which the men were using, needed a skilled steersman to safely navigate the rivers. Holmes did not have enough experienced men to act as a steersman, and he used a big canoe he had built earlier in the year. In the absence of a steersman, one of his men, J. Wilson, steered the large boat. After nearly two weeks of navigating the rivers, they reached a place called Gods Lake, which had a dangerous run of waterfalls. Holmes warned Wilson that he should not attempt the falls without first examining it carefully, but *'they paid no attention to what I said'*. As the large canoe was running Gods Lake, Wilson overturned the canoe in the falls and Holmes recorded on May 23rd: *'I am very sorry to relate a very melancholy accident that happened this morning Ja Wilson upset his canoe in running Gods Lake next to Duck Lake & Peter Moone was lost'*.

This was indeed a sad end to the year at Egg Lake, with a man lost and all the fur bundles soaked in the accident. Holmes employed his men the next day in drying the furs, which took all day until sunset, and it was not until the next day that they were able to resume their journey. Three days later on May

27th, the men made camp about nine miles from Nelson House. Holmes carried on in his canoe and reached Nelson House around midnight where he was welcomed by John Charles and Mr Snoddie. The rest of the men arrived the next day, and after a day's rest John Charles and Holmes set off towards Churchill Factory. Holmes recorded his last diary entry in the Egg Lake Journal on May 29th, 1810. *'This day Self & Mr Charles set out for the factory with 3 boats I have not been down this 4 years.'*

The Hudson's Bay Company Season or 'Outfit Season' ran from June 1st, 1809, to May 31st, 1810, so Holmes would spend some time at Churchill Factory over the summer before returning to Egg Lake for a second season.

Watercolour: Hudson's Bay Company officials in an express canoe crossing a lake. *Source: Library and Archives Canada/Peter Rindisbacher collection/e011161353*

Watercolour: A Hunter-family of Cree Indians at York Fort, drawn from nature. *Source: Library and Archives Canada/Peter Rindisbacher collection/e008299389*

Chapter 6

Starvation

'What to do I cannot tell. If the Indians do not kill some Moose soon we shall surely die'

After spending nearly three months at Churchill, Holmes started his journey back to Egg Lake. The passage took forty-two days, and it was not until August 26th, 1810, that he arrived back at Egg Lake. The men he had left to look after the post over the summer were in good health, but to his dismay, they had made very little trade over the summer. The Indians had been trading with the Canadians at Nelson House, Pelican Lake and near Cumberland House, which meant that Samuel Mowlam and Mr Walter had only managed to trade 90 lbs of meat, 15 lbs of fat, 25 lbs of pounded meat and ten summer beaver furs.

Over the summer the Canadians had made the best of Holmes' absence and had persuaded some of the traders to change allegiance to them, so he set out to Pelican Lake to retrieve his traders, who he felt had been *'debauched thither by the Canadians'*. Holmes met up with two tents of Indians who were with the Canadians but discovered that the Canadians had few supplies other than a little brandy and some ammunition to use as trade. Holmes talked to the Indians and asked them to spread the word that he was back at Egg Lake and instructed them not to bring any goods direct to his house, but rather to leave them in a safe place, and he would then collect them later. In this way, he hoped to gain an advantage over the Canadians as they would not know who had returned to trading with him.

The dispute with the Canadians over their actions in *'debauching the Indians'* started to come to a head on September 14th, 1810. The Canadians arrived back at Egg Lake with six canoes and some hunters that had previously been traders of Mr Snoddie at Nelson House. That evening, one of them came over to the house and told Holmes that the Canadians had forced him to trade with them and that he hated them and would leave them if Holmes would give him 'a little debt'. Holmes declined but nevertheless gave him a little ammunition and tobacco together with a letter to take to Adam Snoddie asking him to take care the Canadians did not go off with the Indian again. Holmes vowed that as long as he lived, he would ensure that the Canadians did not steal any more traders.

It was with this in mind that on August 16th an event occurred which brought the conflict with the Canadians to a serious standoff. On the previous day, two hunters with their families had arrived at Egg Lake and pulled their canoes ashore by Holmes' house. They had a bear skin, two beaver skins, one moose skin, 167 lbs of pounded meat, 70 lbs of fat and 150 lbs of dry meat to trade, which Holmes exchanged for ammunition, brandy, tobacco and some blankets. The Indians then went over to the Canadian house and the master, Mr Chastelain, immediately took one of the Hudson's Bay Company blankets away from one of them and replaced it with a Canadian blanket. He then sent the man over to Holmes to return the blanket to him, with a message that he would no longer be allowed to trade with Holmes. Whilst acknowledging that the man had been a Canadian trader, Holmes reasoned that as he came ashore at the

English house, he was within his rights to trade with him. He decided that action was required. He placed a loaded pistol in his breeches pocket and went over to the Canadian house with one of his men, James Walter, to accompany him. He was met by Mr Chastelain who was initially polite, and invited Holmes to take a seat which Holmes declined, saying *'I am not staying long'*.

When Holmes announced that he had come over for an explanation of why the blanket had been sent back with the Indian, Chastelain flew into a sudden rage and said that Holmes had not acted like a gentleman in coming with one of his men when he knew Chastelain was alone in the house. An argument ensued as Holmes replied, *'I think myself as good a man as you and my man will not touch you'*. Chastelain would hear no reason and retorted that he was as good a man as Holmes. The situation escalated when Holmes reiterated that he was as good a man as Chastelain and that Chastelain should take care if he dared to deny it, for he would strike him for the insult. At this, Chastelain made a sudden dive for the heavy trunk which held his pistols. When Holmes saw this, he decided to strike first and gave him a *'most tremendous blow which swelled up his eye immediately'*. Holmes then hit him on the nose and split his own knuckles with the force of the blow. Chastelain, now injured and bleeding heavily, called for quarter and Holmes ceased his attack and sent James Walter and the Indian back to Bedford House. He helped Chastelain to his feet and turned to leave. As he did, Chastelain drew his gun from the trunk and fired it four times at Holmes at point-blank range, but as Holmes recalled later that day in his journal, *'very luckily it did not fire or he had killed me dead upon the spot like a coward as he be.'*

On the next day, Holmes was apprehensive as he only had

James Walter with him, and all the Canadian men had returned, having been sent to fetch Mr Chastelain's possessions from further along the lakeshore. Holmes was uneasy, fearing that they may *'come over and commit some depredation at my house'*, so he made preparations to defend himself. He loaded three guns with two balls each, loaded two pistols and also made ready with two axes and an axe handle so that if he were attacked, the Canadians would meet with a very warm reception indeed. There was no sign of an approach from the Canadians, and later that day the rest of Holmes' men arrived back, having collected supplies and furs left at the portage some three miles away. Feeling reassured, Holmes relaxed a little, but in the evening feared the worst when he saw all the Canadian men approaching his house without their master. His worries were, however, unfounded, for the men were very friendly and after sharing glasses of rum with him, admitted that their master had behaved badly and apologised for him, saying that he had deserved the beating that Holmes had given him. Early the next morning Holmes was surprised to see Mr Chastelain approaching the house. Holmes invited him in, but Chastelain continued to argue that he was right in keeping the Indian because he was his trader. Holmes repeated that the man had come ashore at Bedford House, not the Canadian house and therefore he was within his rights to complete a trade. He added forcefully that he would not be prevented from acting like this again, whether by Chastelain or his men and that if Chastelain was not satisfied with this, then he should stand up and Holmes would *'give him satisfaction'*, which was an invitation to settle the matter with a duel. Chastelain sensibly remained seated and after a long argument, finally agreed that he had been in the wrong. The two shook hands and according to

Holmes were *'very good friends again'*. Whether this sentiment was shared by Chastelain is not known.

With the arrival of the winter weather in October, survival in these conditions depended on obtaining a plentiful supply of food, both for the men and for the dog teams. Holmes sent one man to overwinter with John Charles at Deer Lake, as the fishing was so bad, he feared he would not be able to catch enough fish to feed the eighteen men and eleven dogs he had at Egg Lake. Along with McKinley, who was to winter with John Charles, he sent three other men and François, a local boy, to take some canoes to Deer Lake, and they were ordered to leave one for the use of Mr Charles. They departed from Egg Lake on October 19th but had not returned by the 30th. Holmes was concerned that an accident had befallen them, as the river seemed free of ice and there were only three places where they would have had to carry their canoes.

Holmes had only four men with him now, and this was not sufficient to look after the fishing nets, collect furs that the hunters wished to trade and keep an eye on the Canadians. He suspected they were trying to set up a new house somewhere between Egg Lake and Pelican Lake in an attempt to increase their trade. It was not until November 2nd that the men finally returned from Deer Lake. Two days after they left Deer Lake the river had frozen, and they could not paddle, but were forced to carry their canoes and goods, walking chiefly through the woods as the ice was not strong enough to support them. They were forced to abandon their supplies of meat and fur which they had traded on the way, in the hope of returning for them when the weather improved.

Holmes had sent two men sixteen miles further upriver to a

place called Three Points to set up a leather fishing tent and to see if they could improve on the poor fishing at Egg Lake. Even with eight nets set he could only catch one or two white fish and a few of other varieties which he said was: *'but little for 18 people and eleven dogs'.* His suspicions about the Canadians were well-founded, for when he sent Andrew Wilson and François upriver to see where they had gone, they were located at their old house at Frightened Narrows, upstream from Three Points, and were catching the fish before they got to Holmes' men in their fishing tent. Holmes again confronted Chastelain and told him that unless the Canadians moved down to Three Points, then he would send his men to Frightened Narrows and set up a rival post. Given Chastelain's experience when the two clashed earlier in the year, he readily agreed and promised they would return from the old house and that Holmes need not bother travelling all the way up there to check. Two days later the Canadians did indeed arrive back at Egg Lake, having abandoned their house at Frightened Narrows.

At the start of December, with food and supplies being at a low level, Holmes sent out three men to collect the meat and furs which François and the other men had abandoned when they were unable to return by river from Deer Lake a month previously. The men arrived at the place the meat had been left but found the meat, the stores and a leather tent totally destroyed by animals. The loss of over 700 lbs of meat, which even in poor condition would have fed the dogs, was a disaster, as they had little in the way of fish or meat left apart from a small quantity of pounded meat and fat. The situation started to improve slightly on December 15th when an Indian arrived to tell them he had killed a moose and wished to trade the flesh.

Men were dispatched to collect it and three days later returned with 200 lbs of moose meat. The overall food situation was not good, however, and on December 29th the Canadians, who were by this point starving, left Egg Lake and embarked on a three day walk to their old house at Frightened Narrows. That morning, Mr Chastelain had visited Holmes and begged him for some breakfast which Holmes provided for him, despite being low on rations himself. Holmes noted in his journal that the fact that the Canadians were starving was their own fault because;

'instead of fishing at the 3 points as we were they went to seek their Indians like mad fools as they are I don't believe the Canadians left this place for the want of victuals for they might have caught fish at the 3 points that would have kept them as well as us if they chose.'

William Auld noticed Holmes' entry when the journals were submitted at the end of the year, and he commented on the discrepancy between Holmes' reports of being starving himself and his report that there were enough fish at Three Points to keep them in food. In the margin of the journal, Auld wrote in pencil: *'A curious confession of himself having sufficient'.*

Holmes recorded his catch of fish for January as follows: *'From the first of January to the 31st only received 72 fish of all kinds from the Three Points for 7 people and 5 dogs. Therefore Gentlemen I leave you to judge our situation.'* William Auld took this as an invitation to make yet another comment in pen in the margin, and this time his judgement was a little more astringent. *'Mr Holmes is the worst steward of victuals alive & we do not believe more than ½ of his scarcity to be real. Wm Auld'.*

It was common practice for company officials to peruse the journals once they were submitted, and decisions could be made on salary and position based on the content of the journals.

Entries in the journals were therefore written in the knowledge that decisions and actions recorded in them would be the subject of scrutiny.

The scarcity of food was, despite William Auld's views, starting to affect the Indians and their ability to hunt and deliver food to Egg Lake. On February 12th, 1811, the mother and a grandson of one of Holmes' traders arrived at Egg Lake and said they were almost starving to death, and that the rest of her family had stopped at the Three Points where the Egg Lake men were fishing. She had brought down what skins they had to trade, which only amounted to twenty-eight beaver skins against the hundred they were in debt for. She said the family was in such distress they had eaten most of their beaver and otter skins to enable them to survive. Holmes decided to call the men back from the Three Points, as they were not catching any more fish. He had no store of meat left at Egg Lake and was sure that unless the Indians killed some moose soon, he and his men would surely die. When the men arrived back at Egg Lake on February 13th the total of their catch was four jack fish, which added to the two that were in his store, was all they had between them for supper that day. Over the next week, there was an improvement in the food stocks as some of Holmes' traders arrived with news that they had killed some moose, although they could not spare all of the meat to trade, as they were so short of food themselves. The men were sent out with sledges to collect the meat, and by February 17th they had collected nearly 400 lbs of meat and three moose skins and brought them back to the house. The next day, Monday, February 18th, Holmes himself set out with two men and the two boys with a sledge each as he had received news that White Bird, one of his best hunters, who he had helped save from starvation the previous season, had meat to trade. The journey was not easy, and it was not until the Thursday of that week that they returned, very much fatigued, to Egg Lake with 179 lbs of green meat, 60 lbs of pounded meat, six moose skins and seventeen parchment beaver skins. During their stay with White Bird, he had said that the Rat River, where he had experienced his best hunting, was totally hunted out and that there was scarcely a beaver lodge left in the whole area. He added that he did not know where else to go to try and hunt and that at the moment it was not in his power to pay any of his debt to the company.

The shortage of food was not confined to Egg Lake. Towards the end of February, three Canadians arrived with a letter from John Charles at Deer Lake asking for provisions to be sent, and for Holmes to send one of his traders to help them hunt food, as they were starving. Holmes dispatched François to Deer Lake to hunt for them and also sent them a little dry meat. He wrote a letter to John Charles suggesting sending one or more of the Deer Lake men over to Egg Lake to reduce the load on their food stores, and he would then send the men over to Samuel Taylor at Frightened Narrows where the fishing and food supply may be better. At Egg Lake, they had only caught ninety-four fish for the whole of February. During March, the hunters continued to bring in skins and furs, but little in the way of meat. The Canadians had started to follow Holmes and his men when they went out on trading expeditions in the hope of finding trade and provisions for themselves.

Holmes was still persuading some of his old traders, who were now with the Canadians, to trade with him as well. On March 15th, he and some of his men reversed the position, by following the Canadians to one of their trader's tents. Holmes was pleased when the traders gave him eleven whole beaver skins, ten damaged beaver skins, one wolverine skin and one parchment moose skin, especially as the Canadians only got five beaver skins. Later in the month, the Canadians attempted to get trade from one of Holmes' traders by following Holmes and his men when they set off with two sledges to collect a debt from one of his traders. Holmes arrived at the trader's tent late at night after a day's journey. The next day he was given twenty whole beavers, thirteen half beavers, fifteen prime otters, five beavers in the coating, one black bear, two cubs, a wolverine, five cats, three deer skins, six moose skins and 30 lbs of green meat. The Canadians who had followed them did not get a single skin of any kind and had to follow Holmes back to Egg Lake, arriving back empty-handed and very much fatigued two days later.

With only two months left of the season, Holmes started to make preparations to organise his men and stocks of furs and skins, ready for transport to the factory in May. On April 1st he visited Samuel Taylor at the new house at Frightened Narrows to check on what he had traded since he set up the trading post. He was disappointed to find that Taylor had only traded sixty beavers, which were mostly from traders who owed a debt to Holmes. The fishing was, however, better than at Egg Lake, so Holmes left one of his men there for the rest of the season. They were still desperately short of food at Egg Lake, where over the month they had only caught a hundred and sixteen white fish and a hundred and ten of all other kinds during March, whereas at Frightened Narrows, there were trout and numerous other white fish. The white fish were generally considered the poorest in flavour and in times of plenty were fed to the dogs. The trout, however, could weigh up to twenty pounds in some rivers and were considered a tasty dish. Once caught, the white fish were speared and cleaned, then split and suspended in lines to dry in the air if there was a surplus, but at present any fish that were caught were eaten straight away, and there were none in store. The local hunters continued to supply a limited amount of meat, but not all of it was fit to eat. On March 22nd, Holmes had sent Osman and Flitt to collect meat from a tent which was a day's journey away. They arrived back with 200 lbs of buck meat, which would have been welcome, but when Holmes inspected it, the buck had been chased by dogs and the meat was bad. Holmes opined that in this season of the year he would eat bad fish but not bad meat, so the journey had been wasted.

Holmes had arrived back from Frightened Narrows on April 9th, and all had been well there when he left. He was therefore surprised when, less than two weeks later, Andrew Wilson arrived with a confused letter from Samuel Taylor to say that 'strange Indians' had arrived belonging to Cumberland House and he needed supplies of brandy and ammunition. Holmes decided he needed to return to Frightened Narrows to 'regulate affairs'. When he arrived, he found that all that had happened was that Samuel Taylor had traded supplies for seventy beaver skins, which were in debt to Cumberland House, and that there had been no reason for him to make the journey. He returned to Egg Lake a week later. The ice there was beginning to break up, but he still had only half a net in the water and was not catching much fish. The prospect of the lake becoming free of ice and being able to fish in open water was at least getting near, and on the 21st of the month, he was able to set a net in the open water. The opening of the lake brought visitors from Deer Lake, and John Charles arrived to collect a twenty-one-foot canoe that Holmes had built for him to take back. He had also built a second which was to go to Cumberland House.

On the last day of May, Holmes and four men set off to Frightened Narrows to deliver the canoe that was to go to Cumberland House. Osman and McKinley were in the Cumberland House canoe and Holmes, Flitt and François in the other. They arrived at Three Points where the men had previously had their fishing tent, and at that point had not encountered too much ice. They camped overnight at Three Points and set off the next day, and although the ice had cleared a little, they had to keep to the shoreline, which made the journey longer and tedious. At about four o'clock in the afternoon, they found their way totally blocked by ice. Holmes attempted to break through the ice to the clear water ahead and had almost got clear when a large mass of ice began to drift down upon the canoe and nearly overturned it. They had reached within five miles of Taylor's house when a solid mass of ice made further sailing impossible. Holmes, no doubt recalling the tragedy of the previous season when he lost one of his men when their canoe overturned, decided not to take the risk of trying to break through the ice again. He ordered Osman to stop and take his canoe out of the water onto the shore, and they left the Cumberland canoe beached, carrying the other with their provisions over half a mile to where they could see more open water. Holmes and his five men then set off in the one canoe towards Frightened Narrows, arriving tired and exhausted but safe at seven o'clock in the evening of June 1st. It was a further two days before the ice cleared enough to send four men to collect the Cumberland House canoe and return it to Frightened Narrows, ready to set off to Cumberland in good time. The lake was still full of drifting ice, and the Indians reported that the route to Cumberland was still blocked with ice, requiring them to carry their canoes over the ice for great distances. Ice or no ice, Holmes knew he had to start the men off on their journey if they were to reach Cumberland House in time, so he engaged a local to pilot the canoes to Cumberland House over the Sturgeon rapids.

Having packed up the skins from Frightened Narrows and seen the Canadians leave for Cumberland House, Holmes set off in his canoe back to Egg Lake on Monday, June 10th, but had to stop his voyage in the afternoon as he was hit by a storm of wind, rain and snow. The storm continued for two days, but he used the time well, putting out three nets and catching sixteen large trout, which he found very acceptable, not having any other provisions. By Wednesday the weather had improved, and he was able to set off early in the morning for Egg Lake. The journey took all day, and he arrived back at Bedford House at midnight, fatigued from steering the canoe and feeling weakened by an illness that had plagued him all winter.

With fourteen men still at Egg Lake, there was a need to build up the food supplies for the last few weeks of the season, but the fishing there was still not good, and the men needed to pack and bale the furs to take down to the factory. Despite the lack of supplies, they were ready to depart on June 14th and set off, leaving Edward Mowatt and François to take care of the house till Holmes returned. They met up with John Charles, Mr Fidler and Mr Sutherland with three boats from the Ile la Cross and sailed in convoy back to Nelson House, arriving without mishap on June 19th.

Holmes had been ordered by William Auld to spend the winter at Sandy Point, where Samuel Taylor had wintered the previous year. Auld had also instructed that the Indian traders from Egg Lake should be sent down to Nelson House. They refused, however, saying that there was nothing to hunt there. Holmes made his last entry in the Egg Lake journal when he arrived at Nelson House predicting that Auld's decision would result in leaving the traders with the Canadians all summer and that this would ruin the trade for the next season. After a short period at Nelson House, Holmes was sent to Frightened Narrows for the season as Auld had instructed. Frightened Narrows, also known as Pelican Narrows, was at the northern end of Pelican Lake and its Cree name was Opawikoscikcan, meaning 'The Narrows of Fear'.

Holmes set off from Nelson House at the start of July in the 21ft canoe he had built at Egg Lake. He was carrying enough supplies to last the winter, taking into account some supplies left at the mouth of the Deer River by Mr Fidler. In addition to these supplies, Holmes also had a small amount of brandy and tobacco. His journey from Nelson House was disagreeable, interrupted by storms of wind and rain and he was obliged to lay up for three or four days at a time until the weather was good enough to travel. This meant that he did not arrive at his first planned stop at Egg Lake until July 13th. There he found Edward Mowatt and François in good health but still short of food because of the lack of fish, which Holmes told them was usual at this time of the year. Holmes spent the day after he arrived repairing an old canoe in preparation for his journey to Frightened Narrows where he was to oppose the Canadians who had once more set up there. He set off on July 15th on his own, but early into the journey he slipped while carrying his canoe over one of the lake portages and damaged it badly. Having spent some time making a repair, he was able to continue on his journey but was delayed, as they had insufficient food and had to stop and set nets to catch fish. They did not arrive at Frightened Narrows till late in the evening of July 20th. Having set up at the house which Samuel Taylor had built, Holmes wasted no time in building an eighteen-foot by sixteen-foot warehouse to store his trading goods and provisions. He then started to contact his old traders, and within a few weeks was having visits from The Moose Hunter, The Spirit and White Bird, who brought green meat, fat and pounded meat to trade.

The trading continued well over August. Having expended all his efforts on setting up the post, it was frustrating when on August 30th, William Osman and Andrew Kirkness arrived in a canoe from Nelson House with orders from William Auld at the factory that they should abandon Frightened Narrows immediately and take all the goods and stores to Nelson House, where Holmes was ordered to take charge. Having packed all the goods and stores, there was not enough room in the two canoes at Frightened Narrows to transport everything to Nelson House in one trip. Holmes, therefore, sent William Osman and Peter Knight with the boat to Egg Lake portages to await his arrival with the canoes. He then sent four men in a single canoe, laden with stores, to the portages with orders to return to help transport the remainder of the goods. The men arrived back five days later, and on September 7th they loaded both canoes and set off for Egg Lake where they arrived after two days' travelling. The boat, canoes and all the stores and goods had then to be carried over the portages and then reloaded onto the boats. Once completed, Holmes carried his canoe over the portages, but had no need of the second canoe so left it on the far side of the portages but burnt it so that it could not *be made use of by the French'*.

Portages Watercolour: Extremely wearisome journeys at the
portages. *Source: Library and Archives Canada/Peter Rindisbacher
collection/e00829943*

It took a further ten days to complete the journey to Nelson
House, and he arrived on September 19th where he found four
families of Northern Indians already waiting for him and
wishing to trade. Holmes was not able to trade with them,
as he had orders from William Auld that he should send any
northern traders to either the factory or Deer Lake to trade.
He reluctantly sent them away without giving them any debt.
The news of Holmes' arrival at Nelson House soon spread, and
over the next week, he had visits from a number of his hunters
including Blue Coat, Red Coat, The Moose Hunter, The Split,
Burnt Neck, The Leaf's son-in-law, The Captain's son-in-law
and Mrs Hawkins' son-in-law. Most of the trade done was of
dry scraps, pounded meat, and fat, with only a few beaver skins

and moose skins. Holmes was concerned that his supply of trading goods was poor, so he *'debted out the Indians that arrived yesterday with as little goods as possible'*. His supply of provisions was also low, and they had suffered a month of poor fishing. He recorded his concerns in his journal entry of September 30th:

'We have had very bad fishing this month only caught 394 white fish none of any other kind which would do little for 9 men besides myself 3 women 7 children and 20 dogs if we had no provisions at the house'.

Trade in October proved to be a little better, with a total of twelve beaver skins, one black bear skin, two swan skins and one duck being brought in, the remainder of the trade consisting of 170 lbs of green meat, 350 lbs of dry scraps, 85 lbs of pounded meat and 57 lbs of fat. By mid-October the lake had frozen over, trapping four of the fishing nets under the ice. They attempted to retrieve them, but two of the nets had been carried away by drifting ice. Holmes sent out six of the men with eight nets for each pair as he was worried that if they did not catch more fish, they would be in danger of starving; they had over twenty nets in the water but had caught only eight hundred and thirteen fish all month. The situation became worse when the weather suddenly improved, and the warmer weather meant that the ice was too thin for the men to go out to the nets for over a week. When they eventually managed to reach them on November 11th, they had only caught two hundred and twenty-seven white fish, the majority of which were rotten, having been in the nets for over a week. Holmes still had four hundred and ninety-six fish in-store, but most of them had spoiled due to the warm weather.

The winter was proving equally hard for Holmes' hunters.

The hunting was poor, and some of them had been starving since the fall. There was little that Holmes could do to help given the poor state of his supplies, but on November 23rd, an Indian arrived who was very unwell and Holmes took him into the house to stay until he was recovered. One of his hunters, The Boss and his family, arrived at the house on December 13th scarcely able to walk because of hunger. They had no snowshoes or anything to make them with, and Holmes had to tell them that he was very sorry but he could not supply them with provisions of any kind as they were so short themselves. The next day, however, he gave The Boss a pair of snowshoes and some netting so that he could make his wife and children some snowshoes. He also gave them a little pounded meat that had gone moldy and would have been intended for the dogs. With no sign of an improvement in the state of the provisions at the house, Holmes was forced to turn away some of his hunters who arrived without providing them with any goods. The Knife arrived at the house on the 19th of the month with his family who were all starving. He said he had not killed anything since the fall when the lake froze over; Holmes traded the furs he brought in but only against the debt that he already owed.

On Christmas Day, the Knife's brother arrived. Holmes described him as being 'nearly dead with hunger'. Like many others, he had no snowshoes and no netting to make any, and he had not tasted anything but water for the last five days. Having given him shelter overnight, Holmes sent him back to The Knife's tent with a pair of snowshoes. The next two weeks saw the situation become even more critical as Nelson House became inundated with people seeking relief from their starvation. On December 30th, Mr Jack Donald, a fur trapper, arrived with his wife, who was the widow of a Mr Harper, together with two of their four children. Holmes described the children as being *'naked and almost hungered to death'* as the family had eaten nothing for the last seven days. They had been forced to leave two of their children about three miles away at the old houses, as they were too weak to walk. Holmes sent a man with a sledge to bring them in. With another six mouths to feed, Holmes realised that unless they were able to get more meat from their local hunters, with the poor state of the fishing and their stores of provision nearly expended, they were all facing starvation.

The first day of 1812 proved no relief from the hardships of the winter, and the local hunter who had arrived unwell on November 23rd died. Holmes recorded his passing in his journal entry with sadness but tempered this with a comment that the hunter had unfortunately died having only paid two half beavers of his debt of about thirty. The true horrors of starvation were brought into stark focus the following week when one of his hunters, The Nest, who he had not seen since the lake froze over, arrived at the house. The Nest had not brought anything to trade, and the only possession he carried was his hatchet. The horrific story he related of how he had survived the last months with no food shocked Holmes, to the extent that he recorded the man's account in full detail in his journal entry of January 8th:

'This day an Indian arrived called the Nest brought nothing but his Hatchet I have not seen him since open water in the fall. He informed me most shocking to relate that he was reduced to such extremity that he said he was obliged to kill his mother an old woman nothing but skin and bone and eat her in company with his wife and 2 children, he then killed the elder son a boy about 6 years aged, he then killed his other son an infant child suckling. Last of all killed his wife made pounded

meat of her that it might be lighter to carry he was perfect in his senses
he said he knew it was not right to act in the manner he had done but
if he had not done it he said he should have died'.

Despite Holmes' horror at hearing The Nest's story, he allowed him to remain at the house for over a month, but in the remainder of his journal entries referred to him as 'The Murderer' rather than The Nest. At the start of February, two boys arrived from Blue Coat's tent and White Bird's tent to ask Holmes to go to them to collect furs and a little meat from them. Holmes set off the next day with three men and a sledge each and reached Blue Coat's tent after a gruelling four-day trek, arriving on February 8th. They had very little food for the journey as the provisions at the house were all but expended, so they were all extremely fatigued by the time they reached their destination. Blue Coat appeared to have fared better than the other hunters over the winter. He had a plentiful store of moose flesh both for his family and to share with White Bird and his family, who had been near to death with starvation until they had the good fortune to come across Blue Coat, who they said had saved their lives. There were six hunters at the tents, and by Holmes' reckoning, two of them were the best hunters between Pelican Lake and Beaver Lake. Despite this, they had only thirty-eight whole beavers, fifteen half beavers, twenty-two otters, five black bears, a cat, five martens and one wolverine to trade between them. Holmes felt they had been put at a disadvantage this winter because the hunters who were trading with the Canadians at Cranberry Lake had broken up and destroyed many of the beaver houses in Blue Coat's hunting area.

Holmes and his men left for Nelson House the next day,

arriving home on the 12th very late at night and again very fatigued from the journey hauling their sledges through the ice and snow. The food situation at the house was still very poor, so on the next day, Holmes sent The Murderer and Jack Donald to the Blue Coat's tent as they had more in the way of provisions. However, given that there were already thirty-one people at Blue Coat's tent, he did not feel he could send Donald's wife and family, for he was afraid that still almost naked, they would not survive the journey. On February 23rd the son of The Knife arrived and said he had left some skins about a day's walk away as he was so starved he could not carry them any further. Holmes sent the men to collect the furs the next day and then, as the provisions were almost exhausted, sent The Knife's son and Mrs Donald and her four children away to Blue Coat's Tent. He wrote his journal on the 26th of February:

'This day sent the Indian away that arrived on the 23rd likewise Mr Harpers wife and 4 children almost naked it fretted me very much to see them in such distress'.

The winter was taking more victims amongst Holmes' hunters, and on the 29th a Canadian arrived from Cranberry Lake with the news that three men to whom Holmes had given debt in the fall had been found dead from starvation. The three had been reduced to eating all their beaver skins and their possessions, such as their snowshoes, the netting from the shoes and an old blanket tent but had finally succumbed. Whether Holmes was now becoming inured to the deaths of his hunters, or whether he was just concerned that his poor trading figures during the season would reflect badly on him, he recorded the deaths in his journal but strangely added the comment *'therefore I do not expect any skins from them this year'*.

March brought little relief from the privations of the winter, and hunters such as The Fathom, who arrived at the house on improvised snowshoes made from two pine boards, were still very short of food. The Fathom had left his wife some distance from the house as she was too weak to walk any further. News reached Holmes that The Bow, The Moose Hunter, The Flag and all their families were starving and had caught very little since the fall, with one of the men having died only three days after leaving Nelson House back in the fall.

At the start of April, events started to take a turn for the better as the hunters began to catch more game and bring it to the house to trade. The Moose Hunter and his family had survived the winter and been a little more successful in hunting, but only traded 93 lbs of green meat. The Blue Coat, on the other hand, was able to supply Holmes with two whole beavers, four half beavers, three parchment moose skins, 237 lbs of green meat and 28 lbs of pounded meat. The other hunters began to drift into the house, and gradually Holmes was able to build up his stock of provisions and trade an increasing number of skins and furs. The fishing in April was still poor and even with twenty nets in the water they caught one hundred and thirty-two less fish than the previous month. Holmes recorded that, without the little provisions that they obtained from the Indians *'we should have been very miserable indeed'*. The situation with regard to provisions remained poor during May, and Holmes was compelled to go out hunting himself, recording having shot five geese on May 19th. With little being brought in by the hunters, he sent six men and two of the women away to live at Stinking River where the fishing was alleged to be better, while the remaining men were planting potatoes and preparing the ground to plant cabbages. By the end of the month, the Narrows opposite the house had become free of ice and they had been able to get two nets set there for the first time that year. On June 8th part of the ice on the lake broke up and Holmes was able to get the people from Stinking Lake to return to the house.

The 1811 to 1812 season was drawing to an end, and the priority now was to prepare everything to ensure that the journey back to the factory was completed safely and without the loss of any of the traded goods. Holmes sent the boy François, six men, three women and five children in the boats to a place whose name he wrote phonetically, 'Puck-a-tar-war-gan', literally 'the fishing place' or 'the net fishing place'. This refers to Pukatawagan, a settlement on the Churchill River, northeast of Nelson House. There they were to catch fish and split and dry them to use as provisions on the journey down to the factory. Holmes was now down to a very meagre supply of provisions, consisting of a little very old pounded meat, and was worried that he had received no news from Deer Lake. This may have meant that the boats, which he expected to arrive from there to convey them back to the factory, had been delayed. Holmes had sent two men in a canoe over to Deer Lake to find out what was happening about the boats. They met the Deer Lake boats at Loon River and returned with them to Pukatawagan where they collected all those who had been preparing fish and returned them to Nelson House on June 27th with 150 lbs of dried fish.

On the last day of June, all the packing was completed, and three men were left to take care of the house with William Osman in charge. Holmes and all the rest of the party set off for the long journey to the factory at four o'clock in the afternoon and by nine o'clock in the evening had reached the second of the portages, where they camped overnight. Their journey over the next week took them through Grenville Lake, Indian Lake and Gods Lake. Each day was a repetition of launching the boats in the early hours of the morning, taking the boats out to carry them over portages and then launching again. By July 6th, the weather was beginning to deteriorate and they were forced to abandon their journey that day and set up camp on an island above Ten Falls. The next stage of the journey was delayed when Peter Knight's boat began to leak, and on July 9th, they had to set up camp early to try and repair it. Having completed the repair, they arrived at a series of four falls. The first three they ran in the boats, but at the fourth, they had to carry the boats and then sailed again until they reached the head of the Grand Falls. There they encountered enormous quantities of ice and had to lower one boat down the falls, with the men walking along the ice pulling the boat along with a long line. They only managed to get one boat down on the 9th and the next day Holmes sent Peter Knight and David Garson out on foot to walk down and report back on how far the ice extended. When the men returned, they said that they had never seen so much ice in the river before and Holmes described it in his journal entry: *'As far as the Lime Kiln there never was so much ice seen in the river in the memory of man at this season of the year.'*

Knight and Garson advised Holmes that they were doubtful whether they would be able to get the boats any further. Holmes decided to attempt continuing, and in a long, slow process they unloaded the boats and then lowered them one by one down the falls. They then tied a rope around each bundle of goods and lowered each of the bundles down into the boats. After a day's work lowering and reloading the boats, they set up camp at four o'clock in the afternoon, afraid of the risk of proceeding further as it grew dark. The next day was a repeat of the previous; unpacking the boats, lowering them over the next set of falls and then repacking the boats and sailing until nine o'clock at night when they set up camp at the Woody Islands, not far from the factory. Holmes' last entry in his journal for 1811 to 1812 records their safe arrival on Sunday, July 12th, 1812: *'Early this morning embarked and arrived at the factory at breakfast time*

John Pocock Holmes'.

Chapter 7

The Murderer

'God forgive me if I judge wrong but I am afraid they have been killing and eating each other'

On July 29th, 1812, Holmes set off at eleven o'clock in the morning from Churchill Factory to make the return journey to Nelson House, his expedition consisting of two boats with twelve men and Mr Williams and Peter Knight. The journey was to prove difficult and take over a month to complete. On the first day, the expedition was beset by fog, and they were forced to set up camp at four o'clock in the afternoon, having only journeyed some five miles from the factory. The days were long and the terrain hazardous, with their day starting at three or four in the morning when they would break camp and set off with the two boats and all their goods. If the weather proved satisfactory, then they would continue until nine at night when they would set up camp and make ready for the next day. On a good day, like August 2nd, with the weather and the river not causing them problems, they could make thirty-four miles in a day. On a bad day such as they encountered on August 5th, they made as little as half a mile. The rivers and lakes were still frozen in places, and they encountered parts of the journey where the men had to carry the goods, wading through ice-cold water and negotiating overhanging ice flows.

After a week of walking, pulling the canoes and sometimes

sailing, they reached the Swallow Falls on Friday, August 7th. One of the canoes, which Peter Knight was steering, had been taking on water all the way from Churchill Factory, and on August 9th Holmes made the decision to unload all the goods from the canoe and take it out of the water to inspect it. They could not find any area of damage and started the laborious job of reloading it. The delay in doing this was compounded by the change in the weather the next day when a rainstorm forced them to halt for three hours, and at six o'clock in the afternoon, they gave up the struggle and camped, still in the rain, at the foot of Four Falls. The next stage of the journey involved an area with ten sets of falls to negotiate. This meant slow progress, and the continuing rain and a strong headwind meant that it took them five days to complete. Setting up camp at two in the afternoon of August 15th after leaving Ten Falls, they now faced a run of five falls which they reached after a further three days, having endured constant rain on some days and strong headwinds on others. The passage through these five falls took them three days. They then had relief as they entered a run of open river and were able to abandon carrying and pulling the boats in favour of sailing from five in the morning till late in the evening, spending the night some six miles above the Sandy Lakes on Saturday, August 22nd. Peter Knight's boat was still leaking, so with a further run of rapids ahead, they unloaded the boat, upturned it and caulked her in the hope of sealing any damaged area. On Tuesday, August 25th they were just approaching the rapids when Peter Knight's boat again took in water. After starting off at five o'clock in the morning, they were forced to stop three hours later to once more unload the boat and try to caulk her again. The prospect of running the rapids with a boat that was not watertight was too much of a risk, and Holmes decided to halt and try and remedy the problem. He recorded the day in his journal with some obvious pride at his own skill:

'Embarked at 5 am arrived at the rapid about a mile from where we embarked we were obliged to disload Peter Knights Boat again and caulk her at 8am loaded and embarked arrived at the… Rapid

Peter Knights Boat still leaky Carried and Launched embarked again pulled against a strong head wind under the lee of an island In the lake above… rapid disloaded the boat again

I am obliged to take on examining the boat I found a seam that had been staved in caulking at the Factory I cut out the board & put a new piece in I caulked it the boat has been thankfully tight ever since.'

Now the boat was repaired the journey went more smoothly, although continuing days of wind and rainstorms meant that some of their days were spent sheltering rather than sailing. However, they were able to sail for the next five days until Sunday, August 30th, when they reached a portage and an area known as the Twenty Pound Rapids, which necessitated more carrying and pulling of the canoes. They had now been travelling for a month and had not seen any other human life for all that time, but on the following day, they encountered their first Indians since leaving the factory. A group of four arrived while Holmes and his men were approaching the Stinking River. They were headed for the French House to trade skins, but Holmes recognised them and insisted that their skins were indebted to him from a hunter named Tooth and took from them eight swan skins, two beaver skins and five pounds of dry meat scraps. Nelson House was now only a day's journey away, and the Northern Indians decided to accompany Holmes and his men to the house. They reached Nelson House safely on September 1st, after thirty-four days of arduous journeying covering some five hundred miles. Arriving at Nelson House at ten in the morning, Holmes found all was well with one exception, which he reported in his journal:

'found all well except Mr Stayner's daughter who died on the last day of July with a pain in the head & stomach'.

This rather detached comment fails to acknowledge that this girl was the third daughter of Thomas Stayner and Ke-che-cow-e-com-coot, Holmes' wife, and therefore technically Holmes' stepdaughter. Stayner had taken the older daughters to England with him when he left Hudson Bay but had left the other daughter with her mother.

The business of trading and moving supplies to outposts was soon back into its normal routine, with Holmes dispatching men with goods for Deer Lake. He tried to persuade the Northern Indians who had followed them to Nelson House to return to Deer Lake, but they were afraid to do so because of the Canadians there, who would not appreciate them having changed allegiance from them to the Hudson's Bay Company. Holmes gave them some debt and extracted a promise from them that they would go over to Churchill Factory in the spring and resume trade there. On September 5th two of Holmes' men arrived back from the tent of Blue Coat with supplies of meat and fat, and later that day another hunter, Red Coat, arrived with a considerable quantity of meat, fat and skins. In addition to the trade, Red Coat also brought news from Deer Lake that angered Holmes. He documented the reasons for his anger in some detail:

'September 6th

The Indians that arrived yesterday informed me that William Loutitt one of the Deers Lake men had taken a woman to wife belonging Andrew Kirkness at this house.

She went with the Indians to live till her husband should arrive I told him at the Houses he was not to have a wife. It was my orders from Mr Auld not to let him have one of any description But in spite of all he had the impudence to take one in consequence of which I was obliged to send William Osman and Francis Laird to fetch her back gave them 7 days provisions which I shall charge to his account Likewise 2 men at 2s 6d per day till they returned which I think he deserves to pay for his impudence it will likewise be a check to others to make them obey their masters orders in future.'

The instruction from Auld about William Loutitt taking a wife *of any description* seem to be specific to William as there had been no objection to Andrew Kirkness having taken a wife. There was no specific ruling from the Hudson's Bay Company about taking a local wife, but the company was concerned at the growing expense of supporting wives and families, and in 1810 had introduced a new form of accounting to try and limit the drain on the profits from this source. The situation with Andrew Kirkness and his wife was, however, a little complicated. The couple were expert fishers, and in the past, Hudson's Bay Posts had been reliant on their expertise to catch enough fish for the traders to survive. In 1810, Andrew and his wife Margaret were at the Hudson's Bay Post at Ile la Crosse, and in July they had an argument which resulted in her leaving the post and going to the North West Company post on her own. A week later, Peter Fidler, the Master at Ile la Crosse, sent two men to the French House to try and persuade Margaret to return. She told them she could not, as the Canadians had threatened to cut off her ears if she tried to leave. The Canadians had realised that Margaret was an expert at fishing and believed that if they could ruin the Hudson Bay's fishing, then the post would have to close. In addition to holding Margaret by threats, they also cut Peter Fidler's nets and made sure he could not access the better fishing areas. Andrew Kirkness was not able to bear separation from his wife, and in the early hours of August 4th, he deserted from the Hudson's Bay Company and took up a post with the North West Company as a fisherman working again with Margaret.

After six months with the Canadians, Andrew wanted to return to work with Fidler at Ile la Crosse, but the Canadians told him that if he tried to leave *they would make every Canadian in the house ravish his woman before his eyes'.*

Three days after this threat, Andrew left the Canadians and returned to Ile la Crosse but without his wife, who had been made to remain following more threats from the Canadians. She did attempt to escape on June 4th but was recaptured outside the post and forced to return to the Canadian House. Fidler and his men, including Andrew Kirkness, were in the final stages of leaving for Churchill Fort at this time, and Margaret was left behind at the Canadian House.

The repeated pressure from the North West Company soon forced the HBC London Committee to order the closure of Ile La Crosse, and in the spring of 1811, it was abandoned. The NWC completed its destruction in the autumn of that year by setting all the buildings on fire. At what point Margaret returned to the Hudson's Bay post is not recorded, but she had been sent to Deer Lake to await the return of her husband from Churchill Factory and had taken up with William Loutitt over the intervening period since Andrew left for Churchill. Holmes would be concerned that, if he failed to resolve the situation, then Andrew might once more leave to be with his wife, depriving Nelson House of their expert fisherman. The men that he had sent to fetch back Margaret returned six days later on September 12th, having persuaded her to return to her husband. Holmes documented the charge he would make to William Loutitt's account in great detail:

'Osman and François 28 lbs of provisions at 6d per pound which comes to 14s 2d.

2 men 7 days labour at 2s 6d per day comes to £2 9s all added together'.

Holmes sent out Kirkness and his wife on September 16th to fish for the house. They returned a day later with thirty white fish, and Holmes ordered that all the nets at the house should be taken up as, even with eight nets, no fish were being caught and he wished the fishing to be concentrated on the fishing places that Andrew and his wife were using.

Holmes' post at Nelson House was opposed by the Canadians, but there were also traders of his own company who were a threat to his trade and endeavoured to persuade his traders to change their allegiance to them. Holmes had several years of experience in dealing with the local hunters and had the advantage of good records and a good memory for old debts. On September 27th a hunter by the name of Mist See arrived at the house, and Holmes recalled that he had given him a debt of good cloth and a blanket in the autumn of 1811, which was equivalent to twenty-six beavers and was still unpaid. Also, the man had a debt of fifty beavers, twenty-seven of which were due to Adam Snoddie and the other twenty-three to someone unknown to Holmes. Since giving Mist See the debt, Holmes had not seen or heard of him and questioned him as to why he had been away from the house so long. It appeared that Mist See had met up with another hunter known as Full Grown Beaver who was trading with Mr Robert Spencer, who wintered at Little Three Points, close to Nelson House. They met up with Mr Spencer, who asked Mist See to trade with him, despite knowing that he was indebted to Holmes and others. When he was met with a refusal, Spencer plied Mist See with brandy until he was intoxicated and then completed a trade for a black beaver parchment, twelve whole and one half beaver, and two jasmine otters. Spencer had informed Mist See that this trade was worth twenty made beavers. Holmes was incensed by this behaviour, particularly regarding getting Mist See intoxicated to make him complete the trade. He made a note in his journal, which was phrased to bring the Company's attention to his concerns:

'He traded them for brandy to my knowledge it is not the first time Mr R Spencer as been guilty of this most shameful trafficking of trading skins belonging to others. This time Mr Spencer can have no excuses for acting in such a shameful or indeed rascally mannered quiet alone no one to molest him by doing so he hurt my trade perhaps my character too but more so your honourable company who must pay for all it is impossible for me or any other persons to make profit in this short times —

While I have the French to contend with on my right hand and Mr Robert Spencer and John Robertson on my left'.

Robert Spencer's trading methods, which included attempting to trade with hunters belonging to fellow traders, offering them bribes of cloth coats if they changed their allegiance to trade with him and using brandy to intoxicate them, angered Holmes. He had reached the point where he declared that he would take the first opportunity to inform William Auld, the superintendent, of Spencer's behaviour and was sure that Auld would be *'highly offended'*.

The supply of provisions at the house continued to concern Holmes. Over the three months from June, they had only caught one thousand one hundred and twenty white fish and four hundred and thirty-five of better quality and he continued to trade small amounts of dry scraps of meat. In an attempt to boost their supply of fish, he sent three men away to fish at Pukatawagan on Monday, October 12th, the very same day Andrew Kirkness returned from Stinking River to report that the fishing there had completely failed. William Osman and Thomas Falkland, two of the men he sent away to Pukatawagan returned on the 19th bringing three hundred and thirty-nine white fish. The journey down from the fishing place to the house involved travelling over the portages. Holmes sent the two back with orders to leave a canoe on the portages so that when Holmes sent men up in a boat to collect the fish, they could use the canoe to paddle across the open water to bring down the fish. When Holmes sent five men to collect the fish some three days later, they found there was no canoe on the portages. The lake had frozen over, and the men at the fishing place could not carry the canoe over the ice. It was not possible to launch the boat, so the men had to return empty-handed. The fishing at the house was not proving sufficient to meet their needs, providing only one hundred and fifty-five white fish and two hundred and fifty-four of all other kinds over the month, and the lake had now frozen over. Holmes sent two men with a tent across the lake to the site of the old houses to see if the fishing was better there. The nets were taken up from the frozen lake, and Francis Laid and his brother Nelson were sent on November 6th to Pukatawagan with three sledges to tell the men there to return immediately with their nets and to secure what fish they left stored there to avoid them being ravaged by animals. The men arrived back from Pukatawagan six days later with the news that they had stored four hundred white fish, and four hundred of other kinds, and in the evening of that day, the two men arrived back from the old houses bringing back their tent and two hundred white fish and four hundred and twenty-four of other sorts. The fish that they had caught this month were now in store in preparation for the next two months when provisions were going to be scarce. The hunters who arrived at the house were now getting short of food, and on November 26th the man called The Boss arrived from Red Coat's tent. He was starving and only had five beaver parchments, a half brown bear skin and one cub, four otters and three common cats to trade. Holmes provided him with a pair of snowshoes, a sledge, some ammunition, ten fish and a little pounded meat and sent him back to Red Coat's tent.

At the start of December, Holmes sent David Garson and the boy François with three sledges and ten dogs to bring back some of the fish stores from Pukatawagan. They arrived back four days later with three hundred and twenty sizeable white fish. The next day, Red Coat and his family arrived. They too were starving and had only brought three beavers, one marten and a few pairs of castoreum, which are the product of the oil glands of the beaver and had been used since the time of Hippocrates in the preparation of a number of medicines. The situation for the local hunters was becoming serious, and Red Coat was ill with a large swelling in his side. Holmes sent his men back to Pukatawagan to collect the remaining fish and ordered them to take Red Coat back with them on a sledge as he could not walk, and to give him and his family two hundred fish and as many heads of jack fish as they wanted. When the men returned, they brought back a further two hundred fish, this brought the number of fish in store to one thousand four hundred and sixty-seven white fish excluding two hundred large jack fish.

With the winter set in, few traders were visiting the house, and Holmes made no trade for the whole of January 1813. The fishing had been poor, and a neighbouring trader, Mr Campbell, had relied on Holmes for fish as he was very badly off for provisions of all kinds. The winter was one of the worst that Holmes had encountered, and the Indians were suffering greatly from lack of food and poor hunting. On February 10th, a messenger arrived from Blue Coat's tent to tell Holmes that they had not found any beaver over the winter and to report that he had found a man starved to death. The features of the corpse were so disfigured by starvation that he could scarcely identify him but thought it was a son of The Rabbit. Holmes sent the men with a sledge each to Blue Coat's tent to collect any flesh and skins they may have. When they returned the next day, they had brought back 200 lbs of green meat, sixteen beaver skins, seventy-three cats and three otters. These were not from Blue Coat but were left there by the three northern traders that Holmes had met on the journey to the house back in September when he had given them debt and sent them back to York Factory. The men reported that there were few hunters at Blue Coat's tent, which formerly had anywhere from ninety to a hundred there.

Holmes was seeing an increasing number of his traders coming to the house in a starved condition and could do little but give them some limited supplies and send them on their way. On February 12th a son of The Knife arrived at the house. He was so starved that Holmes described him as *'nothing but skin and bone'*. The boy said he had left his mother on the portages about seven miles from the house and that she was not able to manage the remaining journey to the house. Holmes sent a man with two dogs and a sledge, a morsel to eat and a blanket to fetch her to the house. When she arrived, she could not stand, and they were obliged to carry her into the house. She was clothed in little but rags, which were not sufficient to keep her protected from the cold. She told Holmes that her husband The Knife was hunting in the Burntwood Lake and she had left two children back at their tent who had nearly died for want of food; she did not expect to find them alive when she returned. The man that had been found dead on the 10th of the month was one from their tent, and she thought there were a further four from the tent who had died from starvation and three who were not able to walk.

Holmes was suspicious of the unusually high number of deaths and recorded in his journal on February 12th: *'God forgive me if I judge wrong but I am afraid they have been killing and eating each other'*.

His fears that the hunters had resorted to cannibalism were at this point conjecture, but there was a common belief that this behaviour, although rare, did occur during times of starvation in the Cree Nation. However, the Cree believed that people who committed such a crime had turned into a Witiko or evil monster, and they should be pursued and killed. Holmes' suspicions of cannibalism would have been heightened by the events of three years previous at James Bay when a Hudson's Bay expedition ran short of supplies having travelled from Rupert House to establish a new trading post. No news was heard of them over the winter, and in the spring a Cree hunter and his wife were sent out from Rupert House to locate them. When they reached the site of the expedition camp, they found only one survivor, the wife of one of the three men in the expedition, Mrs Henry Swanson. On the journey back to Rupert House, Mrs Swanson was said to have become deranged, and the Cree hunter claimed he had killed her in self-defence. A second search party set out to locate the other three missing men of the expedition, Peter White, his wife and William Laughton. White was found to have starved to death, but Laughton had been killed by a Cree hunter who discovered him living off human flesh. Alexander Christie, the superintendent of Rupert House, recorded that he believed that the Cree had murdered both Laughton and Mrs Swanson and would kill even their closest relative *'when they know of their having been reduced to the dreadful necessity of eating human flesh.'*

Holmes had sent The Knife's family back to their tent on February 26th with as much fish and pounded meat as he could spare. His concerns about the real reason for all the deaths increased when on Sunday, April 14th, The Knife's son returned and brought the news that six more had died at their tent. News also arrived that a woman had eaten her mother at Lake La Ronge. The hunting in the area was very poor, and Blue Coat, who arrived at the house on March 20th, said he had only a few skins and some meat at his tent and had only seen two beaver houses since his last visit. Holmes sent four men with sledges to collect the furs and meat from Blue Coat, and when they returned, they had only five beaver, 130 lbs of pounded meat and 164 lbs of green meat. The Bow arrived on March 28th and Holmes followed him to his tent and came back with a further 133 lbs of green meat, 100 lbs of pounded meat, eleven beavers, two martens and three prime otters. The food situation at the house continued to be a problem and another bad month of fishing meant they were short of supplies. Furthermore, because the weather had warmed up, they were not able to store the fish as they had in the winter.

The poor hunting conditions and the lack of food meant that the Indians were being forced into trading with often unscrupulous company traders on poor terms, to ensure that they could get at least some provisions. The wife of a hunter known as The English Talker arrived at the house on April 3rd. Holmes had not seen this family since the fall and enquired as to where they had been. He was incensed to find that they had been to 'Little Three Pointe' where Mr John Robertson traded. The English Talker had only got three martens to trade but cut a beaver skin out of his own coat and traded that to John Robertson. His son had eight parchment beavers, six martens and two deer skins to trade also. The deal that John Robertson made was of brandy, tobacco and ammunition and he had taken the skins for his house when he knew they were owed to Holmes. Worried about his poor trading and what he saw as dishonourable behaviour by John Robertson, he expressed his feeling forcibly in his journal entry of April 3rd:

'If Mr Robertson persists in this kind of traffick or is allowed to do it I shall give up and return home to England such trading as this ought not to be suffered... The truth is if Mr Robertson had acted like the honest man to his company he would have supplied the Indians

with what was sufficient and charged it to Nelson House account. I
have a most miserable trade this year so I may with so many oppositions
but if I had traded part of the Beavers that the Northern Indians
brought here as Mr Robertson has done I should had a tolerable Trade
but if I cannot get a good name as a trader in an honest way I shall
remain as I am an honest trader. Even supposing trading these few
skins did not hurt the company nevertheless it spoils the Indians for
instance one of my Indians comes in with his skins by some accident
or other I affront him in company of which he immediately goes in to
another house and says I am not the only English man in the Country
if he got no encouragement he would not do it.'

Over the next week, a succession of northern hunters arrived at the house all wishing to trade with Holmes. Despite his poor trading over the season, he stuck to his principles and informed them all that he could not trade with them as their furs were owed to Churchill Factory. He agreed to provide them with anything they needed within reason, which he would charge to the factory account, but they must take their trade down to the factory. In acting in accordance with what he felt was his duty, Holmes had turned down the chance of trading to his account a total of one hundred and ten whole beavers, thirty-eight half beavers, one hundred and fifteen pairs of castoreum, thirteen martens, three prime otters and one bear. He documented this all in full, highlighting the contrast between his trading ethics and those of Messrs. Robertson and Spencer. On April 23rd the wife of The Knife arrived back at the house, still in a state of starvation. Holmes gave her provisions and ammunition and told her to go back to her tent and return with her children to live at the house until her husband had completed his spring hunting. She arrived back at the house a week later with her daughter and her eight-year-old son. Holmes called the boy into the house and questioned him about the number of people dying at their tent. Holmes told the boy that if he told him everything that he knew of the deaths, then he would be rewarded with sugar. The boy then recounted to Holmes that there had only been three people who died a natural death and four who had died of starvation, but that the other seven had been killed and eaten by his father, The Knife. The boy added that one of the women killed and eaten had been one of The Knife's wives. Holmes called in the boy's mother and told her what the boy had said, but she flatly denied it. Holmes decided to wait until The Knife returned from his hunting when he would question him directly about the deaths.

With an increasing number of mouths to feed at the house and very poor fishing, Holmes decided to send all the men and women over to Stinking Lake to live until the lake opened up and fishing improved. They remained there for a week until the ice on the lake started to break up, and Holmes then moved them to Pukatawagan as they had caught very few fish at Stinking River, and there were none to be had at the house. They were instructed to split and dry as many fish as they could to provide a store for the summer. Holmes remained at the house and on May 23rd, 1813 recorded in his journal that they had nothing to eat apart from dry pounded meat and had caught no fish worth mentioning, apart from a few grey carp. On May 24th, he heard the Canadians were planning to leave the next day. Concerned that they would plunder any of his goods that they found, Holmes sent William Osman and one Indian in a small canoe to secure anything that his traders may have in the way of trade near the Burnt Wood Portages where the Canadians would travel through. His information proved correct, and on the next day, the Canadians left to journey down to Cumberland House. Having kept a close eye on them during the season, he was confident that at most they had traded only fifty skins. On the last day of May, he was visited by The Knife, the man he had suspected of cannibalism earlier in the year. He confronted him with the information he had been given by the son, but The Knife denied all of the allegations. Holmes however remained convinced that the events had occurred, and sent him away to the North River, which was in the York Factory District. Holmes was sure that if The Knife remained in the Rat River vicinity, the others would capture him and kill him and his family. Holmes only allowed him to take two of his three wives and kept one of them at Rat River.

The season was over at Nelson House, and Holmes wrote his final entry for the season in his journal on the 31st of May: '*My Trade miserable indeed the extreme Indians that used formerly to kill 50, 60, 30, 100 have only killed 8, 10, 15 and the higher only 59. I am in hopes the Canadians will very soon be asked to leave the country, if that should take place as bad as the Rat River is profit would be made.*'

Holmes was to remain in charge at Nelson House for the next season of 1813-14, and on June 1st he opened a new journal book and started his entries for the season.

The start of the season went well on the first day, with thirteen traders arriving together with their wives, all with furs to trade. They brought forty whole beavers, forty half beavers, one hundred and forty-five rats, two black bears, two bear cubs, four moose skins, and one otter. Holmes had not seen three of the Indians since he had traded with them in the fall, and they reported that they were finding very few beavers. Over the next four days, seven northern hunters arrived, and by the end of the week, he had more than doubled the number of furs that he had traded. These trades were to the factory account, and he limited his trading to supplying a little tobacco and ammunition. The people he had sent away to Pukatawagan earlier in May arrived back on June 17th, and Holmes prepared the bundles of furs to go down to the factory. On June 21st, he sent the boats off to the factory with Mr John Sutherland, Holmes having been instructed to overwinter at Nelson House.

The success of Holmes' trading in June meant that his supplies of trading goods were becoming depleted, so he sent two Indians off to Deer Lake for more supplies. They left on June 18th and arrived back eleven days later bringing 8 lbs of tobacco and 5 lbs of powder. The trade with his hunters was poor in July, with only one coming to the house with fat, pounded meat and dry scraps. He was very unwell, and Holmes allowed him to remain at the house for almost two weeks until he recovered, leaving on August 2nd. August proved a better month for trading, with hunters arriving every week. While this was good for Holmes' trading figures, it proved a further drain on his supplies, and on August 21st he recorded his concerns in the journal:

'This day supplied the Indians with Tobacco Brandy, Ammunition & sent them away. If any more Indians should arrive I shall be at a great loss for want of Powder Tobacco and Brandy I have only one pint of spirits in the house not a single load of powder and only about ½ lb of tobacco & small twist of my own and the boats have been from here 62 days and they generally go and return in 50 days.'

During September, Holmes traded once or twice a week at most and gained little in the way of furs and skins. Towards the end of the month, the Canadian traders arrived from the portages, having travelled back from Cumberland House. They had very little goods with them and no blankets, only Buffalo Robes. It appeared that they were going to abandon Nelson House and spend the winter at Indian Lake. When the boats arrived back from their journey to Churchill Factory, they brought back some of the supplies that Holmes had requested but also a letter from Thomas Topping complaining about some of Holmes' trading practices:

'*Churchill Factory 25th July 1813*

Mr J Holmes

Sir

Mr Sutherland with the two Batteaux arrived here on the 5th Inst. By whom we received your acct. papers etc with the Furs collection at Nelson House, we now send you the Goods indented for as per Invoice with various papers containing the amount of your Trade etc.

Upon making up your accounts we cannot help remarking that your expenses far exceeds for the quantity of Furs procured now, that of 1812 when your Trade was considerably larger and in the article of Ice Chisels in 1812 you expended only 5 Chisels and this year in the column expenses we found 66 are deficient, we will thank you to explain the cause of so many being disposed of this year by the first opportunity.

The Northern Indians going to Nelson House are getting debt, this has hurt this Factory very much, they ought by no means to be encouraged to do it and should they persist no debt ought to be given only a little ammunition to make them to reach the factory and without you receive further orders we do hereby request you will use the utmost of your power when you see or hear the Factory North Indians or those who trade with Mr Sutherland to send them to this Factory and on no account to give any debt to any one of them on Nelson House account.

If it is absolutely necessary to leave the present House on account of firewood or living. We have no objection up your going to Puc ka ta wa gan but without real necessity we could wish it was deferred for another year.

The enormous prices of all the Goods must point to you how absolutely requisite it is that the greatest frugality should be exerted by us all. In every department and any post which does not pay its expenses and yield a profit also will not be worth keeping up.

The Goods you debted The Northern Indians with are now sent up and not charged against you so that your remains will remain correct.

We have received a few Furs from Mr Snoddie, and have sent you a list of them, that you may credit the natives who have them.

We here fervently desire that you will send down next summer 24 Hatchet helms for the use of the Factory and the same quantity each year following.

Andrew Kirkhough, may stop at his old wages £20. Per annum or he can return home, we have sent your letters to the superintendent for his inspection and shall defer making any comment on your disposal of Samuel Taylor's property for the present, but it was strange you deferred taking an account of them until the evening of the day after you arrived although you had positive orders to the contrary.

Mr Cameron Costello, writer, is sent up to stay at Nelson House and to render you every assistance he can.

Your changing the manner of keeping the accounts of Twine from Skeines to Pounds I cannot conceive the reason for and beg you will make no alteration on keeping your account without orders.

Wishing you a more successful Trade and plenty of Provision.

I remain Sir your most obedient serv.
Signed Thos. Topping.'

The remarks about his trading with the Northern Indians appear harsh, given that in the Spring, Holmes had declined trade with them and instructed them that they must trade with the factory. This was despite the problems he was having with Mr Robertson and his generally weak trade figures. A second letter from Thomas Topping revealed that the factory had decided to send Mr Clouston Dickinson to live alongside the Northern Indians as an 'outhouse' of the factory, and the letter reinforced the message from that sent in July:

'Churchill Factory 28ᵗʰ August 1813
  Sir,
  The Compy. Ship Prince of Wales Capt Turner under convoy of his Magesty Frigate Brazen Capt. Stirling anchored in the River on the 18ᵗʰ Inst. And sorry I am to tell you the Typhus fever is very bad on board the Prince.
  We have sent you the letters and a copy of the price of Furs for your Government & have sent Clouston Dickinson to settle belong the North Indians as an outhouse from this Factory, you will therefore upon no account interfere with the Northern Indians and should any of them come to your House you must give them every discouragement and send them to Clouston Dickson's House which is established on purpose for their accommodation.
  Mr Sutherland's Nephew is sent up to go to him you will therefore forward him in a canoe with either two Englishmen, or an Englishman & an Indian to Deers Lake immediately.
  The Company having consented to my request to return to England,

I have to inform you that Mr John Charles is appointed to succeed me.
   Wishing you health, plenty & success I remain etc.
   Yours Sincerely
   Signed Thos Topping
   Mr J P Holmes
   Nelson House'

On September 6th, 1813, Holmes and Betsy's second child Elizabeth was born. There was no record made in Holmes' journal of the event, she is however recorded as having been born at *'one of the Hudson's Bay Co's. posts in the interior'*. It is not clear from the journal whether Betsy was living elsewhere when Elizabeth was born. If so, Holmes would not have been aware of the event at the time. However, in a document completed in 1870, Elizabeth gave her place of birth as Nelson River, so it seems that she was born at Nelson House, but Holmes chose not to record the event in the journal. This was not unusual amongst the Hudson's Bay Officers. Peter Fidler, for instance, kept a separate private notebook in which he recorded the details of the births of his fourteen children rather than recording them in the post journals.

The fishing that month was poor, despite having twelve nets in the water, so Holmes sent three men to Pukatawagan to pole fish, and gave them orders to make sure and send the boat back down with the fish before the lake became set with ice. The winter was beginning to make conditions challenging, and at the start of October Holmes tried to persuade some of the hunters to go to Deer Lake in a small canoe to take letters and reports for the factory. They refused, as they believed that although the water was still open, it would soon freeze over and they would not be able to return. Instead, Holmes gave them tobacco and ammunition and sent them to Granville Lake, as he suspected that three of his hunters there were planning to go and trade with the Canadians at Indian Lake. The men were unable to find the hunters but returned to say they had seen a mark that signified that they were not going to the Canadians. The lake was now showing signs of freezing over, so Holmes sent a boat up to Pukawatagan on October 17th to bring back the men and their catch. They arrived at Nelson House two days later with a boat full of fish but had left a large quantity as it would not fit into the boat. The lake by now had a lot of ice, and when hunters arrived to trade on October 21st, they were not able to cross the lake and sent smoke signals from the other side of the lake to attract attention. They had left their canoes about two days' walk away, and Holmes sent a boat across to collect them and their furs and then sent them away the next day. A week later the lake froze over completely.

The winter was again causing hardship to the locals, and they were finding it difficult to hunt enough to get food. On November 19th the old wife of The Knife arrived at the house to say they were starving and had nothing to eat and nothing to trade. Holmes gave her some fish, a sledge and a pair of snowshoes and sent her back to her tent. Ten days later another old woman arrived starving and lame, and Holmes allowed her to stay at the house in the hope she would recover. He could not, however, accommodate all those who arrived in a state of starvation, and as with two who arrived starving on December 1st, he was only able to give them a night's stay and then send them away the next day with tobacco and snowshoes. The river through to Pukatawagan was still free of ice, and on December 1st, François came down the river to inform Holmes that since the lake had frozen over, they had not been able to catch much fish. Holmes sent him back with a message that the men should return and bring the nets and any fish they may have caught. They arrived four days later with the nets and fifty-six white fish, twelve of other kinds and over a thousand that were not fit for use and which Holmes described as *'rubbish'*.

While the Canadians had abandoned Nelson House and moved to Indian Lake in September, they were still a threat to trade. Holmes was keen to ensure that they gained as little information as possible as to where his hunters were and where the Hudson's Bay Company traders were spending the winter. His suspicions were raised when on December 14th, two of the Canadians from Indian Lake arrived claiming that they had come to collect two dogs that they had left at Nelson House in the fall. Holmes rather supposed that they were more interested in finding out what trade he was doing. However, having spoken to them, he believed that they did not know that Hudson's Bay Company had set up a post for the winter a little below them at Indian Lake.

The last two weeks of 1813 saw some trade done, although this was mainly skins and furs and little in the way of meat or provisions, and many of the hunters were still arriving saying that they were starving. When Holmes calculated the fishing total for December, they had been more successful than the previous months of the winter with one thousand two hundred and ninety-nine white fish and one thousand six hundred and fifty-five of all other kinds.

Holmes' health had been suffering during the year, and he had decided to make a request to be allowed to return to England at the earliest opportunity. As the Hudson's Bay ships only sailed once a year, this would not be until the summer of 1814. HBC considered his request and the Hudson's Bay records show that this was agreed: *As ill health is the reason of Mr H. wishing to return we hope the Honble Co. will consent to his recall. Allowed'*.

The first month of 1814 saw the arrival of two northern traders who brought in otters and some green meat, which was to be traded to the Deer Lake account. Holmes gave them some tobacco and ammunition and informed them that William Auld had set up his post at Indian Lake so that in future, they should take their trade to him. He made sure to tell them that when they did want to trade, they should take care not to go anywhere near the Canadians at Indian Lake as Auld's post was at Letter Point, only a day's walk below the Canadians, who were not aware that he was there. Later in the month, Holmes sent Indians across the Lake to hunt at some beaver houses, but they did not catch anything. The people who he had been allowing to stay at the house as they were starving when they arrived had recovered, and he sent them away with provisions to hunt for themselves. One of them had been at the house since November 20th.

February saw virtually no trade being done, only one hunter arrived, and he had brought only twelve whole beavers, seven half beavers, one brown beaver, a marten and one mink. Holmes gave him tobacco and ammunition and sent him back to his tent. With little trade having been done and another month of poor fishing, supplies at the house were running low. By March, the hunters were beginning to make regular visits to the house, bringing not only furs and skins but also supplies of green meat. Some of those who arrived were still starving and had been unwell all winter and unable to hunt. By the end of March and with another poor month of fishing, Holmes recorded that their stocks of fresh fish were almost finished. Over the next two months, as the weather improved, the visits from the hunters became more frequent, with one or two arriving every week. By now they were able to supply good quantities of pounded meat and green meat as the hunting improved.

On May 26th, Holmes set off to Deer Lake in a canoe that he had made in the spring. He took the boy, François, and the nephew of Mr Sutherland with him. The purpose of the trip was to take the packet of letters and papers that should have gone to the factory in the fall. Holmes had not sent it then as Mr Sutherland, when he returned from the factory in August, had informed him that no packet should be sent in the fall. The letter from Thomas Topping in August 1813 had ordered Holmes to send Sutherland's nephew to Deer Lake immediately. This had not been possible because the route had been blocked by ice since September, and even the locals had refused to make the journey. Edward Mowatt was left in charge of the house, and the rest of the men were sent to Pukatawagan to fish with orders to leave as soon as the Canadians did. The journey to Deer Lake was made difficult by bad weather and took seven days, and Holmes did not return to the house until June 12th.

It was now time for Holmes to start making preparations to return to the factory, there to join a schooner which would take him to meet the boat to sail back to England. The men arrived back from Pukatawagan on June 21st, and on the same day, the boat from Deer Lake with Messrs. Sutherland and Richardson arrived, ready to make the journey down to the factory. Holmes left Edward Mowatt in charge and arranged with the hunters that they should continue to trade with Nelson House. He set off on June 25th taking Mr Costello with him and arrived at Churchill Factory on July 5th, 1814, after an uneventful journey, ready to start his voyage back to England.

Chapter 8

A Return to England?

1814 Churchill House

The Churchill House journal kept by Mr Charles recorded Holmes' arrival on July 5th, 1814:

'Late in the evening Messrs. Sutherland, Holmes & Costello arrived from Inland with 19 men in 3 boats'.

The schooner that journeyed between York Factory and Churchill Factory on a regular basis was to take Holmes to York Factory to embark on his voyage home late in September, so Holmes spent the two months at Churchill House waiting for its departure. He was to be accompanied home by Mr Costello, who had come down from Nelson House with him in July. On September 20th, early in the evening, Holmes and Mr Leslie, who was travelling to York Factory to give evidence to William Auld with regard to a dispute concerning Mr Charles, boarded the schooner. Mr Costello had gone up river a few days previously and had not returned, so the schooner set sail in the early hours of the next day without him on board. The schooner was not able to get out of the mouth of the river because the winds were too light. In the afternoon the two men who had gone to fetch Costello arrived, so they took him over to the schooner where he boarded ready to sail as soon as the winds were favourable. However, the wind and weather deteriorated over the next day, and the schooner had to return to its anchorage opposite the Sloops Cove, a situation which Mr Charles described as:'*the more mortifying by the wind being as fair as it can blow if the vessel was only out of the Rivers mouth so that it is only Foul wind in the River*'.

The weather continued to be poor, and the ship sent Mr Leslie over in a boat for more supplies in case they should be delayed on their passage. Eventually, on September 24th, the wind shifted, and four days late the schooner set off for York Factory to rendezvous with the Hudson's Bay ship bound for England with Holmes on board, heading for York Factory and then onward to England.

It was four weeks later on October 16th, late in the evening, that the men at Churchill Factory noticed a fire had been lit across the river. They assumed this was lit to signal them that someone was in need of help, but the weather was so bad they were not able to send a boat that night. The next day a boat was sent across the river which returned carrying Mr Holmes, Mr Leslie and six other men who had all left on the schooner to York Factory. They reported that the schooner had not arrived at the factory until October 3rd, and the ship to England had already sailed. Holmes had missed his chance to return to England that year. The other six men had been sent back because the factory did not have enough supplies to support them for the season.

Having missed the ship, the party had decided to take a boat and return to Churchill Factory. Leaving York Factory on October 5th, they arrived after seven days at Broad River, which was as far as they could sail because of the ice along the coast. They left the boat there and started to walk northwards along the shore of Hudson Bay towards Churchill River. Having reached the headland opposite the house, they lit a fire as a signal and waited for a boat to be sent for them. Once they were safe at Churchill House, they informed Mr Charles that one of their number, the young Mr Costello, had become separated from the party on their journey from Broad River and they had not been able to locate him despite searching and feared he was lost somewhere across the river. Charles was not convinced, given the time that had elapsed since Costello went missing, that he would be found alive. He decided therefore to interview all the men who had been in the party and to ask Holmes and Leslie to give him a written statement of the events so that he had a clear record of what had occurred. His journal record summarized the information given to him separately by all those involved.

The party had left the boat at Broad River on the morning of October 12th, every person carrying his own possessions and bedding on his back with supplies to last them until they reached Churchill River. After leaving the boat, the party were walking with Mr J. Halcrow and Mr Costello going on first and walking along together. Mr Halcrow was the guide, as he was the only one who had walked the road before. But in fact, the journey required no guide so long as the party kept to the coastal edge. Costello had asked Mr Halcrow for reassurance that they would be able to make the journey safely. Halcrow replied that Costello was walking much too fast and that if he continued at such a great rate, he would soon fatigue himself and not be able to keep up with the rest of the party. Costello then said that he would be all right as his load was very light; he had brought only two blankets and a little tea and sugar with him. Mr Halcrow reminded Costello that on the next day his load would be heavier because at the moment Halcrow was carrying both their shares of oatmeal and it would be Costello's turn to carry the load tomorrow. Costello discussed the route they were taking to Churchill Factory and observed to Halcrow that, when he first came to Churchill in the winter of 1813 with a party of Indians and two of his own men, they walked mostly through the woods rather than along the coast, and enquired as to whether they should take that route now rather than going along the shore. Halcrow recalled that he made it clear that the swamp and small lakes in the woods were not frozen over sufficiently to venture on, and that the coast path was the only safe route. Whilst they were discussing the route, they saw a partridge. Halcrow waited to shoot at it while Mr Costello continued on but did not take the route they had been following. Two of the men followed Costello, but Halcrow called to them to all come back. The two men returned, but Costello only turned around, stood still for a moment and then walked on. The men suspected he intended walking on the dry ridges a little further away from the shore, rather than staying on the route they were following, which was wet and swampy. After a short time, they saw him walking on the top of a large ridge on the landside of them but then he went out of view, and they thought he was continuing to go in a parallel direction with them and would soon join them.

The party continued their journey for three or four miles and then set down to rest and wait for the young man to overtake them. They waited for some time, but he did not appear, and they assumed that he must have gone on ahead, so they continued walking until about half past two in the afternoon. They then made camp, in the hope that he might find them before nightfall. They fired their guns frequently, both to shoot partridges and also in the hope that he might hear them. They spent the night where they had camped and the next morning decided that

Costello had probably decided to take the route through the woods and would be waiting for them at Churchill River. The men had neither snowshoes, provisions or sufficient clothing to survive in the winter conditions, should they be unable to get across the river because of floating ice. They were well aware that William Auld and a party of men had been trapped on this side of the river under exactly the same conditions the year before. They decided therefore not to go back and search for Costello but to press on to the Churchill River in the hope of seeing him or overtaking him. When they reached the river opposite Churchill House, there was no sign of Costello, so they lit a signal fire and waited until the next day to be rescued.

Having heard the story of the loss of Costello, Mr Charles organised search parties to try and locate him, which he sent out the next day as soon as he could. One party led by Mr Halcrow, together with a team of dogs, was sent to Broad River where the boat had been left to start a search for Costello. As there was not much snow, the dogs were to be allowed to run free in the hope that they would pick up a scent. Mr Charles hoped that once Costello realised he was lost, he would make his way back to the boat where there were a few supplies comprising two or three hatchets, several buffalo robes and a few personal possessions the men had decided not to carry with them. Another two men were sent directly across to the south side of the river with a tent and supplies and ordered to remain there in case Costello strayed there and perished in sight of the factory as he had neither the means to make a fire nor a hatchet or a gun to make any signal. The men were provided with a plentiful supply of ammunition to hunt partridges for food but also to defend themselves, as Holmes and the other men had reported that they had seen a great number of white bears on their journey from Broad River. Mr Charles recorded his concerns in his journal entry of October 18th:

'… they saw a great many white bears and which we are much afraid will destroy the young man before he is found for although it is the general opinion in this country that this animal will not molest the traveler unless first attacked there is few I believe who would stand to give him a trial unless well prepared to receive him for if you approach them at night in a direction they do not smell they frequently make towards the person till they get the scent & then make off. Yet coming on them suddenly may have a very contrary effect.'

The search for Costello continued over the next two weeks, and on October 30th another fire was observed, over the river at the site where the tent had been left. This was a signal that Halcrow and his men had returned from Broad River. The signal was not a welcome one as the arrangement had been that if Costello had been found then two fires would be lit. The river was now full of drifting ice, and it was not safe to send a boat over to the tent to Halcrow and his men. It was not until November 4th that one of the men from Churchill House was able to find a safe place to cross the river and bring Robert Garrick, one of Halcrow's search party, back to report to Mr Charles. Garrick informed Mr Charles that they had arrived at Broad River on October 25th and searched the whole area. There had been no sign of Costello and the goods and provisions at the boat were undisturbed. They had then worked their way back towards Churchill River, but again found no trace of the missing man.

Halcrow and his men returned to Churchill House bringing the few possessions and goods that had been left on the boat and some meat from three deer that they had killed during the search. On November 8th, four weeks after Costello was reported lost, Mr Charles made the decision that the search was now in vain and Halcrow and his men were sent across the river to bring back the tent which had been left there and recorded in his journal: *'all hopes being given up of the return of Mr Costello'.*

The fate of Mr Costello remained a mystery, but Mr Charles' suspicions that he might have been attacked by bears was given some substance when on November 12th, having observed the tracks of a moose in the woods near the house, he went in search of the animal with Mr Leslie. Their search was interrupted when they heard what they described as *'a horrible noise of growling'* which on closer inspection, came from *'two large white bears'* on the ice fighting over something they had killed, surrounded by a pack of white foxes who were attempting to steal the kill. Charles and Leslie did not have enough ammunition with them to attempt to shoot the bears, so they fired their guns in the air to attempt to frighten them. One of the bears left but the other remained with his prey. The two men retreated to the factory and returned better armed, and with the assistance of Holmes, they killed the bear and were able to inspect what it was eating, which proved to be a seal rather than the remains of the missing Costello.

Holmes, having missed his passage home, was now free to spend the winter with his family and on November 19th, 1814, Charles noted in his journal that:

'Early this morning Mr Holmes with one man and two Indians as guides left this (place) to proceed to the Indian Lake for the purpose of being with his family.'

Having passed the winter at Indian Lake, Holmes returned to Churchill House on July 15th, 1815, when, in company with nineteen men, he arrived with three boats carrying furs from Nelson House, Deer Lake and Indian Lake. They had taken twelve days to make the journey because of the amount of ice in Indian Lake. Holmes' plan was to return to Indian Lake and then to proceed to York Factory later in the year. Two weeks after he left Churchill Factory and returned to his family, Mr Charles received instructions from the Governor, Mr T. Thomas, that he should convey a message to Holmes that he was required to go to Cumberland House rather than York Factory. Charles replied to Mr Thomas on July 28th informing him that they had not received any communication from Indian Lake and had not had a chance to send a message to Holmes and that: *'consequently he will be at YF in the spring as was his intention if he does not change his mind'*.

Holmes did not change his mind, and having arrived back at Churchill Factory, was ready to depart to York Factory on August 1st, 1815, accompanied by Mr Brown and Mr Spence. Having arrived safely at York Factory, he awaited instructions from Mr Thomas as to where he was to be stationed for the next season.

1815 – 16 Split House

In September 1815, Holmes was appointed to take charge of the Nelson River District. He was asked to relinquish one of his best steersmen, William Leith, as he was required to take a boat to the Red River with some of the women and children that had arrived by ship. Holmes' instructions were to take two big canoes and travel from York Factory up the Nelson River to either Split Lake or White Lake, whichever he thought would be in the best interests of the *'Honourable Company.'* Split Lake on the Nelson

River is some one hundred and fifty miles from York Factory and has connections to the Burntwood River and the Grass River. The lake is about thirty miles long, and the journey from York Factory to the Split Lake House was to take Holmes and his men over three weeks. Their journey was made difficult by the cold weather and repeated problems with leaking canoes, so they did not arrive until October 14th, having set off on September 19th. When they arrived at Split Lake they were greeted by John Scott, who had been left there to take care of the house and trade over the summer. John Scott explained to Holmes that he had experienced great difficulty in persuading the Indians to stay at Split Lake to await the arrival of Holmes and his men. Altogether there were fifty-seven men and boys in addition to the women and children at the house. It was common for the Cree families of the area to assemble at the trading posts in the fall and then to leave for their winter quarters during September, where they would spend the winter hunting and moving from camp to camp in search of game to hunt. There was an urgency to get the post organised before the winter set in and the lake froze over, making journeying more difficult. Holmes took an inventory of the furs and provisions that John Scott had traded over the summer and 'debted out' the traders at the house to ensure that they would return with furs and provisions later in the year. There were letters that had been sent down from York Factory with Holmes to be delivered to Nelson House, where Mr John Charles was in charge, and Holmes dispatched Andrew Kirkness with a local pilot to deliver them.

Some of the Cree were settled at the White Lake, which was the alternative site for a trading post that had been suggested, so Holmes decided to set up an outpost there and on October 21st sent

John Scott and James Taylor to set up the post. He provided them with tobacco, brandy and ammunition to debt out the Cree hunters and instructed the men to remain at White Lake to capture any trade from those who passed that way. It was only four days later that the lake froze over and John Scott had not managed to reach White Lake before the ice set in. On September 7th, two hunters arrived who had travelled from White Lake and brought a letter from Scott. In it, he explained that he had been stuck a day and a half's walk from the lake and had met the hunters who were travelling to Split Lake to bring their debts, and they had gone back with him to help him reach White Lake. Holmes had ordered his men to set up nets in the lake to try and get fish for provisions, but the fishing was not very productive, and the nets only provided two hundred and eighty-three white fish over the course of November. The only new provisions that he obtained over the next two weeks was a deer that a hunter had killed half a day's walk up the lake. Holmes and one of his men trekked along the lake and returned with 60 lbs of deer meat. On checking the state of his goods and provisions, Holmes was dismayed to find that when he opened a bale of tobacco containing between 80 and 90 lbs, the tobacco had gone rotten and *'was only fit for manure'*. This was a setback as tobacco was one of his main commodities for trading.

With the winter came poor hunting, and over December Holmes was visited by many families who were starving through lack of successful hunting. John Scott reported back from White Lake that the fishing there was good but that they had seen no Indians as yet so had not completed any trades. In view of this and the lack of tobacco at Split Lake, Holmes sent James Taylor up to White Lake on December 18th to bring back some of their tobacco supplies which he returned with on the

29th. Despite taking up his nets several times to find a better fishing place, Holmes was still not taking enough fish to supply the house, and his provision store was greatly depleted. When hunters came to trade, he was not able to give them provisions even if they were starving and had to restrict his trades to everything except provisions. On January 30th, 1816, he decided to send Robert Garston and Robert Thompson to White Lake until the spring, recording in his journal that: '...*our living being so miserable we cannot all subsist together I have now 3 men here and myself and family'*. The food supply had, by the end of February, become critical, so when a man arrived with 30 lbs of green meat, Holmes wrote that the meat came *'very opportunely as we had not a single mouthful of anything for supper'*.

The supply situation began to improve a little as soon as the weather allowed the locals to resume hunting and Holmes traded for beaver, rabbits, wolves, wolverines, mink, geese, musquash and martens as well as supplies of deer meat, half dry meat and green meat. He also traded for sixty pairs of castoreum. Some of those who arrived told Holmes that the winter had been so bad that they had cooked and eaten most of the animals they had killed as they were starving, so the skins were damaged and not fit to trade. The news from White Lake was not encouraging. Robert Garston and two men arrived from there on May 7th with a letter from John Scott informing Holmes that they had still not seen many hunters and had very few skins. Holmes recorded that he was concerned that the trade for this season was going to be *'but indifferent'*.

It was on May 19th that the ice on the lake started to break up, and Holmes lost no time in sending some Indians down to York Factory to obtain more tobacco to replace his rotten stock.

When they returned on June 9th, it was with only 5½ lbs of tobacco and a message from York Factory that tobacco was very scarce. The season was starting to draw to a close, and Holmes started to prepare for his return back to the factory to be there in time to deliver his furs and skins for shipping on the annual voyage back to London. On June 1st the men arrived back from White Lake with their stocks of traded furs and skins, which as Holmes had feared, was not a great amount.

To prepare for the return journey the canoes needed attention, and supplies of bark were obtained from the Indians to enable repairs to be made. Once the goods were packed and the canoes made ready, then Holmes and his men awaited Mr Charles and the boats from Nelson House to arrive. On June 23rd, 1816, Holmes signed his last entry for Split Lake House as *'John Pocock Holmes — surgeon'* and the Split Lake boats joined John Charles and Richard Sutherland with their three Nelson House boats in the voyage back to York Factory.

1816 – 17 Rock Depot (Gordon House)

Holmes spent the next season at Rock Depot. The exact location of the depot is unknown, but it was situated at Swampy Lake on the Hayes River, somewhere above the Berwick Falls, and there was an associated depot below the falls known as Gordon House. The voyage from York House to Rock Fort entailed some difficult passages along the Hayes River. Peter Rindesbacher, an accomplished artist, documented his voyage along the same route in 1821. His illustrations of the passage along the Hayes River and of Rock Depot itself give a clear impression of the conditions that faced Holmes on his journey to the depot and the conditions under which he was to spend the season.

Watercolour: Difficult voyage up the South-Hill (?) river to Rock Fort in Sept. 1821. *Source: Library and Archives Canada/Peter Rindisbacher collection/e008299430*

Watercolour: Arrival and Stay at Rockfort. *Source: Library and Archives Canada/Peter Rindisbacher collection/e008299431*

Rock Depot was not a trading station in its own right, but rather a changeover point or transfer depot, where the boats from York Factory would drop their cargoes for transfer to smaller canoes that could safely navigate the Hayes River, a journey which was not safe for the larger York boats. Holmes was stationed here in a dual role as trader and surgeon but was not in charge of the depot. The master of Rock Depot was Robert Logan, who had originally been an employee of the North West Company but was persuaded by Colin Robertson to transfer to the Hudson's Bay Company in 1814 and was in charge of Rock Depot from 1815 to 1818. Holmes and Logan journeyed up from York Factory to Rock Depot in October 1816. Holmes did not endear himself to Robert Logan when, on their arrival at Rock Depot, he gave the Indians a dram of rum each. Logan commented in his journal of October 21st: *'Came up with Mr Holmes who gave the Indians a dram, and I was obliged to promise them an Extraordinary dram at night with a weeks provisions'*. As Holmes was employed as a trader and surgeon, he made no direct records of his time at Rock Depot. The post journal records that on December 9th, 1816, he was sent with two men and two Indians to the fishing lake, the Indians were supplied with one pound of flour and the men with a gallon of rum. Logan had supplied Holmes with a hundred and five pounds of flour and fifty pounds of oatmeal since their arrival at Rock Depot. After his departure to the fishing lake in December 1816, nothing further is recorded of his time at Rock Depot and he was next posted to Pelican Lake for the season 1817 to 1818.

1817 – 18 Pelican Lake

The Pelican Lake post, also known as Pelican Narrows, was a fifteen-day journey from York Factory and was situated on the edge of Pelican Lake, which John Franklin described as being set in swampy ground and extending six miles from east to west and eight from north to south, decreasing in width to a mile at the northern end. Holmes served at Pelican Lake as a surgeon, so made no entries in the log for that season. His time there is recorded in the Depot's 'Men's Debt Book' for that year which details the purchases that were made from the Company to be set off against their wages as a debt.

Item	Amount	Price	Debt	
			s	d
A cotton white shirt	1	9/10 ¼	9	10¼
Handkerchiefs Loose	3	4/7	13	9
Hat Fine	1	17/8 ¾	17	8 ¾
Buttons Gilt	3	1/10 ¾	5	11 ¼
Blanket of 2 Point	½	25/7 ¼	12	9 ¼
Rum LJ gall	3/8	6/6 ¾	2	2/3¼

Holmes' purchases were in the main of clothing and material such as:

1818 – 19 Pelican Lake

Holmes was posted back to Pelican Lake for the season 1818 – 19 and his return journey commenced on August 24th 1818 when he set off from Norway House towards Cumberland House, with Mr Thomas Thomas and his family in the company of seven Canadians. On the first day, they made good progress and camped about fifteen miles from Norway House, setting off at five o'clock in the morning on the next day to get an early start. The first part of the journey was along the shore of Lake Winnipeg heading southwest. The currents here were strong and boats seldom ventured far from the shore as the high waves on the lake carried the risk of a capsize. They had only made about three miles when they discovered articles floating in the water that appeared to have come from a canoe that had been lost a few days previously. Holmes left the party and waded along the shore in the hope of finding more of the lost items. After only a mile or so he located boxes of possessions belonging to Mr Rodement and Mr Kingins, and a little further on, a box of private property belonging to John McDougal. One of the boxes contained the packet of correspondence which had been the item Holmes had hoped to find. He sent a man back to Norway House on foot to alert them to the discovery and to send a man and a canoe to retrieve them. Whilst they waited for the man to return, Holmes and Mr Thomas occupied themselves drying out the letters, but made little progress, as it continued to rain throughout the day.

The canoe from Norway House arrived the next day and the packet of letters and other property was loaded onto the small canoe together with a message from Mr Thomas to the Master of Norway House. In it, he suggested that, as the packet of letters for the Red River Settlement needed to be sent as quickly as possible, then they could be entrusted to a Mr DeQuine, who was travelling to Red River if he had not already departed. For the next ten days, their journey was difficult, with a headwind and heavy rain causing them to remain in their encampment for days at a time. Their route took them over eighty miles along the north and west shore of Lake Winnipeg and then into the mouth of the Saskashawan River, and on to the Grand Rapids where the river fell seventy-five feet in three miles. The river here is a quarter of a mile across and the canoes and cargo had to be carried by a portage which stretched for a mile and involved crossing a ravine over a wooden bridge built by the Hudson's Bay Company. They camped on the far side of the portage and managed to trade with some Indians and acquire a second canoe which enabled Holmes to transfer some of the cargo and lighten his canoe considerably, thus making the journey a little easier.

After five days of poor weather, which caused them to remain in the camp unable to get the canoes into the water, they resumed their voyage and, on September 9th, reached the Moose River about nine o'clock in the morning. The supplies were running low because of the delays in the journey, so Holmes left the men at the mouth of the river and set off across Moose Lake to the Hudson's Bay Company post to replenish the provisions. When he reached the post, he found that the men were not due to return to the house until the next day. After an overnight stay at the house, he loaded his canoe with eight sturgeons, 12 lbs of dried meat and ten bales of potatoes and paddled back to the Moose River to join up with the rest of his company. Over the next five days, they made slow progress as the weather was again very poor, giving them only five hours a day of paddling at best, and once again their supplies began to run out. They were saved when on September 14th they encountered some Indians and were able to trade fourteen geese, which Holmes described as *'very acceptable as our provisions all expended'*.

It was on September 16th that they finally reached Cumberland House. The voyage had taken over thirty days, almost twice the duration that they would have expected at this time of year. They arrived at the house at ten o'clock in the morning and found Mr Kennedy, the master of the house, in good health but *'thwarted by a set of drunken Indians'*.

The men remained at Cumberland House for six days and busied themselves repairing the boat that they were to use to travel to Pelican Lake, the canoe being too small to carry all the men and provisions. Holmes and his party set off on September 22nd, and he was not optimistic about the coming season at Pelican Lake, writing: *'I am afraid I shall not be so successful as last year Caliway having seized 11 Indians and forced them to take debt from him that traded with me last year I have only four Indians that I can expect anything from'*.

The journey did not start well. After only a short distance they were forced to stop to repair the boat which was leaking and had taken on a considerable amount of water during the morning. Holmes estimated they had bailed out fifty-one six-gallon kettles of water during the course of the morning. On the next day, having completed what repairs they could, they arrived at the Sturgeon River, named by the Canadians La Riviere Maligne, because of the great number of dangerous rapids as it drops ninety-one feet in twenty-three miles with almost continuous rapids. The boat continued to leak and Holmes became concerned that, despite the men repairing and caulking the boat, it was so old that it would not hold together long enough for them to reach their destination. By September 25th they had reached Beaver Lake, having managed earlier in the day to trade with Indians to get more supplies. They encountered a fair wind and were able to hoist a sail and cross the lake, which is twelve miles long and six miles wide, without incident in about four hours. Over the next two days, the journey involved crossing the numerous portages of the River La Pente where Holmes was able to construct a hoop net and catch eighty fine white fish out of the rapids. This method of fishing resulted in the area being known as the Scoop Rapids as it was possible to scoop fish in the eddies below the Leaf Rapids.

Having crossed all the portages, they made camp on September 28th, some twelve miles away from Pelican Lake. The next day, having started out at five in the morning, they reached the houses after four hours. They were welcomed by Mr Jonas Peck with the news that there was not a single Indian at the place. It appeared that the North West traders had sent men out in all directions and taken all the Indians that they found to their post at Lake La Ronge. Holmes was keen to travel up to Lake La Ronge, but as his boat was in such a poor state and he had little in the way of trading goods, he decided against it. He was convinced that he would see very few Indians during the winter, as the North West Company had sent their men to live with them to avoid them being persuaded to return to the Hudson's Bay Company. However, the North West traders were made aware of his arrival at Pelican Lake by one of their Indians and his wife, who took the news on September 30th. Holmes sent two of his men back to Cumberland House to collect the packet of correspondence, which was expected to arrive in the fall boats, and also to bring back trading supplies. The rest of his men he set to work repairing the houses whilst he dispatched his four Indians that had travelled with him to hunt.

The news of his arrival at Pelican Lake had reached some of the Indians who had previously traded with him, and on October 16th, The Split arrived with the flesh of two moose. The next day his two sons arrived and traded some fresh meat, and over the next three days, The Split's family, including his wife, returned with more meat and skins. As two of the North West men had arrived at the lake, Holmes took the precaution of sending one of his men to live with The Split and his family *'to secure them from the grasp of the N. West merchants'*.

A message arrived from Cumberland House by canoe, informing Holmes that the fall boat had not arrived but was expected any day. This meant that the trading goods he had requested would be delayed, and Holmes was worried that the men would not be able to travel once the ice set in on the open waters. For the whole of November, the house was isolated as the lake froze over. Holmes set fishing nets under the ice, but the ice was so weak that by the end of the month he had to take them up. Over the month they caught six hundred and sixty white fish and forty-three trout with five hundred and eighty-five of all other kinds. Despite the ice, the weather was unusually warm, and only a little snow covered the ground. It was not until December 7th that the two men he had sent to Cumberland on October 1st were able to return, but they did not bring all the things that Holmes had requested or the correspondence packet. He had sent out two men in search of the Indians between Pelican Lake and Lake La Ronge but they returned four days later without success. A week later Holmes and three of his men set off for Cumberland House to spend Christmas there with Mr Williams, Mr Bird and Mr Kennedy. He arrived there on December 18th after a four-day journey and remained there until the 28th when he set off alone back to Pelican Lake. As he neared the woods between Cumberland House and Beaver Lake, he found a track which he followed for several hours until he came across a tent with three Indians who usually traded with Mr Kennedy and one that the North West merchant Mr Caliway had a claim to. Holmes, however, was sure that he had as strong a claim on the Indian's furs as Caliway because the man had traded with Holmes during the last winter season. The Indian had been travelling to Cumberland House in the spring when *'that rascal Frobisher met him, pillaged him of his debt and beat him'*. Holmes took the view that the Indian wished to trade with the Hudson's Bay Company but was being prevented from doing so by the North West traders. He asked him if he wished to travel back to Pelican Lake with him and as he consented, they set off immediately. The journey back to the house took them over five days and was uneventful, apart from the fact that they ran out of food a day before they got back to the house. Their hunger was satisfied, however, when they killed and ate a dog that had followed them. Holmes recorded in his journal *'I doubt I never eat a bit of meat with more avidity nor a better appetite in my life'*.

When they arrived back at the house on January 3rd, Holmes took care to travel through the woods in order to conceal the Indian from the North West men who were at the lake, having arrived on December 21st to pass Christmas, but had not yet returned to Lake La Ronge. During Holmes' absence, The Split had continued to supply the house with furs, skins and meat. The man who had been staying with them now wished to remain at the house so a man by the name of Bernard had been sent back with The Split to live with them. The tensions between Holmes and the North West traders continued and Holmes took great precautions to avoid them knowing his plans. On January 8th 1819 he sent out Lusia, Desham, DeBois and Cadorette to search out Indians between the house and Lake La Ronge, but refused to let them take dogs or sledges as these would be too easy for the North West traders to track. The men set off on foot supplied with tobacco, ammunition and half a bag of pemmican to trade with anyone they might locate.

On January 11th Mr McLeod, the master of the North West House, arrived from Cumberland and paid Holmes a visit. From the nature of the conversation, Holmes deduced that they were not aware that he had taken back their Indian who he met between Cumberland House and Pelican Lake at the end of December. Holmes, however, continued to be wary of the North West men and noticed on January 13th that McLeod had sent two of his men off in the direction of Lake La Ronge and had employed some more of his men to pitch a tent halfway between the North West House and the Hudson's Bay Company House. Holmes, assuming that the aim of pitching the tent was to enable the North West to keep a better eye on the comings and goings at his house, retaliated by sending four of his men out to build a double stockade between the two houses *'to shut up their view'*.

Five days later, two of the men that Holmes had sent away on January 8th to search for Indians returned, requesting that he send dogs and sledges to the other three men who had traded with some Indians and had a number of items to bring back to the house. Whilst this was, at first sight, good news, Holmes was distressed when Charles Lusia told him the full details of the men's expedition. They had met up with a number of Indians five days after they left the house, including The Moose Hunter, who had previously been one of the Hudson's Bay Company traders. Desham, who was leading the party, had traded with all the Indians and given them a little debt, despite the fact that the others belonged to Mr McMurray of Lake La Ronge, and were accompanied by a North West Company man whose task it was to ensure that their furs were only traded with the North West. To make matters worse, Desham had got the North West man drunk and traded all his goods from him. Holmes expressed his feelings clearly in his journal entry of January 18th:

'Desham gave the Indians a little debt for which they gave him all they had after which he would not give them any more but like an ignorant cloth head made the N West man drunk & traded all his furs from him & debauched his wife from him. Also the Oraquios no doubt will have a most lamentable story to tell his master when he arrives at Lake La Ronge. I am really vexed at Desham trading the Martens from the N West man he must have known that they were stolen property which I shall be obliged to give up on demand. I told the men before they went away not to pillage or do any mischief what ever but Lusia having had his wife debauched from him last Fall at Cumberland by Calliway he was determined to retaliate the first opportunity.'

Holmes realised that Desham's actions would cause great annoyance to the North West Company. Lusia informed him that The Moose Hunter intended to leave the North West and return to trading with the Hudson's Bay Company, despite the fact that he was in debt to Mr McMurray at Lake La Ronge. Lusia was dispatched back to Desham, who was about a day's walk away, with two men, dogs, sledges and provisions to bring back the furs they had traded.

On January 21st, Holmes observed that the North West men had found the tracks of Lusia and the sledges, and McLeod had sent three men off in pursuit of them. The North West men arrived back a day later on January 22nd and gave McLeod the news that they had located Desham and the Indians, at which news McLeod set off with three men and three dogs on each sledge at a fast gallop. Holmes had no dogs left at the house and knew that he could not keep up with McLeod if he set off on foot, so had to remain at the house. This, despite knowing that the North West men were, in all probability, going to attempt to redress what they saw as an act of theft of their trader and his goods. It was about sunset when Mr Peck, who had been out hunting with five men, arrived at the house to say that he had met with Desham and the rest of the men who were not far from the house. Desham had asked Peck to request Holmes to go and meet them as he was afraid that the North West men would threaten the Indians and make them go back to the North West House at Lake La Ronge. Holmes and two men set off as fast as they could and found Desham and the Indians about six miles from the house, but McLeod and his men had reached them first and were still there.

Holmes approached McLeod and explained that The Moose Hunter was one of his traders and that the North West had no claim on him. McLeod replied that he was *'a stranger and did not very well understand the nature of the trade'*, but as The Moose Hunter had taken goods equivalent to ten beavers from them last fall at Lake La Ronge, then he would expect him to repay that debt before trading with anyone else. Holmes still felt he was in the right to take The Moose Hunter back to trade with him and grasped hold of him to take him back to Pelican Lake. At this point, the situation rapidly deteriorated. One of the North West men, Joseph Caddotte, came behind Holmes and gave him three heavy blows to his back and head before he had time to turn around. Holmes span round and gave Caddotte a right-handed blow to his left eye, which swelled up immediately, and followed it up with a left-handed blow to the stomach which left Caddotte lying breathless on the snow. Caddotte was not finished with his attack though and, getting up, started to approach Holmes. At that point, Desham, and one of the other men, struck Caddotte heavily with a gun and he fell back to the ground. Caddotte was widely known as a dangerous bully and only nine months previously had been charged as an accessory to the murder in 1816 of Owen Keveny, a Hudson's Bay Company accountant, but had been released 'on recognizance' in the spring of 1818. Caddotte was never brought to trial, but another man, Charles de Reinhard, was found guilty of the murder and sentenced to execution, though this was never carried out. McLeod, taken aback by the assault on Holmes, intervened and reprimanded Caddotte for his actions and apologised to Holmes for the attack. He suggested a compromise, which was for them to settle the matter by asking the Indian which company he wished to trade with and both agreeing that they would abide by whatever his answer was. Holmes posed the question to The Moose Hunter, who replied that as he owed a debt to the North West Company then he would have to go with them. Holmes was true to his word and gave up his claim on him for the present.

McLeod however, pursued the matter and said he believed Holmes had another trader at Pelican Bay who belonged to their Mr Caliway and should be returned. Holmes' reply to this was not as conciliatory as in the previous discussion, and he informed McLeod that the Indian belonged to the Hudson's Bay Company, had been trading with them last year and had come up from Cumberland House with him this season. He added that no person would take his Indian away by force, but if he wished to go elsewhere, he was at liberty to do so. Holmes was still angry that Desham had been stupid enough to get the North West man drunk and trick him into trading the furs which belonged to McMurray at Lake La Ronge. He questioned Desham as to how many of the skins he had traded from him, but Desham had mixed up the skins he traded from the North West man with those he got from others and could not recall the number.

Having returned to Pelican Lake, Holmes was visited by two of the North West men from Lake La Ronge, with news about Holmes' men at Deer Lake. They informed him that the fishing in the fall had failed and the men were starving. The fishing at Pelican Lake was also poor, and McLeod was forced to send three men, two women and five children away to Lake La Ronge as they had no fresh fish and none in store. Holmes recorded that he was not anxious about his own food stocks as he had over five thousand fish in store. Despite the concerns over the lack of food, McLeod visited Holmes on February 2nd 1819 to pursue the matter of the Indian that he believed belonged to Mr Caliway, who he felt would be at a great loss if the Indian was not returned to him. Holmes replied that Caliway would feel no more inconvenience for the loss of him than Holmes had last year from the loss of the Indian that Frobisher took, by force, within a day's walk from Pelican Lake and took to Lake La Ronge. McLeod appeared to be keen to avoid any further conflict and explained that whilst he believed Holmes, he would take it as a favour if his interpreter could talk to the Indian to ask him a few questions. Holmes agreed to this provided that no threats were made to the Indian. Once McLeod's interpreter had arrived, he asked the Indian why he had left Caliway. The Indian replied that he had debt to pay off here from last year and he did not want to return to Caliway at Cumberland House. McLeod thanked Holmes and said he would pass the information on to Caliway, who could now act as he saw proper.

Over the next two weeks, Holmes saw little of the North West traders but on February 15th he saw that Mr McMurray had arrived under cover of darkness at the North West House from Lake La Ronge, accompanied by seven or eight men and another two men who arrived from Cumberland House. Holmes and his men were concerned when they saw that all the North West men were armed with swords and pistols and had hidden themselves and their dogs in the house to avoid raising suspicions. Early next morning, McLeod came over to beg a favour of Holmes, asking him if he would have the goodness to visit a sick woman at his house who they expected would not live. Holmes agreed and, not suspecting any threat, accompanied McLeod to the house. As he entered the house he was confronted by McMurray and twelve of his men. He quickly realised that he had been deceived, but it was too late to retreat. McMurray made him take a seat and, having set three men to guard him, informed him he was their prisoner.

McMurray, McLeod and six men then armed themselves with pistols and went over to Holmes' house where they broke down the door and seized the Indian and his wife who had refused to go back to Caliway at Cumberland House. The man and his wife were *'beaten unmercifully'* as was Lusia's wife, who had refused to go with them. Having beaten and seized their captives the men returned to the North West House where Holmes remained a prisoner. McMurray then started to interrogate Holmes about the martens that Desham had *'traded and pillaged'* from his man on January 17th or 18th. Holmes replied that he was well aware that Desham had got the man drunk and unfairly taken the skins, but that Desham had mixed up all the skins so was unable to tell how many belonged to the North West Company.

McMurray called his man into the house and asked him how many martens had been traded, to which he replied that there were seventy. Holmes, being suspicious, asked him to say how many he had got from each hunter he had traded with. Holmes added up the individual figures, and as this did indeed come to a total of seventy, he agreed to give McMurray that number. McMurray was not however satisfied and said that there was also the matter of an otter that Desham had taken from the man. Holmes replied that this was not true and that McMurray had no right to the otter. McMurray replied that Holmes might please himself but he would be held prisoner until he gave up the otter. Holmes recorded in his journal that:

'to get clear of the rascal I gave him a small shabby Otter but at the same time gave him to understand that I should keep an account of it as property belonging the Hudson Bay Company'.

As soon as the otter was handed over, Holmes was released having been held prisoner for three hours. Before he left, he expostulated with McMurray on the unfair acts of breaking into his house and taking three Indians out by force, but he got little in the way of a reply. The next day McMurray and his men, still armed with swords and pistols, set off for Lake La Ronge, taking the captured men with them.

The disputes with the North West flared up again four days later when the son of The Moose Hunter arrived and asked Holmes to take him in because he had run away from his North West trader. As soon as McLeod became aware that the boy was with Holmes he sent out three men to the tent between the houses, in response to which Holmes sent out four men. Holmes was adamant that he would not give up the boy who had traded two martens with him and wrote: *'I suppose the N West will attempt taking the boy out of my house but if they should they will remember it, I am well prepared to receive them'*

McLeod, realising that Holmes was well prepared and that he would not be able to take the boy by force without a struggle, waited a week and then sent a man over to him with a note asking him to send the boy over to his house so that he could take some articles to his father The Moose Hunter. At the end of the note, he said an answer was *'highly requested by the bearer'.* Holmes found this both impudent and threatening and wrote the following letter in reply:

'Mr McLeod

Sir,

I received your note by the bearer which not only is xxx for its impudence but a kind of threatening not really expressed but left to be understood. Therefore the Indian Boy you are so anxious to get hold of for the purpose of sending a few articles by to his father is only a mear pretext a way of cheating or deceiving me. If you want to send anything to his father send it by your man who I know his going to live with him. The Boy shall not take any thing neither shall he go over to your man was he not inclined. If you want him and wish to have him come here to my House and take him by force now I am at home not as you and McMurray did when I was a prisoner in your House.

I shall then acknowledge you to be a brave young Man & if you think you are not able to do it with the men you have, send for McMurray & his men to support you, I assure you at the same time I shall not send for any more reinforcement, if you do it not I say that both you and McMurray are Pusillanimous in the highest degree

John Pocock Holmes

N.B the N West are some of the hardest rascals that God ever created they will stop at nothing House Breaking, Robbery, Murder etc is all the same to them their morals are deformed to a degree that shocks our every feature and employing itself in the maintaining of tyranny and dissimulation frustrating myself an advocate for truth.'

Despite his letter, Holmes decided to take steps to avoid the boy being taken by the North West. Late at night, he sent him away to live at The Split's tent as he was sure that McLeod would have taken him back to Lake La Ronge if he could have captured him. Over the next two months, there were no more incidents involving the North West traders and Holmes and his men were employed building seven canoes. This involved building the wooden frames, which had to be soaked and bent to shape, a process that could not be completed if the weather was too cold. The skins of the canoes were made from birch bark that Holmes sent the Indians to collect. They brought back large quantities, as much as a hundred fathoms length at a time. By March 18th the last of the canoes were timbered but still required completing, and the next day the ice on the Narrows opposite the house became free of ice and fishermen were able to bring in fish by canoe for the first time that year.

On March 26th the last of the canoes were finished, and Holmes began to pack up his belongings in preparation for the journey back to Cumberland House. He set off the next afternoon at one o'clock with seven men and two canoes and arrived at the Narrows about four o'clock, where they met some of his hunters who told him that the lake was still frozen and it was not possible to proceed. They had to wait until June 2nd when the lake finally broke up and they were able to complete the journey to Cumberland House. They made good progress and arrived there on June 5th but discovered that, because of the delay due to the ice, they had missed the boats from Cumberland which had left two days previously.

1819 – 20 Cumberland House

During the season 1819 to 1820 Holmes had charge of Cumberland House. His arrival on June 5th, 1819, with six men, two canoes and four bundles of good furs was noted in the journal with the comment that he had only had four Indians hunting for him at Pelican Lake, otherwise, he would have procured more furs. William Auld in his entries in the District Journal went into more detail in summarising Holmes' season at Pelican Lake. He writes that Mr Holmes was so late getting on the station that the North West had debauched and drawn away all the Indians from the area, leaving him with only four hunters. He adds that whilst Holmes had not been successful in his trading, he had put the North West to a great deal of expense as they had been obliged to set up a house at Pelican Lake in opposition to Holmes, from which they obtained no benefit. The Governor, William Williams, during his time at Cumberland House had improved the conditions there. He had encouraged the cultivation of the land inside the wooden stockade and arranged for cattle, sheep and pigs to be brought there to supplement the limited range of food that was normally available. The wooden stockade provided shelter for the crops and also protection for the animals and the men against the wolves, which had been known to attack and carry off sheep, and on occasions to attack even armed men.

In March, Holmes and two other men set off for the Whiteys

Narrows, where they were occupied splitting and preparing canoe wood. They arrived back three days later with enough wood for five canoes. Holmes continued to build canoes but also had time for hunting, and on April 10th he shot the first duck seen that year at Cumberland House. Holmes was to record proudly, some thirty years later, that he had built one of the canoes that Sir John Franklin and his men used and also built five pairs of snowshoes for his Arctic expedition. Holmes had his wife and family living with him at Cumberland House, and his daughter Elizabeth, who was then seven years old, having been born at Nelson River in 1813, used to recall her meeting with Sir John Franklin and his men at Cumberland House. During his time at Cumberland House, Holmes appears to have been occupied in a number of tasks including making soap and building canoes. A good deal of time was spent by the men in assisting Franklin and his men who were preparing to set off on their expedition to the Arctic. The expedition had arrived at Cumberland House in October 1819 and remained there until June 1820, when they set off along the Sturgeon River on their epic but ill-fated Arctic Exploration.

There was a lot of building and construction being undertaken during this period. Holmes was a skilled carpenter in addition to his other abilities and is described as *'assiduously employed at Carpenter Work'*. Amongst other things, he was building panelled doors for his own rooms. The fitting out of his room appeared to be a project that occupied many of the men over the month of July. Messrs. Snoddie, Kirkness and Spence were busy building a double stove for the room whilst Mr Sanderson was putting up partitions. Robert Garrick and two boys were hauling lime for the double stoves, whilst Holmes is noted to be working on a chest of drawers. Over the course of a week, the work on the stoves continued whilst Mr Sandison was preparing the room for plastering. The journal entry for July 27th notes: *'Mr Holmes employed as usual'*.

On July 29th, three men and some boys were dispatched to the narrows for some fir to use as laths for Mr Holmes' room *'previous to their being plastered'*. Having gathered the wood for the laths, all the rest of the men were employed in burning lime for plastering the room. The next two weeks saw a continuation of the work on the room with men laying floors, collecting more laths, wheeling barrows of lime and plastering. The room was nearing completion and a good deal of time, labour and expense had been put into the project. It must therefore have been a shock to Holmes when a letter arrived from Governor William Williams dated July 26th, 1820, instructing him to give up the charge of Cumberland House and proceed down to Norway House where he would receive further orders.

The letter from Governor Williams, written at Rock House Depot, appeared to cast doubt on Holmes' ability to continue in charge of Cumberland House, and indeed his whole behaviour as a company officer:

'To Mr Holmes

Sir,

I have appointed Mr Thomas Swaine to take charge of Cumberland House — such instructions as you have received you will hand over to him.-

Impressed with the idea that your long services had been neglected, from partiality or undue prejudices, I was unwilling to abide by any reports of your unfitness for the situation, however I regret to state that your management in the charge, your repeated neglect of duty, and lastly your disobedience of orders, have imperiously called for your removal.-

You will therefore proceed immediately to Norway House, where you will receive an appointment better adapted for your capacity.

Yours Hereafter

(signed) Wm. Williams'.

So it was that five days later, Holmes with his wife Betsy, now six months pregnant, and the two children, George aged ten and Elizabeth aged seven, left Cumberland House for Norway house in a half-sized canoe with James Sandison and three Indians. Holmes' sudden departure from Cumberland House at the orders of the Governor is surprising, given that Colin Robertson, in a letter written from Norway House in 1821, describes Dr Holmes as *'a favourite of the Governor of Rupert's Land, William Williams.'*

However, Robertson's letter throws some light on the events:

'His next favourite was the athletic Mr Holmes a powerful man in his way, and of a very ingenious turn. He often assisted the Governor in Dove tailed work and actually began on a chest of drawers belonging to Miss Fidler. This excited some suspicion and the Doctor was ordered from Cumberland House, and has since been accused of embezzling the Company's property.'

Miss Fidler (Sally Fidler) is the subject of a footnote in Colin Robertson's letters which notes the baptism of two children of William Williams and Sally, one in 1822 and the other in 1823. The letter from Robertson does not make it clear what the 'suspicion' with regard to Holmes and Sally Fidler was. He does record that the charges were dismissed:

'The cause was laid before Mr Gary, who after taking a proper view of the thing decided in favour of Dr Holmes. However the Governor succeeded in procuring the Doctor a passage to England, which deprived the old wife of a husband and the Red River an excellent settler'.

1820 – 1821 Sandy Bar

From Norway House, Holmes and his family moved to Sandy Bar and Jack Head on the shores of Lake Winnipeg and near to the Red River Colony, which was located along the Assiniboine and Red Rivers at the southern end of Lake Winnipeg. Holmes and Betsy had their third child, Charlotte, who was born on September 20th, 1820, and shortly after their three children were baptised on October 4th, 1820, at Red River by the Reverend John West.

Holmes, now aged thirty-six, was preparing to retire from the Company and return to England. His intention was to bring the children over to England once he had settled and got accommodation and employment, and in August 1822 the committee granted him permission to arrange their passage on a company ship. Before leaving for England, he provided funds to support Betsy and his children and settled them at Norway House where they were to remain until they moved to the Red River Settlement.

Watercolour: View of English Minister`s House on Red River,
Summer of 1822. *Source: Library and Archives Canada/Peter
Rindisbacher collection/e008299448*

Chapter 9

Retirement and a New Life in London

'Can any thing be conceived more dreary and disheartening, than the prospect before a young London physician, who without friends or fortune, yet with high aspirations after professional eminence, is striving to weave around him what is technically called 'a connection'?'

Holmes sailed back to England from York Factory on September 11th, 1821, on the Prince of Wales. The ship needed considerable repair before it set sail on the voyage back to England, as it had suffered severe damage whilst traversing the eastern Hudson Strait. The convoy of HBC ships had been nearing the end of their outward voyage to York Factory when, at about three in the morning of July 24th, they had encountered the Lord Wellington, a ship carrying Swiss settlers, in danger of being crushed by ice packs. The Prince of Wales attempted to pull the ship clear using grappling hooks and the Lord Wellington was freed from the ice, but the wind and currents were very strong, and the two ships collided. The Prince of Wales was hit midships, and the side of the ship was stove in over a great length. The Prince of Wales began to take on water at an alarming rate and had to transfer cargo to its sister ship, the Edystone, to lighten the vessel. This allowed the damaged timbers to emerge above the water line and temporary repairs were made. The ships continued through the straits without further incident, and the layover at York Factory gave time for the more permanent repairs to be made.

Watercolour: The ships Wellington and Eddystone in collision, thereby breaking their spars. July 21, 1821. *Source: Library and Archives Canada/Peter Rindisbacher collection/e008299413*

The return voyage from York Factory to England was uneventful, and the ship arrived at Stromness at the end of October. A letter to the Caledonian Mercury reporting the ship's arrival, stated that there were a hundred and fifty Hudson's Bay *'servants'* on board.

Having arrived in London after a period of fifteen years' absence, with no immediate prospect of a permanent position, Holmes was fortunate to obtain employment as an assistant surgeon to Mr William Hutchinson Box, MRCS of Ave Maria Lane in London. Mr Box was the surgeon to Newgate Prison and several other London prisons, with a practice that also took patients from the Ludgate Hill Area. The appointment as surgeon to a prison carried a salary, so was a source of guaranteed income, and allowed for the employment of assistants to help with both the prison work and the day-to-day treatment of patients. The post of an assistant surgeon in a prison was, however, not well paid, and the work included supervising floggings and executions as well as attending to the health of the prisoners. In addition to the care of the prisoners, the prison surgeons would be called on to give evidence in the trials of the prisoners on matters of health. Newgate Prison was where prisoners awaiting trial at the Old Bailey were held, so many of the prisoners were charged with offences that carried the death penalty.

Holmes gave evidence in one such trial on Friday, September 13th, 1822, when Thomas Prior was charged with the wilful murder of his aunt, Elizabeth Martin. Thomas Prior was aged about twenty at the time of the trial and according to the witnesses called, *'had from his infancy been considered a person of weak intellect'*. He was alleged to have stabbed his aunt several times whilst she slept. The judge made it clear to the jury that they were not there to consider whether the prisoner was guilty of the offence, but rather to decide whether he was of a sound state of mind. After hearing evidence from a number of Prior's acquaintances, who all described his strange behaviour, the judge called for a medical opinion on the patient. The newspaper accounts of the trial reported that:

'John Pocock Holmes the surgeon of Newgate stated that the prisoner was a complete idiot. He did not believe that he could answer to an indictment'.

This was an important piece of evidence for the court to hear, as under the 1800 Act 'for the Safe Custody of Insane Persons Charged with an Offence', anyone who was deemed 'non compus mentis' by reason of suffering from a mental insufficiency or a mental perversity, could be detained at His Majesty's pleasure rather than being found guilty of a charge. The term 'idiot' was a well-recognised term that differentiated those with a 'defect in mind from birth' from those classified as 'lunatics' who had a mental illness. After hearing all the evidence, the jury wasted no time in declaring that they found Thomas Prior was *not in sane mind*. Judge Best ordered him to be taken away and to be dealt with as directed by the coroner at Elizabeth Martin's inquest, who had said that if the jury returned a verdict that he was insane, he should be removed to Bedlam to be confined during His Majesty's pleasure. In fact, he was taken to Hoxton House, a private establishment run by Sir Jonathan Miles at Hoxton where he remained for twelve years until he was transferred to the Bethlem Hospital in 1836. His patient records show that he never again exhibited any signs of violence, and by the time of his admission to the Bethlem, he was described as being almost blind and very deaf. He spent the rest of his life in that hospital, dying of erysipelas in 1855.

As well as his prison work, Holmes deputised for Mr Box when he was not able to attend to patients that required urgent attention. He was called to such a case on Wednesday, October 16th, 1822, when Mr Sturtevant, a well-known Glover and Hosier of 36 Ludgate Street, became suddenly unwell. He had returned from a few days in the country and was sitting and conversing with his niece when he suddenly complained of a pain in his chest. His niece immediately summoned Mr Box, but he was indisposed and sent Holmes in his place. Holmes arrived about six o'clock in the evening and recommended treatment with bleeding. He had no sooner commenced the treatment when the patient fell back in his chair and died. Mr Sturtevant's death at the age of seventy-five was reported as *'an awful instance of sudden death'*, with Holmes' name linked to some of the reports.

In 1823, Holmes purchased a lease on 21 Fish Street, Doctor's Commons for the sum of £300 including the cost of repairs. Fish Street was located on the south bank of the Thames and was close to St. Paul's Cathedral. The address of the house in Fish Street is given by Holmes as Old Fish Street or Old Fish Street Hill. Maps of 1830 show it adjoined to a sugar refinery which was on the corner of Fish Street and Little Distaff Lane, with the house facing St. Nicholas Church on the opposite side of the road. To the rear of 21 Fish Street were a distillery and a carpenter's shop, with the White Horse Inn extending from its entrance to the rear of the properties. The map of 1799 shows the various properties in that section of the street.

Maps of Fish Street. *Source: Horwood's Plan of London (1792–9)*
British Library. Source: London Metropolitan Archives

The use of 'Doctors' Commons' in the Fish Street address refers to its location adjacent to Doctors' Commons in Knightrider Street. Doctors' Commons, rather than being a medically related organisation, was the name of an ancient set of five courts to which only law graduates of Cambridge or Oxford University could be admitted. These courts, which occupied a number of sites surrounding St. Paul's Cathedral, dealt with ecclesiastical law, maritime law, wills and divorces.

Within eighteen months of returning to England, Holmes, now thirty-eight years of age, had settled into building a new life in London. He had a post as an assistant surgeon, his pension from the Hudson's Bay Company and a lease on a house where he could start to develop a practice of his own. Holmes now needed to make a decision about the future of his 'country marriage' to Betsy, and the best course of action with regard to their three children. Holmes had gained permission to bring his children over to England. However, as he was technically an unmarried man in the sight of the law and the church, he was free to marry in England despite the fact that Betsy was still alive. This was the situation with numerous Company employees, many of whom returned to England and took an English wife whilst still supporting their previous wife and family that they had left behind.

Since his arrival in London, Holmes had made the acquaintance of a young lady by the name of Charlotte Eliza Bowen, the daughter of Mrs Sarah Bowen. Mrs Bowen was the widow of what she described in an advertisement for lodgers in 1832 as a *'highly respectable clergyman'*, a term that was not perhaps entirely accurate. Charlotte was not yet twenty years old, some eighteen years younger than Holmes and was described as *'a very beautiful and accomplished young lady'*. The gap in ages might have attracted some comment in society, but from Mrs Bowen's viewpoint, the prospect of marrying off her eldest daughter to a professional man would have been a great relief, whatever the age difference. Holmes and Charlotte would have found a lot in common, given that they both came from clergy families and had both been brought up in an isolated rural setting. Charlotte's childhood experiences were, however, a little different from Holmes' because of the poor financial position of her father.

Charlotte was christened by her father, Richard Bowen, who was the curate at the church in the village of Mainstone in Shropshire. He was a graduate of Cambridge University and married Sarah Evans, who was also from the parish of Mainstone, in 1792, his profession being recorded on the marriage record as Clerk of the Parish. He was appointed as the vicar of Myndtown, Shropshire in 1810, and held that position until his death on May 24th, 1820. Richard had inherited some property, and the residual amount from his father's estate in 1801, but the funds raised from the sale of the property were not sufficient to meet the debts of the estate or the annuity of twenty pounds which Richard's sister Rebecca had inherited, together with her father's *'best bed'* and her late mother's *'wearing apparel'*. A farm in Radnorshire which had been left to Richard in the Will had to be sold to pay the debts and meet the costs of his sister's annuity, and the remainder of the proceeds from the estate were placed into a Trust for sixty years.

Charlotte's father met with hard times in the last six years of his life and he had been plagued by debt. In December 1814, Richard Bowen's trustees issued a notice through their solicitor, J. Dickson of Dogpole, Shrewsbury, that if any of his creditors would sign a 'letter of licence' giving him time to pay this debt without the risk of legal action, then the trustees would pay a dividend to those who signed the letter, but no dividend would be paid to any creditors who refused to sign. In January 1815 the 'letter of licence' was signed by Richard Bowen's creditors which gave him a limited time to repay his debts without risk of legal intervention. In May 1818 his Trustee, Lancelott Dowbiggin, placed an advertisement in the newspapers informing his creditors that a further dividend of four shillings in the pound would be paid to them at the house of Mr Thomas Wilkes, Innkeeper, Mardol, Shrewsbury on May 7th, 8th and 9th, 1818. The attempt to pay off the debts was not successful, and in 1819 Richard Bowen was imprisoned in His Majesty's Gaol of Shrewsbury as a 'Prisoner of Debt'. The prisons in England had become overwhelmed by the number of imprisoned debtors, who could remain in prison indefinitely if their creditors so wished. To remedy this, in 1813 Parliament had created a Court for the Relief of Insolvent Debtors, where insolvent debtors could apply to the court for release from prison. The central court was held in Portugal Street, Lincoln's Inns Field, and the scenes in the court were graphically described by Charles Dickens in The Pickwick Papers. He described the court as a *'Lofty room, Ill-lighted and worse ventilated'*, adding *'a casual visitor might suppose this place to be a temple dedicated to the Genius of Seediness'*. His description was based on his experience as a reporter, and also from the time when his father was sent to Marshalsea prison in 1824, when Dickens was twelve years old, for a debt to a baker.

A description in 'The Leisure Hour' gives a clear impression of the process which prisoners were subjected to:

'The object of general interest at the moment is a tall fellow, of middle age, in semi-rural garb, who, trickling with perspiration, and nearly dumb foundered with cross-questioning, bears on his face the expression of a wild animal at bay. He has claimed release from the debtor's prison, where he has been confined; but he cannot account, or he will not account, for fifteen hundred pounds, of which he stood possessed nine months ago, and which, of course, his creditors are anxious to get sight of. He has had complicated doings with some small landed property down in the south; he has bought and sold, mortgaged and redeemed, leased and released, borrowed and paid,

and lent moneys, and has mingled together his transactions in such an inexplicable way, that neither he nor the lawyers can unravel the web. Then, there is, an aunt in the business, who is bedridden and unproduceable, and only speechable at rare intervals she is at the bottom of all the mystery, but she cannot throw any light upon it until she gets well, which won't be, according to appearances, until the nephew is safe out of prison, be that when it may. Meanwhile, the badgered debtor struggles in the toils, and we, willing to escape from the spectacle of his shifts and doubles, and from the suffocation, leave him to make the best he can of it.'

The practical operation of the court was outlined by James Nichols in his publication 'The Practice of the Court for Relief of Insolvent Debtors'. Cases outside London were devolved to other county courts. The Act made provision for hearings to be held in front of a commissioner at a provincial assize court, or by a Justice of the Peace at a sessional hearing near to the gaol where the prisoner was held once the London Court had agreed that the petition for release could be heard and it had been published in the London Gazette. Richard Bowen's case was posted in the London Gazette and was heard at the General Quarter Sessions of the Peace at the Shire Hall in Shrewsbury on Saturday, June 5th, 1819, at ten o'clock in the morning. Sadly, a year after his release Richard died on May 2nd, 1820, and his widow and her two daughters then moved to London where Charlotte met Holmes.

Holmes' relationship with Charlotte grew and, with the agreement of Mrs Bowen, arrangements were made for them to be married in the Autumn of 1823. The marriage ceremony was to be conducted at the church directly opposite Holmes' house in Old Fish Street. The wedding took place on September

15th, 1823, at St. Nicholas Cole Abbey, with Charlotte's mother, Sarah Bowen, giving consent to the marriage and her sister Maria Rebecca acting as one of the witnesses. The marriage had been the subject of a marriage contract issued by the Bishop of London on September 13th, 1823, and this contract was in the form of a sworn statement that there was no impediment to the marriage. It carried a penalty of £200 if the marriage did not proceed because of false information being provided. Charlotte was under the age of twenty-one, having been born in October 1802 and baptised on October 7th, 1802, in Mainstone, Shropshire. As she was a minor, she needed her parents' permission to get married, and the declaration of her mother that she was a widow and the lawful parent of Charlotte is recorded in the church documents. Pupils of Holmes had reported that Charlotte was the daughter of a surgeon and a good surgeon herself. Marrying a woman from a medical family would be seen as an asset by many practitioners, as a wife with a range of medical skills and knowledge would assist in building a successful practice. However, there is no evidence to support the suggestion by Holmes' pupils that Charlotte was a surgeon. There were examples during this period of women taking apprenticeships in surgery, and of the family of surgeons and apothecaries taking a part in running a family practice. Whether or not Charlotte did receive any training as a surgeon, or had contacts with other family members with medical knowledge, she was remembered by Holmes' pupils as a skilled anatomist and a good surgeon who helped to teach Holmes' students basic anatomy and aspects of surgery.

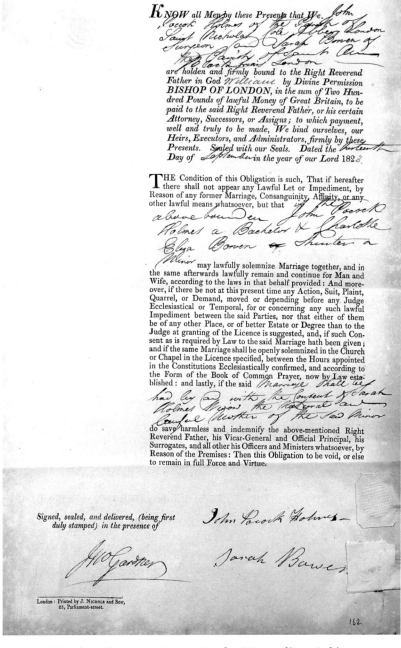

KNOW all Men by these Presents that We *John Pocock Holmes of the Parish of Saint Nicholas Cole Abbey London Surgeon and Sarah Bowen of the Parish of Saint Ann Blackfriars London* are holden and firmly bound to the Right Reverend Father in God *William* by Divine Permission BISHOP OF LONDON, in the sum of Two Hundred Pounds of lawful Money of Great Britain, to be paid to the said Right Reverend Father, or his certain Attorney, Successors, or Assigns; to which payment, well and truly to be made, We bind ourselves, our Heirs, Executors, and Administrators, firmly by these Presents. Sealed with our Seals. Dated the *thirteenth* Day of *September* in the year of our Lord 182*3*.

THE Condition of this Obligation is such, That if hereafter there shall not appear any Lawful Let or Impediment, by Reason of any former Marriage, Consanguinity, Affinity, or any other lawful means whatsoever, but that *if the above bounden John Pocock Holmes a Bachelor & Charlotte Eliza Bowen or Hunter a Minor* may lawfully solemnize Marriage together, and in the same afterwards lawfully remain and continue for Man and Wife, according to the laws in that behalf provided: And moreover, if there be not at this present time any Action, Suit, Plaint, Quarrel, or Demand, moved or depending before any Judge Ecclesiastical or Temporal, for or concerning any such lawful Impediment between the said Parties, nor that either of them be of any other Place, or of better Estate or Degree than to the Judge at granting of the Licence is suggested, and, if such Consent as is required by Law to the said Marriage hath been given; and if the same Marriage shall be openly solemnized in the Church or Chapel in the Licence specified, between the Hours appointed in the Constitutions Ecclesiastically confirmed, and according to the Form of the Book of Common Prayer, now by Law established: and lastly, if the said *Marriage shall be had by and with the Consent of Sarah Holmes Widow the Natural and Lawful Mother of the said Minor* do save harmless and indemnify the above-mentioned Right Reverend Father, his Vicar-General and Official Principal, his Surrogates, and all other his Officers and Ministers whatsoever, by Reason of the Premises: Then this Obligation to be void, or else to remain in full Force and Virtue.

Signed, sealed, and delivered, (being first duly stamped) in the presence of

J. W. Gardner

John Pocock Holmes

Sarah Bowen

London: Printed by J. NICHOLS and SON, 25, Parliament-street.

162

Marriage Contract: *Source: London Metropolitan Archives*

Drawn by Tho. H. Shepherd.

Pl.121

ST. NICHOLAS, COLE ABBEY, FISH STREET.

St. Nicolas Cole Abbey. *Source: Author's collection*

Charlotte moved into 21 Fish Street after the marriage, and the house was to become both their home and the principal location of Holmes' professional work. She would also have been preparing for the arrival in London of Holmes' son George, as arrangements had been made for him to come to England to be educated. George, then aged sixteen, was due to set sail on the Prince of Wales in September 1823, arriving in London before the end of October. The two girls were to remain with their mother at the Red River settlement. On September 10th, 1823, the Prince of Wales, captained by John Davison, was moored in Five Fathom Lake at York Factory, the previous days having been spent loading cargo and preparing the ship for the voyage to England. At seven in the morning, the boats from the factory started to come alongside with all the passengers and their luggage. Soon after, the passengers boarded and the Governor, William Simpson, arrived with the packets for England. He stayed on board until ten a.m. and when he departed back to the factory, he was saluted with the firing of five guns.

George and the other passengers spent the night on board and the next day set sail for England. The voyage went well, and by October 25th the ship was making its way past Gravesend. After anchoring overnight at Blackwall, it arrived safely at the London Dock Basin at five o'clock on the afternoon of Sunday, October 26th. So, after nearly fifty days at sea, George had arrived in London to be reunited with his father and to meet his stepmother, Charlotte. The education of mixed-race children of Hudson's Bay employees in England was for some a success, with the children being accepted as part of the British middle class. Others were reported to have problems adjusting to life in England and wished to return to the place of their birth. There are no records of George's education in England, but it appears that he became a sailor and sadly was lost at sea. Holmes was naturally distraught at this loss and later in life discussed this with acquaintances who wrote: *'He grieved much over the loss of his half breed son George. Scarcely a day passed but he would utter some words of sorrow over his fate'*.

Whilst Holmes was in the process of setting up his own practice at Old Fish Street, he continued in his post as assistant surgeon at Newgate, and it was through this position, in December 1823, that he was called to give evidence in a trial concerning piracy which attracted a great deal of public interest. The trial of Aaron Smith on two charges of piracy commenced on December 19th, 1823, at the Old Bailey. He was charged with having unlawfully seized two vessels off the coast of Cuba during the previous year. Smith was a British subject who had been the mate of The Zephyr, a cargo ship that had been captured by pirates on July 7th, 1822, off the Cuban coast. The pirates had boarded the ship, plundered all the cargo and threatened to burn the captain and two crew members alive if they did not hand over any money the ship was carrying. The pirates then left the Zephyr, but according to the letter written by the Zephyr's master, they *'detained my mate Aaron Smith to pilot their vessel'*. It was alleged that having been captured, Smith then fell in with the pirates and was party to two acts of piracy against British vessels sailing near Cuba. A number of witnesses were called who identified Smith as one of the pirates that had boarded their ship, and gave evidence that he had taken an active part in the events and had injured at least one crew member by striking him with a sword. Smith had eventually escaped from the pirates but was arrested in Havana when one of the crew of a ship the pirates had attacked recognised him. He was duly put in irons and shipped back to London to face trial.

Smith gave his account of the events in great detail to the court, claiming that he had been in fear for his life whilst a prisoner of the pirates, and had only taken part in the acts of piracy in order to survive. He described to the court how he had been tied to the mast of the ship and that gunpowder had been placed on the deck all around him and then ignited, causing an explosion and severe burns to his legs. In addressing the court, Smith stated that he was *compelled by the most cruel torture inflicted upon him by the savagest monster that ever lived to do what he had done'*.

The court, having heard Smith's pleas that he was a victim of the pirates rather than their accomplice, sought to find evidence that his story was true. To this end, they called Holmes in his capacity as deputy surgeon at Newgate to give evidence on any injuries that were present on Smith's legs. Holmes informed the court that when he examined Smith, there was indeed a scorch mark on both legs but he was unable to say whether this was from gunpowder, or a scald, or a burn, but was very possibly the scorch from gunpowder. Having heard all the evidence, the judge instructed the jury to retire and consider their verdict. When they returned at eight o'clock that night they informed the court that they found Aaron Smith not guilty of the charges. Smith was now a free man, and the next year published his account of his experiences in a book entitled 'The Atrocities of the Pirates'. He returned to the sea and eventually became a sea captain, but in 1826 was, bizarrely, again on trial for alleged piracy committed in 1822. Once again, he was acquitted.

The evidence that Holmes gave in the trial partially

supported Smith's account of his torture by the pirates. The court had also asked for a second medical opinion from Mr Boast, a surgeon who was described as having knowledge of the effects of gunpowder in wounds. He stated that he believed the wounds were inflicted by gunpowder because of the '*livid hue of the scars*'. Holmes may not have seen cases of severe gunpowder burns, as those with the most experience of gunpowder burns would have been army or navy surgeons. The burns arising from '*the exploding of unconfined gunpowder*' were described by Dr James Bird in a lecture on burns and scalds as being scorched or blistered in the same way as when caused by boiling oil; it was only where particles of gunpowder had entered the skin that an indelible bluish tinge could be seen. Unless Holmes saw such discolouration and recognised it as being from gunpowder, then he was correct in giving a guarded opinion as to the cause of the burns. It is of interest that another witness at the trial, a '*Serjeant of Marines*', remarked that he had often seen wounds produced by the explosion of gunpowder, and '*knew those on the prisoner's legs to have been so produced*'.

In order to advance his career, Holmes needed to gain a recognised qualification as a surgeon. On February 20th, 1824, Holmes became a Member of the Royal College of Surgeons, entitling him to use the qualification MRCS (London). The Royal College of Surgeons examinations in 1824 consisted of a one-hour oral examination comprising four fifteen-minute discussions with examiners. These examinations were not always as thorough or taxing as might be expected, with contemporary reports of these events giving an impression of a rather lax system. The certificate that Holmes was presented with proclaimed that he was now a qualified surgeon:

'Know all men by these presents: that, we, the court of examiners of the Royal College of Surgeons in London, have deliberately examined Mr Holmes and have found him to be fit, and capable, to exercise the art and science of surgery: we therefore admit him a member of the College and authorize him to practise the said art and science accordingly.

In witness whereof, we have subscribed our names; and have caused the common Seal of the College to be fixed thereunto.'

Having obtained his Membership of the College, Holmes now needed to develop his career to ensure an adequate income. Charlotte did not bring with her a large dowry, given the circumstances of her father's financial problems, and the Hudson's Bay Company Pension of £60 a year would only be paid to Holmes for a limited time. His appointment as an assistant to Mr Box was poorly remunerated and had no prospect of career advancement, so to advance his practice in the competitive medical scene of London, it was important for Holmes to raise his profile amongst the influential professional and City members of London Society. The cultivation of personal connections and obtaining patronage from wealthy patients was a key element in building a successful practice. Social and professional connections in the city could be obtained by membership of societies and clubs, but gaining a foothold in the commercial and government areas of the city would connect Holmes with many influential contacts.

Within the wide range of trade societies in the city lay the key to social and commercial contacts. Membership of a society and its associated Freedom of the City could only be obtained in one of three ways; patrimony, servitude or redemption. To be admitted through patrimony would require proof that the applicant's father was a Freeman prior to the applicant's birth. Admission through servitude was available to apprentices of Freemen, and the route through redemption involved being nominated by two Liverymen of the Guild, being accepted as suitable by the court of the guild and paying a 'fine' or redemption fee. These trade guilds or companies had a long history in the city, formed originally as craft guilds that could lay down conditions of trade by its members, and formed a route to obtaining the freedom of the city. No tradesmen could work within the boundaries of the city unless they were a Freeman, and only members of a guild could become Freemen. The guilds had become an integral part of the government of the city and membership of a guild carried the right to vote in elections and to stand for high civic office.

Holmes resolved to become a Freeman of the City of London through membership of one of the trade societies, the Wax Chandlers. The choice of the Wax Chandlers was appropriate as, in addition to being associated with the trade of beeswax candles, a luxury product compared with animal fat tallow, the Guild was also a minor medical guild through its connection with the medical uses of wax such as ointments, plasters and suppositories. The admission papers dated June 24th 1824 show that he was accepted as suitable for admission into the Company of Wax Chandlers as a Freeman by redemption. Redemption membership was by payment to the Company the sum of forty-six shillings and eight pence. His trade is recorded on the certificate as 'surgeon', and having paid his redemption fee, he was formally admitted to the Guild on June 30th, 1824. In taking the oath of a Freeman within the Worshipful Company of Wax Chandlers, he was joining a guild that had received its Royal Charter in 1484 and had been in

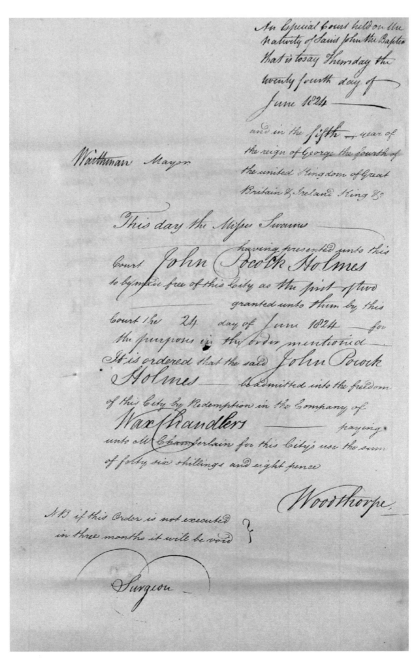

An Especial Court held on the
Nativity of Saint John the Baptist
that is to say Thursday the
twenty fourth day of
June 1824 _____

and in the fifth ____ year of
the reign of George the fourth of
the united Kingdom of Great
Britain & Ireland King &c

Waithman   Mayor.

This day the Misses Swains _____
            having presented unto this
Court John Pocock Holmes
to be made free of this City as the first of two
            granted unto them by this
Court the 24 day of June 1824 ____ for
the purposes in the Order mentioned _____
It is ordered that the said John Pocock
Holmes _____ be admitted into the freedom
of this City by Redemption in the Company of
Wax Chandlers _____ paying
unto the Chamberlain for this City's use the sum
of forty six shillings and eight pence

                                Woodthorpe

NB if this Order is not executed ⎫
in three months it will be void ⎬

            Surgeon ____

Freedom of City. *Source: London Metropolitan Archives*

168

existence for over a hundred years prior to that. The oath that he took had remained unchanged since 1664, and before the court of the company Holmes declared that *'I swear to be true to our Sovereign Lord the King's Majesty that now is and to his heirs and successors; I shall be obedient at all times hereafter to the Master and Wardens of the Art or Mystery of Wax Chandlers, London and to their successors in all matters and things concerning the said Society; I shall not disobey the warning or summons given me by the Beadle or Officer of the same Company without I have a just and reasonable excuse; and for my part I shall observe and keep all and singular the lawful and reasonable orders and ordinances and constitutions made or hereafter to be made for the well ordering and governing of the said Master and Wardens and Society and their successors and shall not do any hurt or prejudice to the said Society but shall let and hinder the same to my utmost power, so help me God'.*

Being a Freeman of the Guild meant that Holmes also became a Freeman of the City of London. The next stage in his membership of the Guild was to progress to being a Liveryman. This required a further vote of the ruling body of the Guild, the Court, and these votes were taken by acclamation, so would be passed unless there was an objection from members of the Court. Being a Liveryman would mean that Holmes was a full member of the Guild, with rights to vote for the Lord Mayor of London and the Sheriffs of the Corporation of London. Holmes became a Liveryman on July 7th, 1824, and at a meeting of the Court was 'enclothed' with a Livery Gown which he was allowed to wear at the next formal or social event of the Guild. Following this, only senior members of the Guild would wear a gown, and along with other Liverymen, Holmes would wear a guild tie at formal events.

By 1825, Holmes was a settled and well-respected member of the local community in the city. On June 3rd, 1825, John Holmes was approached by Mr Acocks, the cheesemonger, whose warehouse at 7 Fish Street was directly across the street from his house at number 21. Acocks asked whether on June 6th his friend Mr Michael Gunston could conceal himself in the surgery to watch the warehouse, as theft was suspected and he planned to try and catch the thief red-handed. On the agreed day, Gunston took up position at 21 Fish Street, and at about half past eight in the morning saw the clerk of the warehouse go to breakfast. Shortly afterwards, John Stretch, who was in charge of the warehouse in the clerk's absence, came to the door and looked up and down the street for about fifteen minutes. He was then joined by a William Palmer, and they entered the warehouse, and soon after, Palmer left and walked down Fish Street. Gunston was then able to see John Stretch climb into the loft of the warehouse and bring down a meat wrapper, which he placed on the floor of the warehouse. He then used a pair of steps to climb and bring down a side of bacon which he put into the wrapper. Palmer then returned, accompanied by a local porter, Thomas Brimble, who entered the warehouse and emerged carrying the side of bacon whilst Palmer kept watch at the door.

Holmes came downstairs into the surgery at about nine o'clock and saw Brimble carrying the bacon down the street whilst Palmer stood at the warehouse door watching. Holmes recognised Brimble, as he knew the family in a professional capacity, having attended Brimble's wife in the past. John Gunston followed Brimble and asked him where he was taking the bacon. Brimble replied that he had been told to carry it to a person called Coomley in Globe Road. A police officer was called, and all three men were arrested and charged with stealing a flitch of bacon valued at forty shillings, the property of David Yates and Thomas Acocks. The three appeared in court at the Old Bailey, the central criminal court, on June 30th and Holmes was called as a witness. In his evidence, he stated, 'I live opposite the prosecutor's ware-house. Mr Acock asked me to let a friend of his watch in my premises, and a few minutes before nine o'clock on the day in question, I came down and saw Brimble go out with the bacon on his back — Palmer was standing at the door.'

Holmes was then questioned by the defence lawyer, who asked whether Holmes knew the prisoner Brimble. Holmes replied, 'Yes, I attended his wife. When Brimble was taken up he was anxious to go on to the place to which he was to carry the bacon, as he said it would convince any person that he was employed in an honest way: he was (I believe) a porter in a nail warehouse in Old-street road.'

The last part of Holmes' reply may have helped Brimble's defence as he claimed that he was paid as a porter to carry the bacon to Coomley's and was not aware that it was stolen. He was told he would receive his pay there, and if he did not receive his money then he was to return and get it off Stretch and Palmer. The jury found Brimble not guilty, but Stretch and Palmer were found guilty. The case was adjourned for sentencing, and on July 30th, the two appeared before Mr Serjeant Arabin, who said that Palmer had received an excellent character witness and the Court would deal leniently with him. Stretch, however, had been transported to Australia ten years previously and then returned to London after his sentence had been completed. Mr Arabin addressed Stretch, who he said had *'recommended his career of guilt, therefore the Court was bound to act towards him with severity, notwithstanding his advanced age.'* Palmer was sentenced to imprisonment for three months at a House of Correction and kept to hard labour whilst Stretch was sentenced to be *'transported beyond the sea for the term of 14 years'*. The court reports in the Morning Advertiser of July 4th noted that *'Upon hearing the judgment, the latter prisoner appeared dreadfully affected'*.

With his surgical and obstetric practice beginning to grow, Holmes was able to take on students, and he had three, one of which was studying at Holmes' expense rather than being a paying student. One student, Richard Peckover, lived with the Holmes family for two years and assisted in building models of obstetric instruments that Holmes was designing. In 1826, Dr Holmes was awarded 'The Gold Vulcan Medal of the Society of Arts' for the design of craniotomy forceps. The Society of Arts, the full title of which was 'The Society instituted at London for the encouragement of Arts, Manufactures and Commerce', awarded both medals and cash rewards (premiums) to a wide variety of areas of innovation and artistic skill. Within the field of mechanics, they awarded prizes for the development of medical, surgical and veterinary devices. The awards were made under the condition that models of the devices were left with the Society, and the inventor relinquished all *'pretensions to patent'*. The medical devices were assessed by the submission of certificates from professionals, and the decisions were *'guided by the written certificates and oral testimony of those, both in and out of the Society'*.

The submission from Dr Holmes was made in 1825 for the 1825 to 1826 session and was accompanied by a number of certificates from some notable professionals, including James Blundell, a pioneer of blood transfusion and midwifery who undertook the first human-to-human blood transfusion. He was 'Professor of Obstetricy' at Guys Medical School, and his commendation of Dr Holmes' instruments was repeated in his lectures and published in his collected lectures in 1834 entitled 'The Principles and Practices of Obstetricy as at Present Taught by Dr James Blundell'. The comments in his lectures expanded on those expressed in his certificate of 1825-26 with regard to the craniotomy forceps which were designed to assist with the delivery of a dead foetus.

'The instrument contrived by Haighton, and much improved by Dr Davis, has been still further perfected by Mr Holmes, of Old Fish Street, a gentleman who, to omit his other instruments, has produced the best pair of craniotomy forceps that I know of, and which I now always use. In his instrument there is no display of elegance, but it is large, strong, and very powerful, not liable when we are using it either to bend or break. Of this instrument, the grand perfection lies in the size and strength of the teeth. On one blade there are three large dentiform processes, very like the incisor of a rabbit, if I may be allowed to make such a comparison; and in the other blade arc three cavities in apposition with these, into which they pass, after thoroughly piercing the bones, so that there is no danger lest the forceps should slip away. Besides these processes, there are several which are smaller, designed to give you a hold of the scalp. To me, however, these smaller teeth, appear to be unnecessary, for if you have a good hold of the bone, the hold of the scalp, not of much importance, will also be secure. The three large chisel teeth constitute, in my opinion, the great excellence of

Holmes's forceps...... The ordinary craniotomy forceps will frequently slip away; I should, therefore, recommend you to use those improved by Mr Holmes.'

A certificate provided by Dr Holmes to the Society of Arts after the award of the medal was from Astley Cooper. A certificate was also provided by John Ramsbotham, a much-respected physician, and his son Francis Ramsbotham, a noted obstetrician who occupied many prestigious posts and who stated in March 1826 that: *'I think Mr Holmes's craniotomy forceps, while they display much ingenuity are calculated to afford the operator great power in his attempts to extract a perforated head through a deformed pelvis'.*

The medal was presented to Holmes at a ceremony held in the King's Theatre, Haymarket on Monday, May 29th, 1826. The medals were presented by His Royal Highness the Duke of Sussex. The audience were subscribers and friends of the Society for the Encouragement of Arts Manufactures and Commerce, and a number of distinguished guests including the French and Persian ambassadors, the latter attending in full national costume.

TRANSACTIONS

OF THE

SOCIETY

INSTITUTED AT LONDON

FOR THE

ENCOURAGEMENT

OF

ARTS, MANUFACTURES,

AND

COMMERCE;

WITH

THE PREMIUMS

OFFERED IN THE YEAR 1825.

VOL. XLIV.

LONDON:

SOLD BY THE HOUSEKEEPER, AT THE SOCIETY'S
HOUSE IN THE ADELPHI; AND
BY ALL BOOKSELLERS.

———

1826.

Transaction of Society for the Encouragement
of Arts & Manufactures

In 1827 Holmes made another submission to the Society for the Encouragement of Arts and was awarded the large gold medal for his improved obstetrical instruments. The submission was in the form of a monograph outlining the improvements he had made to the design of a variety of obstetric instruments, with illustrations of them and certificates from a variety of practitioners as to the value of the improvements.

These successes in his professional life helped Holmes to build up a network of contacts across London and his time with the Hudson's Bay Company had also produced many useful connections. Whilst he was at Cumberland House, he had assisted Sir John Franklin, the well-known explorer, by building canoes and snowshoes, and had maintained his links with officers of the Company such as William Smith, the company secretary. Smith was based in the London offices of the company at Hudson's Bay House on the south side of Fenchurch Street. On entering the hallway of the Company House, visitors were greeted with *'a vast pair of horns of the Moose deer, weighing 56 pounds and various canoes'*. The canoes were on view to anyone attending the annual fur auctions at Fenchurch Street and attracted the attention of visitors, three were exhibited: *'a canoe such as is used on North American rivers, and dragged up the rocks at the different portages, attracts the attention of the spectator; at the other end, a smaller one, suitable for a man to sit in when employed in harpooning seals, catches the eye, while over the door a larger canoe made of bark, in which one of the directors of the company, in days gone by, ventured on many an arduous enterprise'*.

Holmes was to recall with pride that he had built one of the canoes that were displayed. The contribution of John Holmes to the Parry expedition of 1827 is noted in the 'Narrative of an attempt to reach the North Pole' published in 1828.

'*Our provisions consisted of biscuit, made by Mr Le Mann, of the best wheaten flour;* **beef pemmican.** *For this article of our equipment, which contains a large proportion of nutriment in a small weight and compass, and is therefore invaluable on such occasions, we are much indebted to the kindness of Mr J. P. Holmes, Surgeon, of Old Fish Street, who had resided several years in the Hudson's Bay Establishments, and undertook to superintend the manufacture of it. The process, which requires great attention, consists in drying large thin slices of the lean of the meat over the smoke of wood-fires, then pounding it, and lastly mixing it with about an equal weight of its own fat. In this state it is quite ready for use, without further cooking.*'

The Expedition to reach the North Pole was the last great exploration undertaken by Captain William Parry and was planned to attempt to reach the Pole by crossing the ice north of Spitsbergen. This route had originally been proposed by John Franklin, who Holmes had met during his time in Hudson Bay and had built canoes and snowshoes for him. Parry's ship, the Hecla, anchored at the Nore on March 30th, 1827, and set sail on April 4th. Holmes received a letter from Parry inviting him to dine aboard the Hecla at the Nore prior to departure.

Holmes' obstetric practice had been given much publicity with the award of the two Gold Medals, and his skill with his instruments meant that he was called in to advise on cases where the treating doctor was not having success. On June 18th, 1828, he was called to see a patient in St Martin's Street, Leicester Square. When the patient was five and a half months pregnant a fire had broken out in the house next door which had caused her great distress. She had experienced a sudden pain in her left side followed by a violent haemorrhage which had continued to some extent since then. She had been seen by Dr George Darling of 6 Russell Square, an Edinburgh trained physician who numbered the poet John Clare amongst his patients. Dr Darling had prescribed medication for her and advised that she should take cool drinks and remain recumbent, but his regime did not appear to have had any success. When Holmes visited, the patient was swollen with fluid, weak and pale, having lost a great deal of blood. He recalled that *'I entertained a very unfavourable opinion of the case; and my fear was much increased when I reflected that the most judicious treatment that could be adopted had already been put in force'.*

A consultation with George Darling on June 21st resulted in the decision that the only reasonable course was to bring on premature labour. Holmes suggested the use of ergot of rye as a method of hastening the labour, to which Dr Darling agreed. The use of ergot to accelerate labour had been known for many years and was used by midwives and doctors in a form known as 'pulvis ad partum' (the powder of birth). The preparation had been introduced into the American Pharmacopeia in 1820 and then entered the British pharmacopeia, although only the American preparation had a standardised ergot content. Controversy over the efficacy of ergot continued over the remainder of the nineteenth century until the various constituents of ergot were identified and standard preparations of the active components became available. In suggesting ergot in this case, Holmes was aware of the varying views on its safety in obstructed labour which were discussed both in the medical journals that year and in the London Medical Society, of which he was a member. In addition, an influential publication in America in 1822 had warned specifically that ergot should only be used to stop bleeding following delivery and that its use to hasten labour was dangerous. The author had suggested that the powder of birth be renamed pulvis ad mortum (the powder of death). However, following his discussion with Darling, Holmes returned to St Martin's Street and at half past eleven that night gave the patient a wine glass full of infusion of ergot, which he had prepared by boiling up three drachms of ergot in half a pint of water. After some time there had been no progression and, following an internal examination, Holmes repeated the dose, which brought on 'griping pains' and then, at ten-minute intervals, two more doses were given. The patient reported increasing pain and Holmes was able to introduce a finger into the uterus and attempt to rupture the membranes. These were, however, so tough that he did not succeed. The pains continued and soon became so intense that he feared that the uterus would rupture, he, therefore, used his perforating stilet which he had invented in the previous year and was able to puncture the membranes. The pains increased and he used further doses of ergot as the baby started to move along the birth canal and finally, at half past five in the morning, the child was born with a breech presentation. The placenta was delivered shortly after and the patient *'lost not a drop of blood after delivery'*, a circumstance which Holmes attributed to his use of the ergot of rye.

Holmes reported this case in The Lancet the following year, concluding that *'the use of ergot is appropriate when it is desired to produce a premature labour but that cases do exist where this potent remedy may be useless and its action injurious unless the unyielding membranes be perforated'*.

Whilst Holmes was building a good professional reputation

in the city, he still needed to ensure that his patients paid their outstanding bills and, rather than approach them himself, he employed a debt collector. In July 1828, Holmes took one of his debt collectors to court at The Guildhall, a man by the name of William Garstang, who Holmes stated had embezzled some of his money. Holmes informed the court that in March that year he had engaged Garstang to collect some small debts amounting to about £40. Garstang had come with very good references from a trader, so Holmes was content to allow him to visit his debtors and collect the amounts owed. About £6 of the debts had been collected when Holmes discovered that Garstang had not accounted for some of the money he had received. On April 18th, Holmes ordered Garstang to stop making collections and to send in his accounts of the amounts collected but saw nothing more of the man until May 14th, when he met him in the street. Holmes informed the court that when he met Garstang he *'gave him a good shaking and threatened to send him to Newgate if he did not immediately send in his accounts'*, and that, if he had not been in a haste to attend upon a lady who had sent for him, he would have detained Garstang there and then. In June, Garstang returned his accounts together with the original list of debtors, but it appeared he had retained a copy of the list and continued to collect money from those named upon it. On July 8th, Holmes discovered Garstang in the act of trying to collect money from one of the debtors and took him to the constabulary to be charged. The case was heard four days later by Sir Peter Laurie who dismissed the case as, although Garstang had attempted to get money from the debtor, no money had been paid to him and he had returned the accounts as requested in June. Having been released by the court, Garstang visited Holmes the same evening and presented him with a bill of £1 and one shilling for his services. Holmes declined to pay, as the arrangement had been that the payment would be 10% of the money collected and the bill amounted to nearly 20% of the debts recovered. The next day, Holmes took out a charge of embezzlement against Garstang which was heard by Alderman Key. Holmes addressed the court, saying that *'the prisoner was a bad fellow'* and he would like to see him punished, adding *'so would the prisoner's wife'*, a remark which occasioned loud laughter from the public gallery. Garstang's defence was that he did not accept that Holmes had withdrawn his authority for the collections to continue. The magistrate, however, believed that the authority had been withdrawn and that Garstang had received eight shillings from *'a poor man under threat of commencing legal proceedings in Mr Holmes's name'* nine days after the authority was removed. He therefore committed the prisoner for trial.

In addition to his growing surgical and obstetric practice, Holmes was also taking on students for tuition, some of whom lodged with him and Charlotte at 21 Fish Street. The education of medical students in this period was in the main by apprenticeship and attendance at lectures and tuition at private anatomy schools. Holmes is known to have taken on pupils and his reputation gained from his publications and prizes would be an attraction for aspiring doctors. Whether Holmes ran a private anatomy school is unclear, but several events reported in the press with regard to the supply of bodies for dissection brought Holmes' name into the picture in unfavourable circumstances, and suggest that he had a connection with the Webb Street Anatomy School. One of Holmes' students, Richard Peckover, recalled that, as a student, he lived with the Holmes family for a period of two years and that there were two other students with Holmes at the same time, a Mr Bird and a Mr Holman. The name Holman is of interest as during the period that Peckover was a student with Holmes, one of the pupils, a Henry Hale Holme, gained a degree of notoriety. In 1828 he was charged with having taken a head from a grave. The publicity surrounding this case was greater than usual as the head was that of his mother who had died some twenty years previously. Whether this was the 'Holman' that Peckover recalled some thirty years later is unclear, but given the similarity between Holme and Holman then it may be the same student. Holme's defence was that he was studying phrenology and was attempting a scientific investigation of a hereditary disorder. The 'Phrenological Case' as it was called in newspapers across the country, was heard at the Middlesex sessions in November 1828 when Holme and two accomplices were charged with violation of a grave and severing the head from one of the bodies in the grave *to the outrage of public decency'*. The majority of such cases being heard in courts at this time involved 'Resurrectionists' or 'Burkers', who exhumed recently deceased bodies for sale to anatomy schools. Such action was clearly seen as unlawful as it involved 'disinterring a body for gain' and was a criminal offence. The act of disinterring a body was itself only punishable by an ecclesiastical court.

The defence for Holme pleaded that as there was no intent to gain from the action, then the court had no jurisdiction in the matter unless the body had been taken up for *'charm, sorcery and witchcraft'*, an offence created during the reign of King James. The court took the view that if the offence alleged in the indictment, of taking up the body causing outrage against decency and public morals were made out, then the offence was punishable by law. The fact that the head was that of the accused's mother made the case a subject of comment in newspapers across the country, with the court hearings being reported in detail, and the level of public interest high. The circumstances surrounding the removal of the head were heard in detail in the court, with a number of witnesses being called. The vicar of the church at Hendon, a Mr Williams, informed the court that he had been approached by Henry Holme's father, who requested permission to open the family vault in the churchyard the day before his daughter's funeral. Mr Williams had refused the request on the grounds that such an action would require a faculty from Doctors' Commons which was the Ecclesiastical Inn of Court located near St. Paul's Cathedral, where issues regarding opening graves or re-siting graves would be heard.

Mr Williams' evidence was challenged by the defence on the grounds that no evidence had been presented to show that Mr Williams was either a minister of the church or indeed the vicar of Hendon. This challenge was dismissed and was unlikely to succeed as the Reverend Theodore Williams was at the time of the hearing a well-known and somewhat controversial character in London, being of Caribbean ancestry and the wealthy heir to income from slavery. He was in 1832 to be closely involved in the final stages of a murder trial of two infamous London resurrectionists, Bishop and Williams, who were hanged having been found guilty of murder in the 'Italian Boy' case of that year. The Reverend Theodore Williams was involved in taking the confessions of the two men prior to their execution and his role in this was to become the subject of much adverse comment. Even prior to this, he would have been well known in the city for his refusal to ban cockfighting in his parish and his unpredictable tempers, which on one occasion resulted in him smashing a headstone in the graveyard into pieces with his bare hands when there was a dispute over payment of the burial fees. Despite the vicar's reputation of violence and of taking parishioners to court for a variety of reasons, the Holme family decided to open the family vault without his permission to *'collect any scattered bones in the vault and put them in a decent form'*. Witnesses who were passing the churchyard at half past seven on the Saturday the event occurred stated that they observed Henry Hale Holme and his co-defendants opening the coffin. John Connolly, a hairdresser of Hendon, told the court:

'I saw the defendant in the vault; Mr Holme removed the shroud, and after propping the head of the body with a piece of wood, he cut off the head with a knife and put it into a blue bag, after which he quitted the church-yard, with it in his hand; he returned afterwards, and I saw him take a skull from the coffin, on the right-hand side, which was also put into the bag; I could see that there were hair and flesh on the first head he took'.

In deciding on the verdict, the court accepted evidence from Dr Unwin, a physician at the city dispensary, Dr Hume, Mr Stanley of St Bartholomew's Hospital and Dr Drew of Gower Street, to whom Henry Holme had been articled, that he had *'a most admirable character for ardour in his profession, and for general morality and propriety of conduct'*. The case did not fit the usual pattern of 'resurrectionists' or 'body lifters' in this period, given that the act was done in broad daylight and involved the body of a relative. The sale of parts of bodies for anatomical teaching was not a pattern that was commonly seen. Bodies that had been stolen for sale to anatomical schools may have had some parts removed where more money could be made, but this usually involved items such as teeth, as they could be sold to dentists to make dentures. Henry Hale Holme's plea was that the act was in the interest of science, particularly to investigate the phrenology of the skulls to look at any similarities between them with regard to a familial disease that had afflicted both of the relatives he exhumed. A letter was also submitted by John Abernathy, the surgeon, in which he stated:

'I solemnly declare, that I believe Mr Henry H. Holme was influenced in the act for which the present proceedings have been instituted against him, merely by the love of scientific investigation; and that he is by no means deficient in kind feelings, or respect to public opinion. I have known Mr Holme to be a diligent student of his profession during five years, and every thing I have observed of his conduct during that period warrants me in making the above declaration.

John Abernathy

Bedford Row 31st October 1828'

Once all the evidence had been heard, the court deferred a decision to allow the chairman to *'make up his mind as to what sentence to pass'*.

When the court reconvened in December 1828, the chairman was moved towards leniency, his verdict relying on the evidence that the act was done in the name of science. He stated that he was embarrassed in giving the verdict as the act was *'a gross outrage upon public decency'* but as Holme had committed the act under the idea that he was rendering a service to science, he would not *'ruin him by sending him to prison, and under all the circumstances, the sentence he should have was, that Holme should pay a 50 pound fine to the King and his co-defendants 5 pounds each'*. The money was paid and the defendants discharged.

The fact that Henry Holme had also been a pupil of John Pocock Holmes did not emerge during the court hearing, and it was not until January 1829 that the link became public. The unfortunate similarity between Holmes' name and his pupil Holme appears to have led to some confusion and rumour in the city, and indeed in some newspapers, his name was reported as 'Holmes' rather than 'Holme'. John Pocock Holmes was moved to write a letter to The Times, which was published on January 22nd, 1829, in which he sought to distance himself from the 'Phrenological Case'.

'Sir,- Although ignorance may, in some cases, operate as a plea for error, yet what circumstances can palliate the crime of wantonly disseminating an opprobrious imputation, founded on a gross falsehood?

By what strange perversion the name of John Pocock Holmes, surgeon-accoucher, 21, Old Fish Street, Doctors'-commons (who has been in practice more than 28 years), can comparatively apply to that of Henry Hale Holm, a pupil, I cannot imagine; but, Sir, such is the celerity with which detraction flies, that the case which lately appeared before the public, of this young man cutting off the head of his deceased mother, is through the city, attributed to me! And, as a duty which I owe my friends especially, as well as myself, I particularly request of you to insert this correction of so infamous a report in your reputable journal; to which sistement it may not be irrelevant to add, that my father was a clergyman of the Established Church, and his bones, together with those of my mother, who died 12 years ago, now lie in the churchyard of South Leverton, near Retford, in the county of Nottingham.

I am, Sir, your obedient servant.

J. Pocock Holmes,

21, Old Fish Street, Doctors' commons

Dec 24.'

Holmes' annoyance at the confusion between himself and his student soon became of less importance to him when in late January 1829, a fire broke out in the sugar baking factory in Old Fish Street adjacent to Holmes' house. The factory was owned by a Mr Banks who was away at his country house at the time and, in addition to the inflammable nature of the sugar stored there, the factory backed onto a distillery and a carpenter's shop. The fire was noticed at ten o'clock in the evening on Wednesday, January 22nd by the neighbours. It was later stated that the fire had been started by the workers in the bakery leaving their aprons too near a fire. The inhabitants of the street requested the workmen open the factory doors to allow them to assist in fighting the fire, but they were refused entry. The fire began to take hold on the building, and neighbouring houses were at risk. The firemen arrived promptly but were only able to gain access by forcing their way into Mr Bank's private residence in Distaff Lane. Despite the fire engine attending promptly, the two adjoining houses were soon on fire, and the blaze continued until five the next morning when the roof of the bakery collapsed and partly extinguished the flames. Newspaper reports of the fire stated that the fire did not affect St. Nicholas Church which adjoined the bakery, but that the interior of the bakery which consisted of seven storeys was entirely consumed. The ruins of the bakery finally collapsed inwards around half past two in the morning, leaving the giant chimney stacks swaying in the wind and posing a danger to anyone in the vicinity. Constables were posted in the street to prevent locals from straying near to the danger.

Fires at sugar factories were a regular occurrence, with ten serious fires in sugar refineries occurring across Britain in 1829. The process involved, which used open fires, heating pans and ovens, was notoriously dangerous, and it was difficult to obtain insurance against fire for these factories. Banks' sugar factory was insured, though the loss of sugar and damage caused by the fire was estimated to exceed the insured value of £40,000 and was predicted to cause problems for a number of insurance companies across the city who had issued the insurance policies. The fire caused damage to 21 Fish Street, and Holmes recorded that *'it was burnt down all but the back front'*. Holmes obtained a further lease on the building for twenty-one years and repairing the damage from the fire cost him £800.

On Saturday, January 30th, 1830, Holmes was called to a house in Little Carter Lane where he found a woman suffering from a stab wound to the abdomen. Holmes had been called to the house by the woman's son, John Haslam, who at eleven o'clock on Friday night had found his mother sitting in her house with a hand pressed on a wound *'above her stays'*. As there was not much bleeding at the time, they did not summon any assistance. When Holmes examined the wound, he found it was about an inch and a half deep and was told that it had been inflicted on the previous day and had bled considerably overnight. He questioned the woman as to how the injury had occurred, and she told him that her husband, Mathew Carter, had been out drinking during the day and had returned home drunk. She had told him to go to bed and that he was not fit to be trusted with running the fishmonger's shop which he kept. According to her, he then threatened to stab her if she did not leave the room immediately. She did not think he would be violent so remained in the room, but he then took a sharp-pointed table knife and stabbed her. Holmes treated the wound as best he could and informed the son that although the bleeding had stopped, his mother was not out of danger. Mathew Carter was arrested by the watchmen and confessed to stabbing his wife, and the watchmen reported that the neighbourhood had been disturbed by the noise of him beating his wife half an hour before he stabbed her. He was brought before Mr Alderman Winchester who, having heard the charges, remanded him for trial and warned him that being drunk would not excuse him in the eyes of the law. On Monday, February 1st, Carter, who was a constable of the Ward, appeared in front of Sir J. Perring at the Guildhall. The police officer who had the prisoner in custody reported that he had visited Mrs Carter, and she was much better, he also delivered a certificate to the court signed by Holmes stating that he had no hesitation in saying that the woman was now out of danger.

In 1831, Holmes was once more involved in a case regarding Resurrectionists. In January, two graves in a churchyard in Hanley Castle Churchyard in Worcestershire were found to have been disturbed and the bodies removed. Thomas Cale, the Landlord of the Anchor Inn at Upton, which is a mile and a half from St. Mary's churchyard at Hanley Castle, was the agent for one of the coach companies providing passenger and freight transport through the county and on to London. Following the discovery of the removal of the bodies from the churchyard, he recalled arranging for two wooden boxes to be sent on the coach to London on the previous day, January 21st, 1831, the day that the bodies had been removed. The newspaper reports of the event recorded that he particularly recalled these boxes because the two men sending them had borrowed his kitchen poker to hammer on the address labels. The Worcester Herald reported that:

'The respectable and quiet village of Hanley Castle was on Friday morning last thrown into a state of great excitement by the discovery that the churchyard had, in the course of the previous night, been the scene of the revolting practices of 'Resurrectionists,' two graves, one that of a female about 20 years of age the other that of an elderly man (whose remains had been consigned to their last earthly resting place about a fortnight since) having been opened, the lid of the coffins part wrenched off, and the bodies drawn out and carried away. An anxious and active inquiry was immediately set on foot by the resident Magistrate and the parish officer, and it was discovered that at an early hour the same morning, two packing cases had been taken by two men, strangers, to the house of Mr Cale, of the Anchor Inn, Upton-upon-Severn, where a booking office is kept for the Worcester coaches. Here they coolly nailed on the cards of the address with Mr Cale's kitchen poker, and left them to be sent on to London.

They were addressed to Mr Naylor, Mr Holmes, Old Fish St, Doctor's Commons…'

Thomas Cale decided to set off to London in pursuit of the packing cases and took the Sunday night mail coach to try and trace what he suspected were the bodies from Hanley Castle churchyard. Once in London, he sought the help of the police in the form of John Richmond, the street-keeper of Newgate Street. Street keepers were appointed in various Wards of the city, as were beadles, constables, patrols and watchmen, according to the size of the Ward. These officers were in addition to the general police of the city, and by 1829 the Metropolitan Force established by Robert Peel was gradually replacing the older Ward based force. John Richmond was based at Newgate Street and is mentioned in a number of cases of the time as being responsible for arresting thieves in the area. Newgate Street is close to Ludgate Hill where there was a famous coaching inn, the Belle Sauvage, and also close to Doctor's Commons where the boxes had been addressed to. John Richmond would have had local knowledge of the likely destinations of bodies destined for 'anatomising' and took Mr Cale across Newgate Street to St. Bartholomew's Hospital. St. Bartholomew's was one of the many sources of income for resurrectionists and is mentioned as such in the diary written by a resurrectionist over the period 1811 to 1812. The area surrounding Newgate Street and the Old Bailey has been described as 'the hub of London resurrection culture' north of the Thames. The proximity to St. Bartholomew's Hospital may have been a key factor in making this area and the public houses surrounding it a centre for storing bodies in transit and meeting places for gangs of resurrectionists.

Enquiries at St. Bartholomew's failed to locate the bodies, so Richmond next escorted Mr Cale to the Belle Sauvage coaching inn at the foot of Ludgate Hill. This was one of the principal destinations for coaches from outside London and the final London destination for one of the Worcester carriers. The packing cases loaded at Upton would have been taken to Worcester and then transferred to a London bound carrier to be deposited at a coaching inn and then transported to the delivery address. Cale and Richmond learned that the two cases had been left at the Belle Sauvage by the Worcester coach and one of them had been taken directly to Mr Holmes' address in Old Fish Street, the address label on the second case had been torn off, and it had been forwarded to the White Horse Cellar in Piccadilly, another main coaching inn where packages would be left for onward delivery.

Cale and Richmond went direct to Doctor's Commons, and at Holmes' house in Old Fish Street, they found one of the packing cases. It was unopened, and John Pocock Holmes is recorded as stating that he was not aware of the contents and he *'readily surrendered the case to John Richmond'*. The second case which had been delivered to the White Horse Cellar was no longer there, but Richmond located it at a police station in 'B' division, where it had been sent by *'a gentleman of the navy, residing in Pimlico, it having been sent to his house from the White Horse Cellar by mistake as part of his luggage.'*

The two cases containing the bodies were loaded into a hackney coach by Cale and Richmond and taken to a magistrate at the Guildhall for permission to release the bodies to Mr Cale. The magistrate, Mr Alderman Smith, gave permission for Cale to return the bodies to Upton and commended him for his *'prompt and voluntary interference'*. Mr Cale then returned to Upton and arranged for the bodies to be returned to their graves in Hanley Castle. Newspaper reports of the time stated that the bodies were those of a female aged twenty and an elderly man, they were named as a Miss Smith, a lady of fortune who had died of consumption, and a Mr Colston. In fact, the body of the female was that of Mary Colston aged twenty-two of Newbridge Green who had been buried on January 11th, but the identity of the other is not known. As a result of the publicity surrounding the Upton Resurrectionists, Holmes was moved to write yet again to the newspapers to protest that he was not connected with the event other than by error. He wrote to the Morning Herald:

'The body taken to my house had been sent by some impudent resurrectionist, who may have known me at the schools, and took

the liberty of directing it to my own house, to be left till called for, supposing doubtless, some of his men would fetch the box away, and that I should never know what it contained.'

Thomas Cale told the magistrate that he did not know who the two men were but that he would recognise them if they returned to the area. An arrest was made in the case several weeks later in Birmingham, when John Watts, a *'noted rifler of graves'*, was apprehended on suspicion of being involved in the disturbance of the graves at Hanley Castle. When Watts was taken into custody, a letter was found in his possession, the contents of which were published in full in the Worcester Herald, and the writer of the letter was identified as *'a medical pupil in London'* and the intended recipient as *'his father, a surgeon of considerable practice and eminence, in Birmingham'*.

'Dear Father — it appears that the man Watts, and his partner here, made a sad mess with the last packages they have sent. This morning two constables from the country called on Mr Holmes, the surgeon, to who the parcels were directed, and saw there the first box which they immediately recognised from the following circumstance. It appears that Watts and the other man went to the house of the constable in the country, and actually borrowed the man's poker to nail on the direction to the box, and thus they (the officers) learned where the parcel was going to. The next day it seems part of the coffin, and a crow bar, were found in the burying ground, and the grave was open. This, of course led to a suspicion as to the contents of the box; and immediately the constable set off for London, and detected, as I have mentioned, the first box, which contained a young female subject. This they took away with them and requested Mr Holmes to be at the Guildhall at twelve o'clock: he accordingly went and waited till twenty minutes past, when, as these officers did not make their appearance, he

left, and has heard nothing more of the affair, it being now four o'clock.
We have heard nothing of the second package, and it is probable it has
been either stopped on the road, or at the office in London. Mr Holmes
is a man of a very strong mind; he does not care a farthing about this
discovery, which is so far fortunate, but we must alter the direction:
— for the future tell the men to direct to Mr Smith at Mr Saunders's
18 Devonshire Buildings, Great Dover Road, London. — They must
have managed most wretchedly to go to very constable's house, and to
leave the grave open. They must keep out of the way, as the officer says
he knows one of them, and will soon take him into custody. Which it is
I do not know, but if they do not mind they will get taken.

I write in haste, therefore excuse this scrawl.

Yours Ever

R.D.G

London, Jan 24, 1831'

The initials R.D.G. and the link of his father, being *'a surgeon
of considerable practice and eminence, in Birmingham'* identifies the
writer as Richard Dugard Grainger, the head of the Webb Street
School of Anatomical Studies. His father was Edward Grainger,
a surgeon in Birmingham. Richard's elder brother, also named
Edward, founded an anatomy school in London in 1819 and
moved it to Webb Street when it became a great success with
nearly three hundred pupils. Richard took over the running of
the school in 1824 when his brother died at the age of twenty-
seven from consumption. The Webb Street School is recorded
as having great favour from the resurrectionists, and the steady
supply of bodies endured its popularity with students. Richard
Grainger dealt fairly with the suppliers of the bodies and in his
evidence to the select committee in 1828, which recommended
alterations in the law to allow access to bodies for anatomical

study, he described how he had taken care of the families of resurrectionists whilst they were in prison. On one occasion, had spent £50 to keep a man's wife and family and also paid him a '*solatium*', compensation for his time in prison, on his release.

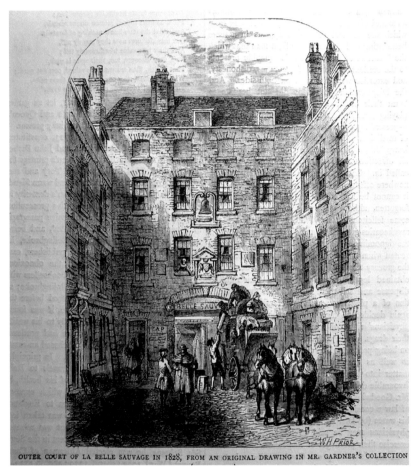

OUTER COURT OF LA BELLE SAUVAGE IN 1828, FROM AN ORIGINAL DRAWING IN MR. GARDNER'S COLLECTION

Belle Sauvage Inn. *Source: Author's collection.*

Chapter 10

'Diseases incident in females.'

In 1831 Dr Holmes published his monograph on '*Diseases incident in females*'. This included an appendix on his improvements to obstetric instruments, which is an expansion of the document he submitted to the Society for Arts when he was awarded the Gold Medal.

The monograph was respectfully inscribed to Holmes' professional brethren with the hope that it would '*facilitate their control over the diseases of females, by shewing to the public the dangers of delay and the power of early remedy.*' The introduction to the book set out in detail the reasons why Holmes felt it important to write on what may have been thought of as an indelicate subject. He denounced some of the popular publications written by those who wrote for the public because they lacked the knowledge or qualifications to write for the profession and instead, he attempted to position his monograph as being on a different level. He outlined the reasons that he has decided to publish a treatise on the diseases of the female, despite the fact that some may have felt that a subject of such delicacy would be better left to a private consultation.

His first point was that, if a work of this kind was to benefit females, then that benefit superseded other considerations of delicacy. Secondly, he believed that few women had recourse to advice from an experienced doctor and often relied on advice from what he described as *'officious old women, whose dangerous practices are pointed out in succeeding pages'*. His final point was that many women were not aware of the danger of neglecting certain incipient disorders and therefore did not consult with doctors. He believed that a written treatise could be read in private, without witnesses, and would then prompt the sufferer to seek medical attention at the earliest opportunity. The style of his book was intended to inform and educate, and he made no apology for using ordinary anatomical terms but explained that *'the grossness of the subject cannot be altogether concealed, and nothing but a conviction of the extreme necessity of the work could have induced me to compose it'*.

In the short introduction to the work, he set out his concerns about the modern styles of dress and tight lacing on the female constitution, and also laid blame at the feet of society for not encouraging sufficient exercise and proper diet in young ladies of 'good society'. He based his views about the effects of a sedentary lifestyle on female disorders on his experiences as a Hudson's Bay surgeon, claiming that: *'During my residence abroad I was at one time confined to a situation where I had the opportunity of observing the diseases of some thousands of savages, and I found scarcely an instance of maladies of this sort amongst the whole number'*.

Continuing his argument that these diseases are almost peculiar to civilised life, he argued that whilst they are single, women occupying *'the lowest sphere of life, such as domestic servants'*, are often free from the complaints he will discuss. However, once married, despite having frequent pregnancies and easy deliveries, they were not able to rest in bed after being delivered, in contrast to *'more respectable females'* and therefore were more liable to *'relaxations and displacements'* and *'still graver maladies as old age advances upon them'*.

The classification of diseases which Holmes adopted in his book was to look at the maladies through the following three life stages; young females, middle-aged women and old age. He acknowledged that the division was not very accurate and that most complaints could occur at any age, but he hoped the arrangement would allow him to develop his ideas in a clear manner for the general public.

Holmes' chapter on the diseases of young females dealt with problems of menstruation. The first complaint which he discussed was when *'the usual periodic profluvium does not come on at the proper time'*. He reassured parents and practitioners that the normal occurrence of the menarche takes place at various ages and stated that it was often at fourteen or fifteen but frequently not until the age of eighteen or nineteen. His advice to parents and practitioners was not to take any action if the first period was delayed unless there was evidence that this was affecting the girl's health. Indeed, he stated that attempts to hasten the onset of the periods in these cases using stimulants would be harmful, and warned against the traditional treatment by *'all nurses and good women'* who administered Pennyroyal and other herbs to force a period, and when this did not work, called in a doctor to prescribe even larger doses. Rather than the use of such stimulants, he advised the use of his plan of treatment which involved *'abstracting from the arm a quantity of blood sufficient to remove urgent symptoms'*. If this was not successful, then he advised the application of *'some dozen leeches to the inside of the thighs, a situation that should always be preferred for the local attraction of blood in uterine diseases'*. If, after a month or two, there was still no period then he recommended commencing a system of constant purging with *'drastic cathartics'*, adding that *'the warm hip-bath forms also in these cases a very useful expedient.'*

Where a delay in the onset of periods was associated with general signs of ill health, Holmes advised a more active approach to restoring the general health. This involved *'inducing the regular daily action of the bowels, and by exciting the appetite by gentle bitters'*, he would use *'diffusible stimulants'* and exercise, to the extent of inducing slight perspiration. Holmes reinforced his views on the use of forcing medicines, stating *'I have never seen any effect produced by their use. I have seen, however, abundance of cases where their employment in the place of the constitutional plan recommended above has been followed by long continued and distressing disorder. I lay it down therefore, as a rule in all cases of retention of the menstrual profluvium never to exhibit emmenagogues'*.

His rule about never using emmenagogues (a substance that stimulates or increases menstrual flow) was, however, relaxed in cases where the periods had started normally but had then stopped. He considered that using his constitutional approach was the first step in these cases, but that if that should fail then the use of emmenagogues may be justified but only on an intermittent monthly basis. He also advised using low doses of the medication but increasing their effect by the use of opium to avoid the medicine passing too readily from the bowel. His choice of drugs in these cases included aloes, hellebore and drastic purges. He specifically recommends ten drops of Tinctura Lyttae, a tincture of a cantharide similar to Spanish Fly, combined with fifteen drops of Sp. Terebinthine (Oil of Turpentine) three to four times a day. In desperate cases, he would use electrical stimulation in addition to his medication regime. The application of local stimulants is included in his advice on treating this disorder, and amongst the agents, he suggests for injection into the vagina are ammonia, ether and gin.

The other disorders which Holmes included in those related to young females were *'inordinate and painful menstruation'* and *'scanty profluvium'*. He acknowledged that most practitioners would class inordinate and painful menstruation as one entity, but he believed that these were two separate issues, as pain could occur with or without excessive menstrual flow. He described those patients who had excessive profluvium with no pain as being *'usually of a delicate constitution, who indulge in late hours, taking large quantities of warm tea, lying late in bed of a morning, and other follies of fashionable life. I think those who have light hair and fair complexion suffer more than brunettes, but I do not perceive that I am corroborated in this opinion by any other author'*.

His treatment in these cases was to prescribe rest during the menstrual period and cold bathing and the application of astringents in the time between periods. Where the excessive menstruation was associated with pain, Holmes would treat the patient with bleeding *'in the first instance, from the arm, and afterwards by leeches to the pudendum, about three days before the profluvium is expected… here all astringents, whether local or general, do much mischief'*. Where pain was the only complaint, then his recommended treatment was bleeding by leeches and the use of ergot of rye, which he described as being *'the most successful agent that has been introduced into practice'*. Holmes summarised the chapter with some key points which he directed towards the popular reader.

- *'It is dangerous to trust to the prescriptions of mothers or nurses, or the still more dangerous prescription of the* chemist 'over the counter'.'

- 'That under all circumstances regularity of diet exercise etc will do more to assist nature than any specifics.'
- 'There are inflammatory states in which the attendance of a medical man will relieve much immediate pain, and probably future suffering.'
- 'Nothing is a commoner cause of suppression than damp feet, which should therefore be especially guarded against.'

The second chapter in Holmes' book focussed on the diseases of middle-aged and married females. The most frequent complaint which he encountered in these women was leucorrhoea, which he defined for the reader as being: *'an increase of the moisture which is natural and proper to the passage leading to the uterus; this increase being so great that an actual profluvium occurs, very irritating and disagreeable to the patient, and which engenders great debility and other constitutional disturbances'.*

Holmes discussed at great length the importance of an internal manual examination of patients to ensure that a correct diagnosis was made. He acknowledged that women may *'betray the utmost aversion to it when first proposed'* and that a young or inexperienced practitioner may be persuaded to prescribe without undergoing such an examination. The consequences of such behaviour, he points out, could be that a tumour or inflammation may be missed for many months or years, which could have been treated at an early stage if the examination had been performed. Whilst Holmes places the responsibility for insisting on an examination with the practitioner, he also counsels women against allowing their modesty to compromise their health: *'although sufficient admiration cannot be paid to feminine delicacy, a lady should recollect that if the instinctive feeling of modesty which is natural and proper to her usurps such an ascendancy as to be opposed to all reason and discretion, to her own health, and to the happiness of her family, it ceases to be a virtue; it becomes at least a weakness, perhaps a crime.'*

Whilst Holmes throughout his book attempts to be frank and describe in great detail the symptoms and causes of diseases, there is one aspect of the subject matter which he appears to have difficulty in approaching directly. In his discussion of leucorrhoea, he acknowledges that this can be related to severe infections. There was a clear awareness of the effects of sexually transmitted diseases in these late Regency and early Victorian ages, and efforts were made to combat a rising number of cases through addressing the issue of prostitution. However, the centrality of the family as a unit and the unwillingness of society to acknowledge that respectable and sometimes eminent married men were customers of the sex trade meant that the key issue of identifying the source of female sexually transmitted disease was not openly addressed. Holmes was no exception to this reticence. He acknowledged that this was a delicate subject but expressed the view that severe inflammation of the vagina is the same whether it results from *'common causes or improper connections'*. He advises the young female and the practitioner not to attempt to determine the exact cause of any such infection *'for they cannot be ascertained with any certainty, and nothing can be more foolish than to wreck domestic happiness on mere suspicion and surmise'*. The method of treatment of leucorrhoea, which Holmes used when the discharge was clear in nature, and he felt it was the result of cold and fatigue, was to prescribe a smart purgative, a low douche and warm *'fomentations'*. After a week of this treatment, he then advised sponging the hips with cold water and the use of an astringent. In cases where the discharge was purulent, then Holmes insisted that this could be due to an ulcer or a tumour rather than simple inflammation and he was adamant that *'no medical man is warranted in prescribing until he has ascertained by examination, the source of the profluvium in question.'* Once he had eliminated ulcers or a tumour as the cause of the discharge, then he would embark on a course of treatment which he described as *'tepid injection, warm bathing, purging with calomel and rhubarb, rest, temperance, and strict abstinence from the nuptial bed, are requisite in all cases, then these may be added local bleeding, by cupping or leeches, and when the uterus seems chiefly affected, blisters to the lower part of the abdomen or groins.'* Where the discharge appeared to be related to inflammation of the mouth of the uterus, then Holmes' treatment was modified to include an injection being *'thrown into the vagina, composed of three drachms of laudanum, and half a pint of warm water'.* Whilst removal of the symptoms was one of the aims of the treatment, Holmes was concerned to remove the cause of the problem to avoid a reoccurrence. He advised a number of ways of reducing the risks of a further episode, including *'cold bathing, bark and steel, with good air, nutritious diet, and plenty of exercise'.* He added the proviso that *'during the whole course of the treatment an absolute separation from the husband should be enjoined.'* The prescription of 'bark and steel' refers to the use of iron sulphate, which was contained in many of the remedies advertised for 'female conditions' such as 'Pennyroyal and Steel Pills' and to Jesuit or Peruvian bark, from trees of the Cinchona genus which contained quinine and was used for the treatment of fevers and headaches.

Holmes' final paragraphs in this chapter concern the treatment of miscarriage or threatened miscarriages. He makes it clear that he feels that an intervention in a threatened miscarriage is important as *there is no certain method of ascertaining at first whether the miscarriage may be prevented or not*. Holmes' first line of treatment was to try and stop any haemorrhage, and he would use bleeding, an enema, laudanum and an astringent such as superacetate of lead, or his favoured astringent, sulphate of zinc. When the haemorrhage was to such an extent that life was threatened, however, he would attempt to induce an abortion using methods such as ergot of rye combined, if necessary, by a manual induction of labour using his specifically designed stilet. The appendix to his book contained the details of these instruments. His stilet was a modified form of the traditional instrument used to puncture the membranes. Holmes' modification was to convert the sharp-pointed and unguarded stilet into a trocar by containing it within a cannula or metal tube. The trocar could be safely introduced into the uterus, and then a bolt was pressed which would drive the stilet out of the protective tube, this would penetrate the membranes and was then returned back into the cannula by a spring to avoid any damage when the trocar is withdrawn.

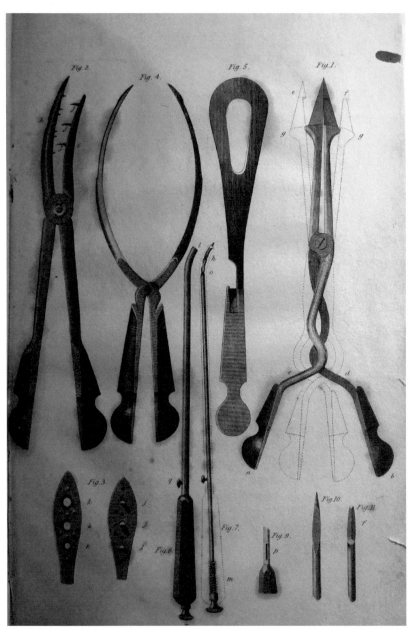

Engraving of Holmes' instruments. *Source: Popular Observations on Diseases incident to Females. J.P.Holmes (1831)*

His treatment of cases of severe haemorrhage using ergot and perforation of the membranes had seen success, as in the case he reported in June 1821 when he was consulted by Dr Darling.

The final advice which Holmes offers in this chapter is with regard to the management of the time after a successful birth. He warns against the practice of confining a woman to her room for a month after delivery, and then exposing her to the atmosphere, *'and above all to the atmosphere of a church'*. He also advises against keeping the patient in a warm bed for too long a period of time as this *'at once relaxes and debilitates'*. Instead, he suggests that the best practice is to spend a considerable period of time lying down on *'a firm elastic sofa for the greatest part of the day'* for the first month after delivery. He warns that *'there can be no doubt that all the displacements, and many of the fatal diseases which afflict the aged female, owe their origin to neglect, in this particular, — to the absurd custom of making one period the signal for a return to those habits of which the manifest tendency must be to prevent contraction, or in other words, the return of the constitution, and the parts affected, to their natural and healthy state.'*

In the third chapter of his book, Holmes turned to the matter of *'affections afflicting persons in advanced life'* in which he discussed three main topics: *'the grand climacteric'*, displacement of the organs and tumours. With regard to the grand climacteric, or 'the turn of life', Holmes recommended a conservative approach. Where the periods gradually subside, allowing the constitution to be *'insensibly prepared for important alteration'*, then no intervention is required. Where the periods suddenly stop, then he advised intervening with emmenagogues and bleeding to continue the periods, however slight, for two or three months. He strongly advised women whose periods have stopped to note any changes in sensation or function after this time, as he believed that changes in weight or fulsomeness may precede the development of a tumour or a displacement of the organs. Holmes provided a variety of suggestions for managing displacements of the organs. He distinguished between a prolapse of the uterus, where the organ remained in the body, and those cases where the uterus protruded externally. In a case of an internal prolapse, he would confine the patient to a sofa, administering *'alteratives and aperients'* and introducing astringents to cause the vagina to contract and provide support. Where these measures were insufficient, he advised the use of a pessary as a mechanical support for the prolapse. His descriptions of the various forms of pessaries available ranged from the pomegranate steeped in wine, which was described by Hippocrates, through to the French varieties made of elastic gum stuffed with wool or horsehair. He took the opportunity in this chapter of introducing yet another of his inventions: a pessary made of elastic gum and distended with air, *'after the manner of the air-cushion used for travelling'*. This, he stated, gave lightness and firmness and had the advantage that the bulk of the pessary could be easily diminished for the purpose of insertion and removal. The treatment for an external prolapse followed the same pattern, with the use of injections of astringents to increase the tone of the vaginal wall, and pessaries being used either as temporary or permanent support. Holmes was clear that the most important part of a consultation was the examination of the patient and distinguishing between a prolapse of the uterus and a prolapse of the bladder, and he gave clear directions as to how to distinguish the two.

The diagnosis and treatment of tumours occupied over

half of Holmes' chapter on diseases in the older age group. He classified tumours as being either malignant or *'susceptible of cure'*. Those which he saw as curable included a variety of polyps of the uterus or vagina which he felt were *'easily curable if the surgeon is aware of their existence'*, and he devoted several paragraphs to the diagnostic marks of the types of polyps he had encountered. The treatment, however, was of one type, namely to *'pass a ligature around the polyp, an operation not of a very formidable description'*. The remainder of the chapter concerns the management of malignant disease. Holmes described two operative procedures, firstly the removal by ligation of a tumour of the uterus which has the nature of a *'cauliflower excrescence'*. Whilst reports of such procedures had been published in 1828, the view was that ligature alone was not sufficient and that the neck of the uterus should be removed in addition. A more radical removal of the uterus by vaginal hysterectomy without anaesthetic had been performed in 1827 by Dr Blundell, who had provided testimonials for Holmes' instruments. Holmes praised this operation as a major advance in treatment: *'Never perhaps was there a greater triumph achieved by surgery over human malady than when a woman, from whom our countryman Dr Blundell had succeeded in completely extirpating a diseased uterus, recovered'*. Holmes counselled against the indiscriminate use of this operation, particularly in the hands of young or inexperienced surgeons, who he felt might subject their patient to *'the torture of the knife'* when *'extensive disease had rendered any attempt of the kind perfectly futile.'*

Holmes wrote passionately about the importance of palliative treatment in cases where a cure was not possible. He urged his professional readers not to undervalue the great importance of a palliative approach and to accept that a patient labouring under a necessarily fatal disease can, by art, have their pain abated within very supportable limits and their life prolonged. Holmes' support of the concept of palliative treatment is summarised in his final sentence on the matter:

'Surely then to relieve pain and distress, although it pretends not to so dazzling an object of attainment as perfect cure, is nevertheless not to be despised or neglected by the medical philanthropist.'

Many of the views expressed by Holmes on the treatment of diseases of the female are ones which would be shared by many of his contemporaries. His skill in inventing new and modified instruments and his championing of the importance of palliative care does, however, make him stand out as an innovator, and he emerges as a caring and skilful practitioner with a high degree of respect from his colleagues.

Chapter 11

The Courts and the Profession

In the same year that he published his book, Holmes became involved in a very public and well-publicised dispute between two factions of the medical profession. The dispute centred on an action for libel taken by Dr Francis Ramadge FRCP against Michael Ryan, the editor of the Medical Gazette, and Thomas Wakely, the editor of The Lancet. The dispute followed the deaths of two patients; Miss Cashin and Mrs Colin Campbell Lloyd. Both were treated by one Mr St. John Long, a controversial character on the London medical scene and a former artist and portrait painter. He changed careers to medicine in the 1820s despite not having any formal training or apprenticeship, claiming to have discovered a cure for consumption. He gave his qualifications as MRSL and MRAS and these were given in full, in a publication defending his treatments, as being a member of the Royal Society of Literature and a member of the Royal Asiatic Society. Membership of both these societies was in fact open to all.

His treatment, which consisted of inhalations of gases and 'friction' with a secret compound to produce an open wound to allow the disease to escape, achieved great publicity and he was able to move his practice to Harley Street. The death of the two patients resulted in two trials for manslaughter. The trial on October 30th, 1830, with regard to Miss Cashin, who was only twenty-four years old, ended in him being found guilty of manslaughter and fined £250. Miss Cashin had been treated by him at the request of her mother because she was concerned that her daughter might develop consumption. Miss Cashin's younger sister aged sixteen, had been examined by Mr Long, who had diagnosed an untreatable case of consumption but assured Mrs Cashin that he could prevent the development of consumption in the elder girl by use of his secret remedies. The post-mortem found that the girl was *'free from all disease, save that occasioned by the wound in the back'* which was the result of Mr Long's application of his secret remedy. The court heard that, on being shown the wound on Miss Cashin's back, he had said that *'the wound was going on remarkably well'* and that *'he would give a hundred guineas if he could produce similar favourable signs in some other of his patients'*.

The second patient, Mrs Lloyd, was from a well-known London family and was treated by St. John Long for consumption using his usual methods. She died on October 6th, 1830, and the post-mortem was said to show her death was a result of the open wound caused by his treatment. The family engaged Wakely, the editor of The Lancet, to represent them at the inquest, where the jury found St. John Long to be guilty of manslaughter. A second trial for manslaughter was held at the Old Bailey on February 19th, 1831, after St. John Long had been the subject of a police search when he failed to attend in court. At this appearance, he was, however, found not guilty, and the charges were dismissed.

The result of the court hearing was met with outrage from some sections of the medical community, but some support was present both from his patients and very publicly from Dr

Ramadge. A letter from him to St. John Long was published on April 12th, 1831, in the Sunday Times supporting both Long's action in the Lloyd case and his general professional behaviour.

This letter was the subject of adverse comment by Ryan in a leader in the Medical Gazette on April 23rd, 1831, but the events which followed Ramadge's letter were to have repercussions in the London medical world for the next two years. The publication of the letter in support of St. John Long resulted in a long editorial by Ryan, who described the letter as an *'open defence of a notorious quack and convicted felon — in unprofessional advertisement of himself — in slanderous imputation against others — and in sneering derogation of the body to which he himself more particularly belongs.'* Ryan then called upon the College of Physicians to expel Ramadge, *'who, to use his own words, has 'openly, fearlessly, and after deep deliberation,' published a letter in open defence of a notorious quack and convicted felon.'*

The outrage of some of the profession with regard to the letter was such that an extraordinary meeting of the London Medical Society, of which Ramadge was a member, was called in May 1831. Present at the meeting as a member of the Society was John Pocock Holmes, who seconded a vote to expel Ramadge. The vote took place using a ballot box with voting balls. Holmes was to recall in his evidence to the Ramadge v Ryan trial in the following year that *'there were twenty-three balls in the box, and one in his favour.'* Ramadge took great exception to being expelled from the society and wrote a letter to the Sunday Times to complain about the society. Holmes was moved to reply, and his response appeared in the Sunday Times on June 19th, 1831:

'Mr Editor, — As I was the person who first proposed the expulsion

of Dr Ramadge from the Medical Society, I feel myself called upon to defend its members against his unfounded accusations. There is only one part of his letter which requires or admits of a reply, the remainder being entirely composed of downright boastings of his own and St. John Long's merit, without the least attempt at proof. But he says that the members of the society acted in a manner worthy of an alehouse club, and that 'not one member of eminent reputation or high standing in the profession voted against him'. I am not competent to dispute with Dr Ramadge, touching our resemblance to an alehouse club, as I have not had the honour of belonging to such a society, but to the latter part of his assertion I reply by an unqualified contradiction. A large proportion of the society was present, several of the oldest and most respected members, many of talent and repute, and there was but **one** *vote against his expulsion. — I am, Sir, &c.*

J.P.Holmes, Surgeon

21, Old Fish Street, Doctor's Commons'

It was the letter from Ramadge, and the subsequent articles and letters in the medical press, which were to bring Holmes into the middle of a series of libel accusations, resulting in him appearing as a witness in the libel trial of Ramadge v Ryan. However, the subject of the libel action was not the comments in the letter in the Sunday Times, but rather a letter printed in The Lancet in 1832 and copied and expanded upon by Ryan in the Medical Gazette, which bought Ramadge's professional competence into doubt. The letter published in The Lancet titled 'Result of upholding a quack' gave an account of the case of a patient, Miss Bullock, who had been treated by Ramadge. Having reprinted The Lancet letter, Ryan developed an editorial around the text of the letter, which focussed very clearly on Ramadge's support of St. John Long. According to the author of the letter, a dispute had arisen between Ramadge and a Dr Tweedie over the correct method of treatment, and during the disagreement, Dr Tweedie had expressed the opinion to the patient's family that *'Dr Ramadge's conduct (with respect to supporting St John Long) had been such that no medical man of respectability could call him in or consult with him without injuring himself in the eyes of his bretheren.'* Dr Tweedie was reported by Ryan as saying that he bore no private pique against Dr Ramadge. He believed him indeed to be clever, but his character, with regards to the above transaction, rendered it imperative for all medical men to decline acting with him. Ryan quoted Ramadge as replying that he was *'a gentleman by birth education and profession'* but that Dr Tweedie was neither.

Ryan's editorial concluded:

'Let him be warned in time: he takes upon him to defend this nefarious quack and man slaughterer, in the face of the whole profession. Let him take warning or we will not spare him.'

Ramadge initially brought a libel action against Wakely for the original publication of the letter in The Lancet. The case was widely reported in the professional and lay press, and the outcome of the case, when the Jury awarded one farthing to Ramadge, was seen by many in the profession as a vindication of the views expressed by Ryan in his editorial. The case was heard on June 25th, 1832, and Holmes attended to listen to the case, as he was due to give evidence in the Ryan case the next day. As Holmes was leaving the court in the company of a Mr Hooper, they encountered a person who informed them that he was to be a member of the jury in the Ryan case the next day, and commented that he was surprised at the smallness of the damages awarded against Ryan. He added that if he had been on the jury in the Wakely case, he would have given larger damages. Holmes was later to state that the person also commented to the effect that he would *'take care that the verdict did not go that way'*.

The Ramadge v Ryan trial was duly held the day after the Wakely case. Holmes was called as a witness and gave evidence with regard to the meeting in Bolt Court, Fleet Street, where Ramadge was expelled from the London Medical and Surgical Club. The court proceedings were taken down by a number of shorthand writers and published in detail, both in the Legal Examiner, in Ryan's Journal and elsewhere. Holmes was questioned as to whether Ramadge abused any persons at the meeting. The report of his evidence published in Ryan's Journal recorded his evidence in detail, together with the shorthand reporter's comments. In reply to the question, Holmes stated:

'that a resolution was read to Dr Ramadge and he made his defence; the balloting box went round, and the result being announced, Dr R. snapped his fingers at them, and said he did not care a d----- for them, and afterwards compared their meetings to pot-house assemblies. [The witness seemed extremely indignant at this conduct, and was so warm and vehement in his description of it, 'suiting the action to the word,' that he threw the court, bar and auditory into a fit of laughter. — Rep.].'

The trial was widely reported in the professional and popular press and resulted in a flurry of comments when the jury found in Ramadge's favour and awarded damages against Ryan to the value of £400. The comparison with the nominal damages of a farthing against Wakely appeared difficult to reconcile with the facts. Following the trial for libel against Ryan, a meeting of the medical profession was called on July 27th, 1832. At the meeting, it was proposed that the verdict was in its results *'severe and oppressive'* and that the article by Ryan was *'actuated entirely by a strong feeling for the honour of his profession'*. A final motion was proposed by Holmes to the effect that *'under the circumstances, we are of the opinion that the profession at large should be solicited to contribute to defray the expenses imposed upon the defendant by a verdict which has been received with such universal surprise, and that a Committee be forthwith appointed to carry this resolution into effect...'*. The committee was appointed at the meeting and Holmes was elected as a member of the committee. Appeals were placed in the lay and professional press requested subscribers to the fund. Lists of subscribers were published in The Lancet and various newspapers, with Holmes subscribing two guineas, and the total raised from forty subscribers was one hundred and forty-nine pounds, eight shillings and ten pence.

Holmes had revealed to Ryan the content of the discussion he had with the juror with regard to the Wakely case. Ryan was clearly annoyed that Holmes had not disclosed this before the trial had ended, as he felt that the juror would have been removed and the damages may have been considerably less. Holmes and Hooper attempted to remedy this by gathering information that Ryan could use to request a retrial. They managed to identify the juror as Mr John Minter Hart, of 19 Mornington Crescent. Holmes and Hooper interviewed Mr Minter Hart at his office in George Street, Hampstead Road. This interview took place in Mr Minter Hart's private rooms on October 31st, 1832, and Holmes reported that Minter Hart admitted he had commented on the decision in the Wakely case, but also stated that he knew something which would get a new trial for Dr Ryan. What he disclosed to Holmes and Hooper was that he had been struck off as an attorney in 1831 following charges of fraud. Minter

Hart stated that if this had been known at the time of the trial, he would have been removed from the jury. Holmes and Hooper reported to Ryan the content of the interview with Minter Hart and swore an affidavit with regard to the events. Ryan then used this to attempt to gain a retrial, on the grounds that one of the jurors had prejudged the case before hearing the evidence. The request for a retrial was heard on November 15th, 1832, and the affidavits from Holmes and Hooper played a key part in the hearing. Holmes and Hooper swore that Minter Hart had fallen into conversation with them after the Ramadge v Wakely trial and that he had confirmed in their interview with him that he had used the expressions that Holmes had reported to Ryan. An affidavit by Minter Hart in conjunction with a Mr John Colman, who stated that he was present at the conversation between Minter Hart and Holmes outside the court, was submitted to the court. In it, Minter Hart and Colman accepted that the conversation as reported by Holmes and Hooper had occurred, but with the exception of the phrase, *'I will take care the verdict does not go that way'*.

The counsel for Ramadge addressed the court with regard to the evidence of Holmes and Hooper:

'...Mr Hart was not only borne out by his own affidavit, but was supported by the conduct of the deponents themselves, who, although they were witnesses in the cause — were parties to a subscription raised in order to defray the expenses of the £400 verdict — and formed part of the body of medical practitioners ranged in battle array, to destroy Dr Ramadge for his advocacy of Mr St. John Long — had never mentioned what they had heard, either to Dr Ryan or to the attorney in the cause, when an objection might have been made, but had kept it locked up in their own breasts until the cause was lost,

and damages, in some way commensurate with the injury sustained, had been awarded; and they found it necessary, as a dernier resource, to rake up something to disturb the verdict, and the fertility of their imaginations had presented this as the most probable ground. Was it likely, had such a conversation occurred, that they would not, zealous as they were in the cause have immediately communicated it?

The utter improbability of the course they adopted, at once invalidated the accuracy of their statement; to say nothing of the fact of their afterwards going to Mr Hart, to endeavour to refresh his memory of a circumstance which they did not themselves by any means feel certain had ever taken place.'

The judge summed up his findings of the hearing by stating that he accepted that the affidavits from Minter Hart and his colleagues fully answered any issues raised by Ryan's counsel and that he saw no reason for disturbing the verdict. The treatment of Holmes' evidence by the court was personally embarrassing for him and, more importantly, left Ryan with the prospect of paying a large sum of damages, in addition to the extra expense of the appeal hearing.

Despite his involvement in these high-profile trials, Holmes still had time for family and local political matters. Charlotte's mother, Sarah, was living near Bedford Square, London, and Holmes inserted an advertisement on her behalf, which appeared in The Times on June 30th, 1832, offering accommodation for one or two ladies or gentlemen stating that:

'The widow of a highly respectable clergyman, living in the vicinity of Bedford Square, would be happy to receive into her family, as INMATES, one or two ladies or gentlemen, who would be treated most liberally, meet with an elegant home, and have an opportunity of mixing with select and agreeable society. For address apply at Mr

Taylor's, 30 Upper Gower-street: or to Mr Holmes, surgeon, 21 Fish Street, Doctors' Commons: or Moor's Library, Store Street, Bedford Square'.

Mr Taylor of Upper Gower Street was the Bookseller to the University of London and Moor's Library was a popular subscription library owned by R.P Moore.

In this same year, a major change occurred in the electoral system of the country in the form of The Reform Bill of 1832. As a prominent householder in the Fish Street area, Holmes was involved in the plans to celebrate the passing of the Act. The Act gave the vote to all householders who paid a yearly rental of £10 or more and changed the boundaries of electoral areas to organise a fairer distribution of constituencies, removing those which had only a few voters but were able to elect two Members of Parliament. The celebration of such a momentous occasion was felt by many to call for an 'Illumination'. These events, where all houses and shops would display lights and illuminations, were often accompanied by riotous behaviour and damage to property when the celebrations got out of control. The initial rejection of the Reform Bill by the House of Commons in 1831 had resulted in riots across the country, with mobs having to be controlled by the police, and damage occurring to the homes of prominent politicians who had opposed the Bill. London had escaped the worst of the rioting, but there were concerns that an illumination might result in further episodes of uncontrolled mob behaviour. There was a long history of such celebrations being accompanied by bonfires, sporadic rowdiness and window-smashing of houses that did not illuminate. A letter to The Evening Standard in 1832 expressed the view of many householders and tradesmen.

'TO THE EDITOR OF THE STANDARD

July 2 1832

Sir, — As I find we are forced by the press to illuminate for the passing of the Reform Bill, I should like to know whether, to please a mob, I must return from the sea side to take care of my property, and put myself at risk of setting my house or furniture o fire, for which I find no remedy from the insurance offices; and if my windows are broken I must mend them at my own expense. As I do not like any of these things, pray tell me how I am to avoid them; probably there may be yet time to get the act of parliament revised, which was intended to protect the lives and property of those who are adverse to this kind of rejoicing.

Pray let us have a little instruction from you on this head, as several young householders of my acquaintance are very much in doubt.

If my house is not lighted up and is attacked by a mob in consequence, am I justified in firing a pistol or blunderbuss for the protection of my property, there not being time to get the assistance of the police.

Yours A Tory'.

The concerns of London householders and tradesmen with regard to the proposed illuminations resulted in the formation of a movement to celebrate the Reform Act in a more appropriate way. It planned to benefit the poorest citizens of the city who the Reform Act had still left without a vote. John Holmes was one of the voices within the Bread Street Ward giving support for this idea, which proposed an alternative to illuminations, instead raising funds to build commemorative Alms Houses to provide homes for *'aged and decayed freemen and householders of London and their wives or widows, of good character and repute, in reduced circumstances through casualties of fortune or visitations of Providence.'.* The organisers of this plan hoped *'to induce the people in general to subscribe the money which they would have wasted in the glittering follies of a night to the establishment of a humane Institution, which reason could approve, and charity consecrate, as a lasting memorial of their united triumph over an absurd and dangerous custom'.*

On November 16th, 1832, a meeting of the householders of the Bread Street Ward was held at the White Horse Tavern to discuss the Alms House proposal. The meeting, chaired by Alderman John Ansley, discussed the plan and passed a motion stating that: *'This meeting is extremely grateful that the evils of a Public Illumination, on the passing of the Reform Bill have been avoided, and is highly desirous of assisting the noble and praiseworthy object of establishment of Alms houses, as the most rational, beneficial, and permanent mode of celebrating that important event.'* Holmes proposed a motion that *'the contributions of the inhabitants, and occupiers of premises within the Ward, be respectfully solicited in aid of the said object'.* His motion was seconded by Mr C. P. Bousefield and resolved unanimously.

The proposal to found the Alms Houses resulted in the formation of the Institution of London Almshouses, which Holmes became a member of. The Institution raised sufficient funds to purchase land in Brixton and build sixteen Alms Houses. The ceremony to lay the first stone of the buildings was held on June 7th, 1834, at Park Hill, Brixton and was followed by a dinner at the London Tavern, Bishopgate Street. Holmes continued to be a supporter of the Institution and was one of the members of the Institution who sold tickets for the ceremony and the dinner, held on the anniversary of the Reform Bill gaining Royal Assent. The ceremony was performed by Lord John Russell MP, a leading proponent of reform whose ideas had formed the basis of the Reform Bill and who had been tasked with managing the progress of the Bill through Parliament.

In November 1832, the Ryan case once again came to the forefront of the medical press. Failure of the appeal for a new hearing for Ryan left him with the prospect of paying £647 in damages and costs in addition to his own costs, which he estimated to total £1,000. The events in court, with the acceptance of Minter Hart's affidavit and the rejection of the affidavits by Holmes and Hooper, had caused some degree of embarrassment to Holmes and Hooper. An editorial in the Medical and Chirurgical Journal outlined the nature of the affidavits and laid out some of the criminal charges that had been brought against Minter Hart in the past. The editorial set about trying to show that the evidence from Holmes and Hooper was in fact correct and that the word of Minter Hart and his associates was not to be trusted.

'...we are induced to lay before our readers the following statement. We are urged to this conduct very strongly by feeling that Mr Holmes and Mr Hooper are on our account, placed in a very awkward situation with the public; and we, therefore, deem ourselves bound to render them such assistance as may be in our power to set the right, not only with the world at large, but what is of infinitely more importance to them, with the members of their own and our profession'.

John Minter Hart was later tried for another case of fraud in 1833. His conviction was reported by Ryan under the title of 'Beauties of the Administration of Justice', and he commented, 'Minter Hart, gentleman attorney, but struck off the roll, aided by three of his company, denied, it is needless to say on oath, that which was sworn by Mr Holmes and Mr Hooper, two very eminent *surgeons, whom to name is enough'*. Minter Hart continued to act as a money lender, and in 1836 was convicted of another fraud and sentenced to transportation. He is reported to have died in 1837 aboard the transport ship on the way to Sydney.

Away from the complex world of medical politics, Holmes continued to run his medical practice and provide assistance to the local community. In the absence of any organised emergency medical systems in Victorian London, the burden of responding to accidents often fell on any practitioner in the vicinity. Holmes was often called on in such circumstances, and his success in one case led to the story of his actions being printed and reprinted in many London newspapers. The Morning Post of November 15th, 1833, was the first to carry the story. According to the report, some workmen were engaged in repairing gas pipes at the bottom of Lambeth Hill when there was an escape of gas from the pipe. Three of the men were *almost suffocated by the escape of the impure gas which remained in the pipe and fell down apparently lifeless'*. The report continued to praise Holmes: *'They were taken up and carried into the White Hart public house, when Mr J. P. Holmes, surgeon, Fish-street hill, who was immediately sent for, promptly attended and, after upwards of half an hours laborious and incessant application of restoratives, animation sufficiently returned to allow of their being removed to their respective homes, where they linger in a very precarious state'*.

In addition to being a resource for the local community for medical assistance, Holmes was also active in local politics and, as a Freeman of the City, was eligible to stand for election to the Council of the City. In December 1833, two vacancies arose in the Bread Street Ward for Members of the Common Council of the City of London. The annual elections of Common Councillors were held traditionally on St. Thomas' Day and took place in the locations where each Ward normally held their meetings that were known as Wardmotes. The Bread Street Ward included Fish Street, which made Holmes eligible to stand for election as one of the Ward representatives. There were two vacancies following the resignation of two of the Council members, Mr Legg and Mr Hallan. Three candidates stood for election to the two posts, Mr Holmes, Mr Cope and Mr Williams. Holmes was one of those elected to serve but his pleasure at being elected may have been a little tainted when the Wardmote recorded the view of one of the members who regretted the retirement of Mr Legg, commenting *'respectable men are now retiring because the Common Councils of the present day were becoming inundated with men of a different character'.*

The Court of Common Council. *Source: Author's collection*

Chapter 12

Challenging the Profession

Francis Ramsbotham, the noted Lecturer in Obstetrics at The London Hospital, was the subject of a letter that Holmes wrote to The Lancet in 1834. Transcripts of Ramsbotham's lectures had been published in the Medical Gazette earlier that year and Holmes was clearly rather upset that the published lectures failed to mention the advantages of his obstetric instrument. In a long letter to The Lancet headed *'Ignorance or Forgetfullness, or something worse, of F.H.Ramsbotham'*, he complained that in a lecture on June 7th, Ramsbotham had failed to note the important improvements which Holmes had made to the craniotomy forceps. This, he stated, was despite Ramsbotham having written a letter of support for the instrument to support Holmes' submission to the Society for Art. Holmes stated that if this was done through negligence, then *'he is liable to censure for having abandoned his pupil's interests'*, adding, *'if… intentionally, in that case his conduct deserves pubic reprobation.'*

This very public confrontation with an eminent physician may appear to be disproportionate to the possible effect on Holmes of not being mentioned in the lecture. The remainder of the letter, however, colours in the background of his annoyance, which hinges on a much greater issue in 1834; the battle for supremacy between the members of the Royal College of Surgeons and the Physicians in the field of obstetrics. Holmes' letter makes it clear that Ramsbotham could hardly have forgotten him. Holmes had recently complained to a committee of the governors of the Royal Maternity Charity about their policy of appointing surgeons as assistant accoucheurs to their physicians, of whom Dr Ramsbotham was one. Holmes' argument to the charity was that *'it is presumptuous and foolish for a physician accoucheur to claim any superiority over the surgeon, whose education and employments are better calculated to instruct him in midwifery, than can be the scholastic attainments which often lead to the acquisition of degrees.'* Holmes continues in his letter to The Lancet to attribute the lack of recognition of his instruments by Ramsbotham to be due to *'the unwillingness to do justice to the surgeon... which influences more or less the conduct of all physicians.'*

The committee to which Holmes had complained was formed in 1834 by the Royal Maternity Charity. Its purpose was to decide whether there was any need for physicians of the charity to have any assistance from surgeon accoucheurs who would be members of the Royal College of Surgeons or Licentiates of the Apothecaries Company. The committee decided to appoint two or three surgeons as assistants to *'help'* the physicians. This period from 1834 started a great divide between the physician obstetricians and the surgeon accoucheurs which continued through the next decade. In 1847, Dr Blundell, a physician to the charity, summarised his position with regard to surgeon assistants:

'I cannot coincide with their views in wishing to be placed upon an equal footing of rank and remuneration with the physicians... responsibility should rest with the physicians, the surgeons being only required to attend urgent cases in the unavoidable absence of the physicians.'

In 1835, Holmes was elected to a more senior position in the Wax Chandlers Guild, becoming one of the two Stewards of the Guild who represent the Liverymen at the Guild Court. They would attend the Court meetings but would not have a right to vote. His medical practice continued to flourish, and he was developing a reputation for his expertise in managing diseases of the chest. The treatment of tuberculosis of the lung, termed consumption, was a source of controversy. Some physicians claimed that it was not possible to recover from it and that any claims to success in treatment were due to the diagnosis being incorrect. Holmes' view differed from this, and he recorded the treatment of a number of patients who he believed met all the criteria for a diagnosis of consumption and who had recovered following his treatment.

One of his patients, a Miss Ledger of Stockwell Place, had been unwell for a period of two years with a number of symptoms which were felt to be diagnostic of consumption, yet she had not experienced any blood in her sputum. Her younger sister had died in March 1834, and her father, concerned that she had the same disease, requested Holmes to treat her. Following the course of treatment, he wrote at Holmes' suggestion to describe the effects of the treatment.

Mr Ledger wrote to Holmes on July 4th, 1835:

'To J.P.Holmes, Esq.

Dear Sir, — In reply to your inquiry respecting my daughter and my opinion as to the efficacy of your remedy, I do not feel qualified to venture an opinion as to the nature of her complaint, but have always believed it to be similar to that which proved fatal to my younger daughter in March last (viz. consumption). My daughter had not been in good health for the last two years, being troubled with cough, great expectoration, and general debility, which was only temporarily relieved by medicine, and shortly after the death of her sister she became much worse, so that we were extremely anxious and fearful of the result. Upon the application of your remedy, by friction and by inhaling, she has in a very short time been most wonderfully benefitted, she has recovered her health and spirits, and we have every reason to believe her cure is effected.

With such as result, I cannot but have a most highly favourable opinion of the remedy you have applied; and likewise of your great skill and attention manifested during the progress of its exhibition. And I remain, dear Sir,

Most Gratefully,

And respectfully yours,

George Ledger

Stockwell Place, July 4ᵗʰ 1835'

Holmes' practice drew patients from the local area around Doctor's Commons and St. Paul's, but as his expertise in treating diseases of the chest became more widely known, he began to expand his territory to south of the river. There was great competition for patients within the City of London area, and a successful practitioner would rely on word of mouth and success in treatment in a specialised area to ensure that patients would consult him, even if they were in the territory of a rival doctor. Holmes did receive unsolicited letters of thanks from grateful patients. Mr E. Peters of 32 Old Change, a street just around the corner from Old Fish Street, wrote to him on June 2ⁿᵈ, 1835:

'Sir,- Having in September last taken a severe cold, which lasted for some weeks, and brought on disease of the lungs, with a cough and shortness of breath, expectoration, with much weakness, and the loss

of appetite, occasioned me to try means for relief, but without effect;
and at last my friends considered me in a precarious state, (this was
the latter end of March,) they advised me to apply to you for medical
assistance; and the means that you used have brought me to perfect
health. I therefore feel it my duty to return you my sincere thanks for
your kindness, and the speedy recovery you effected, which took place
after only a month's application of your liniment to my chest.

I hope, if any of your patients are labouring under the same
complaint, they will not fail to use the same means, which I feel
confident will speedily restore them to health.

I remain, Sir,

Yours most respectfully

E Peters

32 Old Change, June 2ⁿᵈ 1835'

Whilst Holmes was building a reputation for his expertise
in treating chest problems, he also saw patients with more
general problems and took on cases where other professionals
had failed to gain any success. In March 1835, he had taken over
the treatment of a Miss Webb, the eighteen-year-old daughter
of John Webb, the Landlord of the Half Moon Public House
at Dulwich. Miss Webb had been treated for eighteen months
by *'an experienced physician of considerable reputation'*. When
Holmes attended her, she reported that she had suffered from
a violent cough, loss of weight and poor appetite. However,
her main concern was violent headaches with lancinating pains
from her head through to her limbs, particularly on the left side.
Holmes treated her for five months and recorded that by the
use of his liniment and friction she had been completely cured.
Whilst Holmes did not believe that her symptoms were related
to any problem with her lungs, he did suggest that where oral

medications had failed, then applying his liniment to the skin using friction could produce good effects in obstinate diseases of the body at large. Holmes recognised that patients would prefer the ease of taking medications by mouth rather than by rubbing and inhaling, and for that reason had not used the application of liniments extensively but reserved the method for cases where other treatments had failed.

During 1836, Holmes continued with his letters to the press where he felt that they had misrepresented his views or commented adversely on his work. In a letter to the Editor of the Morning Advertiser, he wrote with regard to an article which had appeared on Saturday, August 13th extolling the virtues of a pamphlet written by a Mr Coulson on *'Deformities of the Chest'*. The article warned, amongst other things, against the severe dangers of tight corsets. The editorial review acknowledged that little in the publication was new knowledge to the medical profession but saw it as *'eminently useful to mothers, and those entrusted with the care of children'* and warned of the dangers of lacing.

'We trust that the exposure here given of the injurious and often fatal effects of stays and tight lacing will powerfully contribute to induce a discontinuance of a practice which, in squeezing the body out of the limits of nature to the compass of a vitiated fashion, so frequently superinduces the deformity, diseases, and death of the miserable victim exposed to the barbarous infliction.'

Holmes had written to the Editor in August 1836 to complain about the praise which was given to the publication in the Morning Advertiser. Holmes wrote that the publication *'does not appear to contain anything new, or any old thing stated with particular force'* and *'exaggerates the ill effects of tight lacing'*. He suggested that there were several errors in the Coulson publication and that their dissemination in the press would do more harm than good, writing *'I do not mean to say that extremely tight lacing is not occasionally prejudicial; but I contend it is only one out of many causes tending to such an effect, and that it is very mischievous to direct the minds of parents to this cause only, and thus to divert their attention from these three main agents, air, diet, and exercise, by which the development of a robust frame can alone be effected'.* His letter was not published but was replied to in the form of a 'Notice to correspondents' published by the Editor. This stated *'We have not space for Medical dissertations, and therefore cannot insert any of the controversial letters sent to us on the subject of the notice of Mr Coulson's treatise. Mr John Pocock Holmes does not seem to be aware that his doctrine would go to the length of preventing all medical publications which do not embrace the whole science'.*

Holmes was, during this period, working on the production of a book on chest complaints. He may have felt that Coulson was a rival for recognition of expertise in the field, which provided Holmes with a significant number of patients and income. He had previously written on the subject in his book on female diseases. His views expressed in his correspondence to the Morning Advertiser followed the general theme of those in his publication: *'Considerable stress has been laid on the form and texture of the female dress, as prejudicial to the general health, and therefore as a remote cause of the complaints in question. But I conceive this accusation has been made on somewhat unjust grounds. Then again as to tight lacing, which has received so much animadversion, I cannot believe it produces the serious effects which have been attributed to it.'*

In addition to treating patients with symptoms of bronchitis and consumption, Holmes was treating an increasing number of patients who had multiple symptoms. His treatment regime focussed on the use of his liniment or embrocation but was coupled with general health and dietary advice. His bedside manner was robust and positive; his patients remarked on the effects of his advice and in their letters to him showed that they recalled word for word what he had said to them. William Cranmer, who Holmes treated for a period of six months from December 1835 and who lived at 17 Old Change, Cheapside wrote to Holmes on Christmas Day 1836 to express his gratitude for *'the kindness and attention which you displayed towards me, during a long and tedious illness'*. When Mr Palmer first consulted Holmes, he had been suffering since August 1835 with *'a dry hacking cough, which continued to get worse with me until November, when I began to expectorate a thick greenish substance, particularly disagreeable'*. This was followed by *'violent perspirations, horrible dreams, short unrefreshing sleep, a strong disposition to vomit, and a violent nervous excitement in the morning, accompanied by a most intolerable thirst, which no liquid seemed to have the slightest effect upon. These symptoms were succeeded by general debility, an oppressive languor took complete possession of my frame, my flesh wasted away with amazing rapidity, my colour became sallow, sickly hue, my eyes sunk considerably into my head, my tongue and mouth assumed a nasty brownish yellow appearance, my extremities became cold and powerless'*.

Holmes, when he first saw Cranmer, told him:

'You have been far, far too long in coming; but I have cured a man who was in a worse state, if possible, than you are; and if you will strictly attend to my instructions, I have no hesitation in saying, I will cure you'.

After a month of treatment with no improvement, Mr Cranmer was in despair and told Holmes that he thought that his constitution was completely broken up. Holmes replied: *'If this will not cure you, nothing on earth will, Persevere and I will answer for the result'*. After a second course of treatment, Cranmer started to see an improvement and, in accordance with Holmes' instructions to change his diet, within six months he found his strength returning and the excessive thirst had gone. When he wrote his letter at the end of the year, he informed Holmes that *'I am this day as healthy and hearty as ever was, to the no small surprise of my friends, nearly all of whom had in their own minds quietly consigned me to the tomb in the March preceding'*.

Whilst Holmes was congratulated by Mr Cranmer on the success of his treatment, a clue to the true nature of his illness may have been given in the penultimate paragraph of his letter:

'It is but justice here to add that being connected with the printing business, I was of necessity compelled (when my strength permitted) to follow my occupation in a very large office, which was over heated with steam during the day, badly ventilated, and had from forty to fifty gas jets burning every evening; and I am firmly of opinion, that the noxious effluvia arising from this combination of causes, materially retarded my recovery, if it did not foster and nurture the disease itself'.

The printing industry was becoming well recognised as contributing to occupational health problems, including lead poisoning. As early as 1786, Benjamin Franklin had written of his experiences working in a printing shop in London, and expressed the view that the risks from lead were not only from lead particles on the hands of workmen but also in the *'danger from the Effluvia'* resulting from the small lead melting furnaces in the print shops. Chronic poisoning from lead is an insidious disease, presenting with an ashen pallor, fatigue, loss of appetite, sleep disturbance, nightmares, coated tongue, chronic bronchitis, headache, irritability, slurred speech, convulsions, nervous excitement, anaemia, vomiting, numbness and tingling in the extremities and kidney failure with excessive thirst. Mr Cranmer displayed many of these symptoms and appears to have improved with a period of convalescence away from his place of work with its lead fumes, poorly ventilated atmosphere, steam-driven printing presses and gas lighting polluting the air with carbon monoxide. Adults with moderate exposure to lead often recover when they are removed from the source of the lead exposure, and it may be that Holmes' advice on diet, rest and convalescence away from the printing offices may have been more effective than the application of his inhalant regime.

Another patient, Mr John Hargreave Junior of 1 Ivy Lane, Newgate Street, was effusive in his praise for the treatment he had received from Holmes. He had consulted him on May 2nd, 1836, suffering from pains in the joints, headaches, night sweats and a severe hacking cough, producing copious amounts of a yellowish mucous which had been persistent for over four years. Despite treatment by various surgeons over the years, his symptoms had only had temporary relief, but after nine to ten months of using Holmes' regime of friction, liniment and inhalation, he wrote to say that he had recovered his usual good health and was now as well as at any time in his life. Mr Hargreave wrote:

'I am at a loss of words to express my feelings sufficiently, for the solid benefit that I have received at your hands; as I am certain that it is entirely your superior judgment and skill, that enables me, at the present moment, to write this humble tribute of the high esteem in which I shall ever cherish the recollection of your name to the last day of my existence…'

He concluded his letter with the wish that:

'you may long live to have the opportunity of saving many from a lingering state, almost worse than death.'

On May 23rd, 1837, Holmes attended the annual ancient custom of the tradesmen of the Bread Street Ward as they all sat down together for a dinner at the Gerard's Hall Hotel. The Gerard's Hall Hotel, located on the south side of Basing Lane and Bread Street, had a coffee room, a ballroom, good wines, beds for seventy-eight guests and an ancient Norman Crypt. Amongst the hundred or more who were present were members of the Common Council of the City of London, of which Holmes was a member. After what was described as a most sumptuous dinner, the evening proceeded with great hilarity until a late hour. Holmes' duties as a member of the Common Council included membership of council committees. He was a member of the Committee of Coal and Corn and Finance, which in 1836 had been tasked with considering a major change to the administration of the Poor Laws within the city, following the publication of the Poor Law Amendment Act in 1834. A special committee, which included Holmes, was formed to consider the issues and, following its report to the Common Council, an order was made in January 1837 to amalgamate all the Poor Law Unions of the parishes of the city into one common fund to be named the City of London Union.

Holmes had now finished writing his second book, 'A treatise on certain methods of friction and inhalation in consumption, asthma and other maladies', which, when published, was well received in the profession and was referred to as 'Holmes on Asthma'. The foreword to the book explained that one of the aims of the publication was *'to recommend to public notice a method of introducing medicine into the system'* and to *'demonstrate the particular efficacy of certain remedies known to himself exclusively'.*

Holmes devoted over ten of the fourteen pages of his foreword to a defence of his decision not to reveal the nature of the *'certain remedies'.* He states that he sees the main objection to his book will be that he is using a *'secret agent',* a practice he acknowledges as being seen as unacceptable by the medical profession and viewed with suspicion by the general public.

The practice of advertising, selling and using 'secret remedies' had of course been one of the key elements of the profession's attacks on St. John Long in 1831, which Holmes had taken a key role in. His reasons for not publishing the details of his remedy are set out in detail in the preface. Holmes lists what he believes are the three main objections that would be raised to his decision to keep his treatment secret.

Firstly, that the evidence produced by an author of a method that is not publicly available in favour of himself is probably weak and has not been subjected to external review. His response to this objection is that his book contains testimony from his patients that the treatment was effective, and that the patients have appended their names and addresses to their letters. The second objection that he anticipates is that a surgeon in the age of enlightenment would naturally wish to promulgate the information on the treatment to benefit as many people as possible. It might be thought that such an altruistic action would also enhance the surgeon's reputation and fortune. Holmes writes *'This the author denies, from observation on all that has occurred around him during the thirty years he has been engaged in medical practice. Neither in medicine, nor in other sciences generally, does fame or fortune attend the disclosure of important discoveries,* however valuable they may ultimately be allowed to have been'. The only beneficiaries of such disclosures, he feels, are those opponents who adopt the treatment and ignore the fortunes of the inventor.

The final objection that Holmes believes could be raised, is that the members of a dignified profession should hold themselves above the lure of fame and fortune and, in the spirit of philanthropy, make all their discoveries available to the world at large. Holmes responds to this by reminding those who are wealthy and have substantial benefit from inheritance or accident that they find reasons not to share them with the poor and needy. He opines that the reasons they put forward for withholding their wealth apply equally to an inventor such as himself, who conceals for his own benefit a discovery made by his own mental exertions.

The objections and arguments which he lists are, he says, *'in the light of the pleading of an advocate, who states all the arguments by which a cause ought to be supported, and who knows they cannot be broken down by his opponents; but may still retain doubts in his own breast as to the merits of his own client.'* In the same manner, Holmes confesses that, however much he is able to justify his actions in keeping his treatment secret, there are two main reasons why he does not reveal the remedies with which he has had so much success. Firstly, that the promulgation of his remedy would place it in the hands of inexperienced medical men who do not have the extensive knowledge and experience of use of the remedy as himself, and that this could prove injurious to patients. Secondly, that there are *'particular private reasons'* why one of the substances used cannot be revealed, as any such disclosure would involve a breach of private honour.

He adds that the author will have to be contented with the ill-opinion of any persons who doubt his motives until *'a few years shall permit him to vindicate himself by a full exposition of his views and his remedies.'*

The treatment method which Holmes describes in the first chapter of his book relies on the use of friction and inhalation to deliver his remedies. He argues that there are many examples of the use of medications applied to the skin or inhaled, which have beneficial effects when the use of the same substances by mouth is ineffective. He develops this theory and expands it to explain the reasoning behind his treatment methods, which is that *'almost all medicines, whether purgative or otherwise, may be made to operate by application to the skin; few, however, acting when merely placed in contact with the surface, most requiring active friction to be employed, and others remaining inert unless the cuticle has been previously removed by blistering or similar means'.* The use of friction may, according to Holmes, be considered in three different ways. The use of simple mechanical friction with no added use of medical or surgical applications, friction combined with substances which have a local irritating effect designed to *'bring about a translation of disease from the interior to the exterior of the body',* and finally, friction with agents which can be absorbed through the skin and carried to the general circulation to produce *'salutary changes in remote organs'.*

The use of blistering by skin irritants or heat was widely believed to be effective, the irritant being applied to the area of skin that covered any affected internal organ. Holmes discussed the various theories underlying this method of treatment and raises several objections to them. He dismissed the theory that a blister on the breast area relieved internal inflammation of the heart and lungs by drawing blood to the surface from a diseased organ, as no direct communication between the vessels of the heart and lungs and the skin of the breast had been found. Theories that relied on the blister to attract 'nervous matter' away from the diseased area through the nerves up to the skin and away from the body he dismissed for similar reasons, that the nerve supply of the lungs and heart had no direct route through to the skin over the breast. His only concession to the nerve theory was that it could be correct, *'supposing the nervous influence to be capable, like electricity, of traversing contiguous structures without being confined to the tract of the nerves'*. He states, however, that *'As I have not the leisure or inclination to follow out investigations of a purely theoretical character, I shall confine myself, therefore, to a practical history of the actual facts and symptoms that are observed to follow the different kinds of cutaneous irritation'*.

The range of substances that Holmes describes as being used to produce cutaneous irritation reveals the scope of his therapeutic armamentarium. These include:

- The cantharides, which he describes as efficacious despite the fact that when absorbed they produce unpleasant effects.
- Direct cautery by the use of potash, silver nitrate and tartarised antimony.
- Direct burning with hot irons, a practice which he does not profess to admire or adopt but which he acknowledges may be fair to try when a disease is so progressive that delay in treatment through the use of more conventional methods would be a risk to the patient.
- Fused potash, which is used by applying adhesive plaster over the skin with spaces cut in it where the potash is

applied and then a second layer of plaster is put above to seal in the caustic substance. This method he usually restricts to those who have a long-standing illness with not much in the way of active symptoms.

- Silver nitrate or lunar caustic he applied in the same manner as fused potash. Holmes notes the value of the use of lunar caustic for the treatment of erysipelas, a skin infection also known as St. Anthony's Fire.

- Tartarised antimony mixed with an ointment is described by Holmes as having been *'long employed by myself'* for removing neuralgic pains and pleurisy. In using this treatment, Holmes would continue the application of the ointment until a crop of pimples resembling the pustules of smallpox appeared. From this point, he would adjust the frequency and strengths of the applications depending on the condition of the patient. If continued for too long, then large malignant-looking boils would be formed which required time and great care to heal. For this reason, Holmes advises against the use of this preparation by *'quacks or incautious people'*.

Holmes' main topic in his first chapter was the use of substances applied to the skin, which are then absorbed to produce general internal effects. The action of some substances through absorption was well recognised at this time. The 1837 Pharmacopeia of the Royal College of Physicians notes this effect with some ointments such as potassium tartrate of antimony, which it states is absorbed if used over a large extent of surface and may produce vomiting. Holmes lists a number of remedies which he has observed are absorbed from the skin and act as forcibly as if ingested, including opium, belladonna, digitalis, croton oil and other purgatives, iodine and the most well-recognised treatment of the period, mercury ointment. He also experimented with some substances which had been advertised as being effective through skin absorption. In cooperation with Dr Turnbull, he gave an extensive trial to the use of veratrine by application to the skin. Turnbull developed two preparations of veratria, one in an alcohol base and the other in an ointment which was to be rubbed into the affected part for five minutes, or from that time to three-quarters of an hour. Both preparations were contained in the Royal College of Physicians Pharmacopoeia for the treatment of muscle paralysis and neuralgia. Holmes' findings from his trial of veratrine were that it had no effect other than as a counter-irritant. This view was echoed by the editor of the Pharmacopoeia, who compared its properties with the ancient use of Squill for treating similar diseases and wrote that he *'ventured to affirm that he who will introduce scillitina externally, (although he will only be a humble follower of Hippocrates), will affect as many cures as are ordinarily effected by the other new active principles'.*

Holmes' experiments, using a variety of substances applied to the skin with friction, induced him to use a number of combinations which he stated had not previously been employed by practitioners, and which, for the reasons he outlined in his preface, he did not wish to describe in detail. He did, however, state what he felt were the two main principles to be employed in the use of substances applied by friction. Firstly, that the friction should be applied over as extensive a surface as possible and, secondly, that the friction should be continued for a long time at each treatment and repeated many times. Within his book, Holmes discussed the various forms of disease that he believed he was able to treat using his method of friction and devotes a chapter to each. These diseases include consumption, rheumatic afflictions of the chest, bronchitis, asthma, haemorrhage from the lungs, some forms of heart disease and obstinate diseases of the whole body. His description of the treatment of consumption is prefaced by a detailed discussion on his views on the diagnosis of the disease. He recalls that previously, physicians relied on the nature of the sputum to make the diagnosis. If the sputum was easily mixed with water, then it was assumed that this was pus and was diagnostic of consumption. If the sputum floated in the water, then a diagnosis of catarrh of the lung membrane was made, a disease that was serious but not necessarily fatal. It was, however, conceded that there were many cases of catarrh which exactly resembled consumption. The general view was that consumption was never cured and that those who recovered had suffered from chronic catarrh mistaken for consumption. Holmes challenged the view that the disease was incurable. He drew on evidence from Laennec, the inventor of the stethoscope, who is recognised as one of the first to develop a unified description of the disease, Dr Davies, a Lecturer at the London Hospital, and Louis, a Parisian physician. From these sources, he developed a set of key diagnostic factors that he believed identified consumption and differentiated it from chronic catarrh and other less serious infections of the chest. He described a number of cases where his treatment had been successful, including that of Mr William Whittle of Archway Cottage, Upper Holloway who he had treated in 1836. Mr Whittle wrote as follows:

'Dear Sir, — It is with pleasure I give you this certificate of the extraordinary cure you have performed upon me, by the external remedies you have used. My cure was hopeless, and I considered myself, as well as did all my friends, past the hope of again resuming any business. I was reduced by a continual cough, with great expectoration of yellow matter frequently streaked with blood to such a state of emaciation, that I could not walk up a flight of stairs without resting several times; a complete loss of appetite, night sweats, a constant action on the bowels, and every distressing feeling I can describe. In a few weeks after you attended me, I experienced great relief; entire restoration of my health in a few months; and I am now able to walk many miles or drive in my usual manner. My appetite is perfectly good, and my strength restored.

I am quite willing to certify this to any person who may be anxious to know the particulars. I was attended by Dr Simple and Dr Sir C. Scudamore previous to your seeing me, but was gradually sinking under all their efforts.'

The symptoms that Mr Whittle described such as debility, night sweats, and diarrhoea are compatible with those listed by Davies as diagnostic of consumption. The description of the symptoms of consumption by Louis includes a cough, sputa of greenish-yellow colour, tinged with blood, hectic fever with exacerbations chiefly in the evening, emaciation and diarrhoea. Holmes opined that the widely held view of consumption as never being cured was an 'injurious dogma' and that he had successfully treated patients whose symptoms were identical to those described by Laennec, Louis and Davies and that they had, in all probability, suffered from consumption. He is careful to point out to the reader that not all cases can be relieved, and that when consumption is diagnosed in its later stages, the patient may be 'beyond the reach of art'. Holmes' views on consumption reveal the breadth of his reading and knowledge, together with a courage to challenge widely held beliefs. Whilst acknowledging the progress that had been made by pathologists in describing the post-mortem changes in consumption, he called for the same degree of enthusiasm and skill to be invested in experiments in treatment, and a constant search for new agents and new ways of giving treatments. Holmes was also of the view that it was important to undertake research into why the disease appeared to resolve spontaneously in some patients. He felt that if more effort were employed in investigating cases where patients had recovered from the disease, then this might enable the profession to develop treatments that assisted *'these natural efforts'*. In addition to understanding the natural history of the disease, Holmes outlined the importance of increasing the profession's knowledge of the cause of consumption. Holmes discounts a number of theories of causation current at the time; the view that the common cold is a cause he describes as fallacious, adding that some inflammations seen to occur during the course of the disease are accidental and unconnected. He notes that some of the factors which were often said to be a cause of consumption such as exposure to the open air, or breathing atmosphere impregnated with animal or vegetable substances in a state of decomposition do not induce consumption and indeed *'persons habitually exposed to such influence are remarkable for their freedom from consumption'*.

Holmes' final conclusions of the possible causative factors of consumption include:

- Impure air from too many people breathing the same atmosphere.
- Scanty and improper diet.

It would be another forty years before Heinrich Koch, having isolated the tubercle bacillus, was able to demonstrate what had previously been a conjecture; that the disease was infectious. Holmes' ideas on the key factors of causation, which were at variance with the more general view in Northern Europe of the disease being a heritable condition, or related to pollution of the atmosphere, had been correct in principle, as was his view that the disease does show a natural resolution in a proportion of cases.

Chapter 13

A Royal Connection

In 1837, the country went into mourning for the death of King William IV. He had no surviving legitimate children and the crown passed to his eighteen-year-old niece, Victoria. She was not to be crowned until the following year but started to attend events before her coronation.

On November 9th, 1837, the Guild Hall was the venue for the annual banquet held by the Lord Mayor of London. The 1837 banquet was notable as it was attended by Queen Victoria and this was her first attendance at such an event since coming to the throne. Holmes, as a member of the Guild of Wax Chandlers, received an invitation to the event. The details of the day were recorded by the newspapers and in a report, produced for the Court of Mayor and Aldermen, from the various committees which had been charged with the organisation of the event. As the Lord Mayor was a member of the Guild of Wax Chandlers, the members of the Guild had the honour of attending the Mayor in the procession to Westminster and earlier in the day had *'serenaded the neighbourhood with the national anthem at break of day'*.

The visit of the new Queen was a major event for the city. The newspaper reports give great detail of the parade to the Guildhall and the enormous crowds who witnessed the spectacle. The city was decorated with flags and illuminated signs, and because of the large crowds expected, there were one thousand three hundred and fifty Police on duty with over six hundred of these being special constables appointed for the occasion. Queen Victoria left Buckingham Palace at two o'clock, and the procession of royal carriages with an escort of one hundred Horse Guards made its way through the streets to Temple Bar and then on to the Guildhall. When the Queen arrived at the Guildhall, she was escorted to her retiring room to make herself ready for the banquet. Her time in the retiring room may have been longer than anticipated by the organisers; a misfortune occurred with her elaborate dress as she was stepping out of the carriage at the Guildhall. Some of the diamonds on her 'stomacher' became detached and fell to the ground, but were quickly retrieved by the royal attendants-in-waiting.

Detailed accounts of the subsequent banquet which Holmes attended were published in many newspapers, with lists of the lavish menu and vast quantities of food provided. A contemporary account was recorded by one of the guests, William S. Samuel, in a letter to his brother-in-law written the week after the event. He gives a more animated account of the banquet than that provided by the reporters of the papers.

'Now to tell you about the tables, its unpossible, you would not believe that it was real you would think it was paintit in Such bewtifwl way it was laid out and ornamented — the Disert, and Every thing was on table with Wine at ones — 1 Soop Plate and 2 flate ones, all Best Chiney, a Napkin and a long Bill of fair in Each Plate. I gote 2 of them, Mother shall Bring with when she comes...'

The ornate menus or 'bills of fair' were obviously a treasured memento of the event and Holmes' copy was found in his possessions after his death in 1858, some twenty-one years after the banquet. Holmes' menu was kept by Dr Hallock, the pharmacist who arranged for his care in the days before his death in Evansville, Indiana. The menu and the invitation to the banquet then passed to Hallock's daughter when he died in 1886 and were displayed in an exhibition at the Evansville Library in 1923. A full description of both the menu and invitation is given in an article in the Evansville Courier of February 4th, 1923, and provide valuable information on what part Holmes took in the event.

The menu is described as:

'a large card of heavy Bristol-board, once presumably white but now yellowed to a tan-colour, shows high relief embossing at its top the municipal arms on shields of pretense, with crest, supporters and motto 'Domine Dirige Nos' (God direct us). This is balanced on either side by two other engraved coats-of-arms, the four possibly representing heraldic bearings of the officials' families, although this is a mere surmise. No less than seven varieties of copper-plate characters are displayed in the nine lines of text reading

Admit

Dr J.P.Holmes (this name is written)

(in his Mazarine Gown) and a Lady

To the Dinner at Guildhall

On Thursday 9th Nov. 1837

No 454 is written in the lower corner and its opposite boasts a heavy wax seal and the dashing signature of Thos Corney, Chairman.'

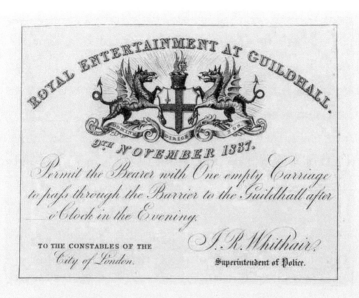

ROYAL ENTERTAINMENT AT GUILDHALL.

9TH NOVEMBER 1837.

Permit the Bearer with One empty Carriage to pass through the Barrier to the Guildhall after ____ o'Clock in the Evening.

TO THE CONSTABLES OF THE
City of London.

J. R. Whithair?
Superintendent of Police.

INSTRUCTIONS FOR CARRIAGES TAKING UP.

The Carriages of the Nobility and Gentry are requested on coming to the Guildhall on the Evening of Thursday the 9th of November 1837, to take up, to remain in Princes Street and Moorgate Street with their Horses Heads towards Cateaton Street, there to wait till called for.

Admission Ticket to Royal Banquet. *Source: Reports relating to the entertainment of Her Majesty the Queen 1837*

The requirement to wear a 'Mazarine Gown' shows that Dr Holmes was a member of the Court of Common Council of the City of London Corporation. The Common Council of the City of London is the lower chamber of the Corporation, which is the longest continuous democratic body of any city in the world and records of the Common Council exist with that name from 1367. Holmes, as a member of the Wax Chandlers Guild, was eligible for election as a member of Common Council for the Ward in which he lived. Old Fish Street was within the Castle Baynard Ward, which covered the area of London around St. Paul's. In addition, the records of the Wax Chandlers Guild show that in 1825, he was one of the two members appointed as stewards of the Guild with duties of attending the Court of the Guild to represent the members.

Holmes would have received a detailed set of orders and regulations together with his invitation to the banquet. These regulations, which applied to the admission of the members of the corporation and their ladies, included instructions on subjects such as appropriate clothing and the directions for carriages bringing the members to the Guildhall.

- That every member of the Corporation who attends shall be at liberty to introduce a Lady.
- That no Lady be admitted unless personally introduced by the Member to whom the Ticket is addressed.
- That no Lady can be admitted in a black dress, nor any Gentleman in a black or coloured stock or cravat.
- That every Lady who intends to be presented to her Majesty must bring with her a card, with her name plainly written thereon; but no other Lady other than the Wife of a Member of the Corporation can be presented.

- That every member of the Corporation do wear his gown and be expected to keep his seat, during the whole period of her Majesty's remaining in the Hall.
- That every Gentleman admitted into the Guildhall, if not wearing an official costume, or a naval or military uniform, must be dressed in a Court suit, with bag and sword.

As a member of the Common Council of the City of London, Holmes and his lady were amongst the group of dignitaries who were instructed to *form themselves into two lines on each side of the passage through the Guildhall, and on each side of the passages from the top of the steps to the Council Chamber (exclusive of the doorways) to witness the arrival of the QUEEN and her progress through the hall to the Council Chamber; and that immediately Her Majesty shall have passed they retire to their respective seats in the Hall'*.

Having witnessed the entry of the Queen, Holmes and his lady guest, who was presumably his wife, Charlotte, would have retired to the main hall. Seating plans for the banquet, showing the various tables allocated by Ward to the members of Common Council, were contained within the report on the event to the Court and Aldermen. Six tables were placed in the western end of the hall extending into the doorway for the Common Council and their ladies; the allocation of places to the Wards is shown in an illustration from the report. The scene at the banquet with the tables can be seen in contemporary engravings depicting the Royal Banquet.

No. VII.

ARRANGEMENT OF THE GENTLEMEN OF THE COMMON COUNCIL AND THEIR LADIES,
IN THE BODY OF THE GUILDHALL,
On the 9th of November, 1837.

Seating plan at Royal Banquet. *Source: Reports relating to the entertainment of Her Majesty the Queen 1837*

From his seat in the Great Hall, Holmes would have had a similar view to that which Wilfred Samuel described in his letter to his family:

'*...the Platform on which all the great people sate, was abut ½ of the Hall, and the other halfe for Such like me and greater People, the one End of the Hall Halfe way up with all looking glass and the other halfe Illuminated Well come Queen Victoria... all the way along Each Side of the Hall was Illuminated from top to Bottom, the whole was gass.*'

The gas lighting system for the banquet was specially installed and included some impressive features. The grand eastern window above the Royal Table was '*sheeted over with iron, in order to effect the safe introduction of gas. The illumination above the throne was of a size that extended over the whole of the window; it consisted of the royal initials in jets of gas, based upon an arabesque scroll of great elegance, surmounted with the word*

WELCOME ..the sides of the Hall were illuminated with gas jets in the several compartments of the building, with a double row of gas lights along the whole of the cornice. From which hung numerous flags and banners, with the Royal and City Arms and other devices.'

The menu for the banquet was described in detail in an Evansville Courier article of 1923:

'The bill-of-fare demands a sheet of thick glazed paper some ten inches wide and unrolling to a length of more than two feet before all the items are listed. A broad fanciful border of gilt surrounds it, with armorial bearings of the United Kingdom and of the 'City' at top and bottom. The printing is grandiloquently headed

'Royal Entertainment

In the Guildhall of the City of

London

On Lord Mayor's day 1837

The Right Honourable John Cowan, Lord Mayor'

The food for the four long tables in the body of the hall, which is where Holmes was seated, is listed in the report to the Court of the City:

THE FOUR LONG TABLES
IN THE BODY OF THE HALL

72	Tureens of Turtle	16	Dishes of Shell-fish
16	Pullets	60	Jellies
16	Boiled Turkeys	20	Blanc Manges
16	Roast Capons	20	Dishes of Tarts creamed
20	Dishes of Fowls	20	Orange and other Tourtes
20	Pigeon Pies	24	Dishes of Mince Pies
16	French Pies	16	Ditto of Potatoes
20	Hams	16	Ditto of Salads
16	Tongues		

REMOVES

20	Roast Turkeys	4	Leverets
24	Pheasants	8	Dishes of Wild Fowl
8	Pea Fowls	16	Ditto of Partridges

DESSERT

32	Pines	24	Ornamental Savoy Cakes
80	Ice creams	28	Dishes of Dried Fruit
80	Dishes of Grapes	20	Ditto of Preserved Ginger
16	Ditto of Apples	12	Ditto of Brandy Cherries
28	Ditto of Pears	4	Ditto of Olives

WINES

Champagne	Hock	Claret
Burgundy	Madeira	Port
Sherry		

The menus varied in quantity and quality for the various tables, ranging from the Royal Table to the General Bill of Fare. Holmes, seated in the body of the hall, had the third-best menu after the Royal Table. The menu was extensive with some dishes served as 'removes' — dishes that are taken off the table after the guests have been served. The wine appears to have been the same for all the tables, although it may have varied in age and quality between the tables, depending on the rank and station of the guests. There did not, however, appear to be any restrictions on the quantity consumed. Wilfred Samuel reported:

'as for wine, there were gentlemen with wans (wands), they askt what wine they wished besides plenty on table, only name (it) and it was sent'

'I drinked I should think about 15 to 18 glasses Wine, Shampane, Carrett, Hokey and Sherry, about a quarter past 11 I was a little Queerish, So I thought Best to go'.

Holmes was not alone in treasuring his invitation to the banquet and the menu as mementoes of the day. The organisers of the banquet had anticipated that the invitations particularly would be kept as souvenirs and arrangements were made to ensure that the guests could retain their tickets. The report to the Council gives details of the design of the tickets:

'the tickets were severally numbered and sealed with the seal of your committee and signed by the Town Clerk; and we have much satisfaction in stating that, in consequence of the great anxiety expressed by many of the guests to retain their tickets as a memorial of the day, care was taken to preserve them uninjured, and that after the entertainment, the ticket of each guest was returned.'

A number of souvenirs of the grand occasion were produced, with engravings of the procession through the city being published in many newspapers and a commemorative medal being struck.

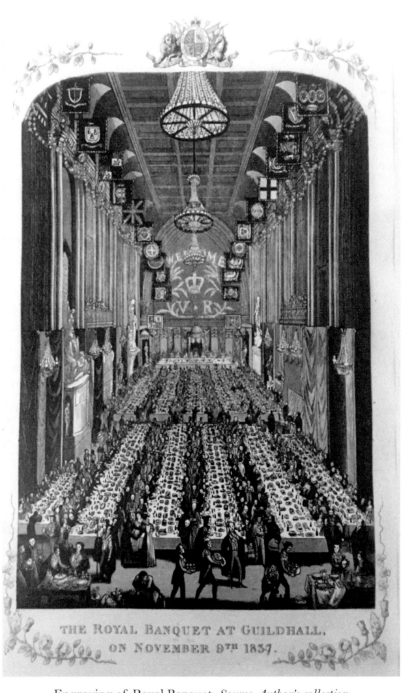

THE ROYAL BANQUET AT GUILDHALL,
ON NOVEMBER 9TH 1837.

Engraving of Royal Banquet. *Source: Author's collection*

Following the events of the Royal Banquet, the Court of the Bread Street Ward met to appoint the Ward Officers for the coming year, and a notice posted in the London Courier on December 22nd carried the following tribute to Holmes, who retired as a member of the Court.

'It was resolved unanimously that the inhabitants of this Ward beg to offer their unfeigned thanks to David Cracklow Esq and John Pocock Holmes Esq., two of their late Representatives in the Court of Common Council, for their attention to the interest of this Ward during the time they were members of that Court, and hope that they will experience in their retirement the comfort they so eminently deserve.'

Away from the pomp and ceremony of the Guildhall, Holmes continued to be involved in high profile cases involving medical evidence.

On July 13th, 1838, the trial of Mary Stewart was held at the Middlesex session. Stewart was charged with keeping a house of ill fame at 26 Portland Place, Charlotte Street, and the prosecution was brought by the Society for the Prevention of Juvenile Prostitution, an organisation founded to campaign against the 'horrible and abominable' system of enticing young girls into prostitution. The case was heard by Mr Serjeant Adams and a full bench of Magistrates. The case for the prosecution was presented by Mr Bodkin and Mr Ballantine with Mr Phillips and Mr Clarkson appearing for the defence. Mary Stewart, who appeared in court *'gaudily attired and conducting herself with much effrontery'*, pleaded guilty to the charge of keeping a common brothel. The case hinged on the testimony of Martha Bull, a young girl who informed the court that she was sixteen years old when she heard from a friend that she could obtain employment at Mrs Stewart's house. She claimed that when she visited Mrs Stewart's house in Charlotte Street, Mrs Stewart had taken her clothes away and dressed her in finer and better dresses and then gave her *'a book of an infamous description in which there were various pictures to read'*.

The opening address at the inaugural meeting of the Society for the Prevention of Juvenile Prostitution in 1835 had described exactly such a method being used to entice young girls into prostitution. A young girl is watched on the streets and then *'decoyed under some plausible pretext to an abode of infamy and degradation. No sooner is the unsuspecting helpless one within their grasp than, by a preconcerted measure, she becomes a victim to their inhuman designs. She is stripped of the apparel with which parental care or friendly solicitude had clothed her, and then, decked with the gaudy trappings of her shame'*.

Martha Bull's evidence to the court described her entry into prostitution as following exactly this process. Her ordeal continued when Mrs Stewart brought a man to the room who gave her wine to drink and asked her if she understood the book Mrs Stewart had left for her to read. The court was then given a detailed account of how she resisted his advances but *'in consequence of her resistance and screams Mrs Stewart again came into the room and held her until the person had accomplished her ruin'*. On the next morning, Mrs Stewart told her to ask the man for twenty shillings *'as it was my first time'*. Mrs Stewart took the money and said she would buy Martha new clothes with it. Martha said she stayed at the house for a week and *'saw a great many gentlemen as many as two a day'*. She then returned to her home at 26 Ray Street, Edgware Road and only visited Charlotte Street to *'see gentlemen'*. She told the Court that she had been under the protection of the Society for some time.

Mr Serjeant Adams commented that if all the facts in the affidavit were correct, then Mrs Stewart was fortunate that she had not been executed as a felon, as it was a case where the severest vengeance of the law was demanded. Mr Bodkin for the prosecution said that the prosecution brought by the Society was aimed to put a stop to the abominable and horrid system which had been adopted by such persons as the defendant. Mr Phillips addressed the Court and expressed the hope that the Court would allow the defendant to give an answer to the charges as she did not deny her guilt, but did deny that the aggravated circumstances mentioned were true.

The Court was also presented with medical certificates relating to Mary Stewart's health, which the defence wished the Court to take into account when passing sentence. The Chairman and magistrates retired to consider what sentence ought to be passed and when they returned, Mr Serjeant Adams addressed the Court:

'It has never been my duty since I had the honour of occupying this chair to pass on any individual a sentence under circumstances so painfully distressing as those which the case of the defendant has attended. In the first instance the offence which she is directly charged is not the main feature of her crime. That is of a singularly aggravated and abhorrent nature. She is however represented by a medical certificate to be visited by a disease which is one of the most painful in character and one which sooner or later would terminate fatally.

It is particularly distressing to discover that a woman who is afflicted with such a dreadful disease is, although in all probability, even on a rapid road to her end, could be engaged in bringing to utter ruin here and hereafter females of a tender age.

If it should turn out to be, as had been stated, that the disease was upon her, the fact would become known to the surgeon of the prison, and then there was a power elsewhere to soften down or alter that part of the sentence which it might, in her situation, be improper to carry into effect. But sitting here, as the court does, in the performance of its duty, to pass judgement in a case, where the best interests of society had been threatened—where every principle of morality and of virtue has been violated, it is necessary for the public good that it should take care and not permit itself to be influenced by any other feeling than such as justice demands.'

Before passing sentence, the Chairman added that he was afraid to pursue the subject further, lest his feelings should induce expressions from the lips of the Court which might not altogether be consistent when it was considered that they came from the judgment seat. He then passed a sentence of twelve months imprisonment in the House of Correction, and to be kept to hard labour, and at the expiration of that period to enter into her own recognisance of £300 and to find two sureties in £150 each, to keep the peace for twelve months.

Later in the year, the sentence was appealed against in a petition to Lord John Russell, the Home Secretary. The petition challenged the sentence on the grounds that the evidence presented had been false. The Home Secretary passed the matter back to Mr Serjeant Adams, who undertook a review of all the evidence presented. He concluded after several days of investigation that the statement provided by Martha Bull had been false. She was in fact aged seventeen and she had been involved in crime and prostitution previously and had come directly from a brothel when she gave evidence in court. He concluded that *'the whole of the evidence adduced at the trial had been a gross fabrication'.* Given this, and coupled with his review of the medical certificates which stated that Mary Stewart was suffering from *'an incurable distemper — a cancer in the breast — which would most probably end in death if she were incarcerated for any length of time, or at all events would become greatly aggravated'* had convinced him to submit a recommendation to the Secretary of State for diminution of the sentence to six months. The Secretary of State accepted the recommendation and the sentence was reduced. The Surgeon's certificates were from Sir Astley Cooper, William Coulton, consulting surgeon to London Lying-In Hospital, William D. Cordell, 29 Bread Street Buildings and J. P. Holmes, 21 Old Fish Street, Doctors' Commons. The certificate from Holmes dated September 11th, 1838, informed the Court that he had been treating Mary Stewart for a cancerous tumour of the right breast for the previous three years and that, in his opinion, the complaint was of such a nature that it would at *'no distant period terminate fatally'.* He stated that he felt the distress of mind and confinement she was now enduring must *'hasten the termination of her existence'.* Holmes signed the letter with his usual signature but attempted to add weight to his opinion by adding that he was the author of the popular book, 'Observations incident to Females'. The certificate from Astley Cooper dated August 23rd, 1838, was shorter, and he restricted his comments to the diagnosis and prognosis, stating: *'Having examined the Breast of Mary Stewart I have not the smallest doubt of the Tumour being of a malignant kind to which her life will fall sacrifice.'*

The reaction of the press to the diminution in sentence was dramatic. The Weekly Dispatch on Sunday, December 10th carried an article headed *'The Wretch Mary Stewart'*, which suggested that the decrease in her sentence was engineered by 'aristocrats' who had benefitted from her services.

'To what beastly aristocrat does she owe her liberation in return for the gratification of his brutal passion? It is perfectly clear to us and must be palpable to every man of sense and observation, that the discharge of this wretch is attributable to aristocratic influence alone. There was nothing in this case that could, under any conceivable circumstances warrant the remission of her sentence to the extent of a single hour.'

The view that Mary Stewart's cause had been championed by her wealthy clients was also expressed in a letter written to Lord Russell on August 22nd, 1838, by an anonymous writer signing himself *'a father'*. The writer informed Lord Russell that although the reasons given for leniency were ill-health, this was a pretence, as her health had improved whilst in prison. The letter continued to say that if her liberation by *'unjust favours'* should occur, then the proceedings would be in the Public Papers. The author added a footnote to the letter, stating that the parties using her house were, of course, a little interested in obtaining her release, and indicated that he knew who they were, partly naming them as Lord G- and A. Mr Serjeant Adams felt compelled to make a statement in Court the following week, setting out the reasons for the decision to remit part of the sentence, and dismissing any suggestion that there was any other influence on the decision other than the fact that fabricated evidence had been presented.

The dismissal of all of Martha's evidence did appear to be mainly based on the fact that her involvement in crime and prostitution was greater than she had disclosed in court, rather than any evidence that Mrs Stewart was not involved in procuring children for prostitution. Michael Ryan, in his book on prostitution in London published in 1839, remarked in detail on the case and commented that *'the prisoner deserves the most severe punishment. Mr Talbot has shewn me a large collection of the most infamous of books, prints, and portfolios found in her house; and there is not the slightest doubt that she is a most abandoned profligate wretch'*. However, medical evidence from Holmes and others does appear to have been taken into account when reviewing the sentence, whether or not there was pressure from wealthy clients.

Commemorative Medal. *Source: Author's collection*

Chapter 14

A Natural Death?

In November of 1838, Holmes' wife Charlotte was taken ill. She had apparently been 'delicate' for some time, and on Sunday, November 18th she suffered a large haemorrhage from the bowels. On the following day, a Dr Clutterbuck was called who prescribed bleeding as a treatment, Holmes himself performed the bleeding but Charlotte died about an hour after the treatment had been given. Dr Henry Clutterbuck MRCP had come to the attention of the medical profession following the publication of a treatise on fever in 1807 and a second publication on the prevention and treatment of typhus fever in 1819. Following the publication of his treatise on fever, Clutterbuck's reputation and practice steadily increased, and he soon gained a reputation as one of the foremost physicians in London.

Henry Clutterbuck. *Source:. Wellcome Collection*

His use of bleeding as a treatment for fever was not universally accepted, and commentaries on his publication suggested that *'we are not sure that Dr C. has not sometimes been led to the use of venesection when it was far from beneficial'*. An inquest was held at the White Horse Inn, Friday Street, Cheapside on Tuesday, November 20th. The coroner recorded that the inquest and post-mortem examination had been held at the request of Dr Holmes:

'for the purpose of clearing his own character and that of Dr Clutterbuck from blame, a great sensation having been created in the neighbourhood, from a report that Mrs Holmes had been improperly treated.'

The inquest had a number of witnesses, including Frederick Wallis, described as an assistant to Dr Holmes, and Mr Sheene of Charterhouse Square, who conducted the post-mortem examination. The post-mortem examination had shown *'an unusual vascularity in the brain, the heart was a little soft, the lower bowel was extensively ulcerated, and the inner membrane full of blood, and was more than usually fluid'*. Mr Sheene was questioned by both the coroner, Mr Payne, and one of the jurors as to the significance of the haemorrhage and the treatment by bleeding. Mr Sheene replied that he *'could not say that the effect of bleeding was sufficient to cause death'*. The treatment by bleeding for internal haemorrhage was a common practice. In response to the juror, he stated that:

'The body was very full of blood, but could not say if there was sufficient remaining to sustain life. The cause of death was one of those casualties which the medical profession had not been able to discover'.

The newspaper report of the inquest commented: *'The testimony of several other surgeons who witnessed the post mortem examination corroborated this last defence'.*

Henry Clutterbuck was also called to give evidence and stated that *'he had ordered bleeding which was his usual practice in the case of internal haemorrhage. He believed that the deceased had died of apoplexy'*. The use of bleeding in a case of haemorrhage was advocated by Clutterbuck in one of his lectures on the Theory and Practice of Physic delivered at the Theatre, General Dispensary, Aldersgate Street in 1826, and published in The Lancet, as were the whole series of his lectures to students. His views, as expressed in his lecture, were a little more cautious compared to his statement at the inquest. Whilst recommending bleeding as a general treatment for haemorrhage, he gave a number of warnings about the risks of its use.

*'If the haemorrhage be accompanied by **pyrexia**, and if the habit of the patient is at the same time strong, **bloodletting** and the usual antiphlogistic treatment will be indispensable. If on the contrary, the haemorrhage occur in a patient of weakly habit, though with febrile symptoms, we should be cautious in using bloodletting…'*

'In some cases of haemorrhage, the system is not only weak, but there is great laxity of the solids altogether: the pulse is soft and unresisting, the flesh everywhere loose and flabby, and the extremities cold. In such cases, bloodletting would be highly injurious.'

The coroner addressed the jury and gave his view that, from the evidence, it appeared every attention had been paid to the deceased by her medical attendants, and the rumours of improper treatment were contrary to the facts. The jury, having considered the evidence, returned a verdict of 'Natural Death'.

Charlotte died at the age of thirty-six on November 14th, 1838, and she was buried on November 22nd in the middle aisle on St. Nicholas Cole Abbey, the church where they had been married only fifteen years previously. Charlotte's death at thirty-six would not appear as unusual in 1838 as in modern times. The death rates for men and women in the age group thirty-five to forty-five during the period 1838 – 1845 were around fourteen per one thousand of the population for women and eighteen per thousand for men. Common causes of death in adults were typhus, consumption, dysentery and cholera epidemics. A typhus epidemic did occur in 1838 in London, but most of the newspaper reports of deaths from typhus were reported as such or as fever. The cause of typhus was not known at that time and contemporary publications on the disease reported that *'in addition to the recent loss from this malady, of many valuable members of society, there have been in London no less than five distinguished members of the medical profession who have fallen victim to Typhus'* and that *'...those predisposed to typhus fever are persons who, aborigine, profess an unusual degree of mental sensibility; those whose natural inclination leads them to deep consideration of abstruse subjects; and those whose station in life gives rise to much mental anxiety'.*

The verdict from the inquest of death by natural causes was a common one where there was no evidence of violence or specific disease. The accuracy of diagnosis and the lack of any confirmatory testing at these times meant that some cases of homicide were classified as death by natural causes or 'a visitation by God'.

Chapter 15

Remarriage

Holmes would have gone into mourning for a period of time following Charlotte's death. The etiquette for mourning in this period was not, however, as strict as in the later Victorian era, following Queen Victoria's prolonged period of mourning for Prince Albert. In the Regency period, women were expected to undergo an extended period of mourning, lasting normally a year and a day. Certainly, a period of nine months prior to remarriage ensured that any children born after the death of the husband were not the offspring of the deceased. On the other hand, a man might marry after a relatively short period, without any degree of approbation from society. The remarriage might be due to the need for a wife to manage domestic functions and care for any children, as the husband may have been the only wage earner.

Holmes remarried on May 23rd, 1839, exactly six months after the death of Charlotte. He was married at Islington Parish Church to Edith Bothilda Horneman, the daughter of the former Danish Consul General. Edith was twenty-three when she married, and Holmes was over twice her age at forty-eight. Edith Horneman came from a distinguished Danish family. Her father, Henry Frederick Horneman, had his appointment as Danish Consul-General to London approved by the Prince Regent on July 23rd, 1814. Henry was born in Copenhagen in

1776 and married Jane Hammond from Bromfield in Shropshire around 1801. They had six sons and four daughters, two of the sons died before the age of one, leaving eight surviving children of which Edith Bothilda, who was born in Lambeth, Surrey on June 13th, 1808, was the fifth eldest. Her oldest sister, Pauline, was born in 1801 and her youngest sibling, Axelina, in 1816. Edith's father had died in 1825. His family had some inherited wealth and Edith had some significant personal wealth.

The Marriage Register gives Edith's address as 70 Islington Green, and there were a large number of witnesses to the marriage, including her brothers, Frederick and Ferdinand, Ferdinand's wife, Emma, and their two-year-old daughter, Emma Caroline, who signed with an X for her mark on the marriage certificate, Edith's sister, Louisa, and three others, John Brown, William D. Cordell and Charles Alaster Latham.

The Brighton Patriot on May 28th, 1839, recorded that *'Mr and Mrs J.P. Holmes left the Gloucester Hotel on Saturday for a continental tour.'* This tour would have been their honeymoon which, by the 1830s, had become a standard part of the marriage ritual, with a continental tour being popular with those from wealthy professional backgrounds. Brighton had become a popular staging point for trips to Europe with regular sailings to France. One of the companies operating at this time was the General Steam Package Company which advertised twice-weekly sailings to Dieppe and Le Havre on the steamship Belfast. The railway line from London did not reach Brighton until 1841, so the newlyweds would have travelled by coach after their wedding the previous week. On their return from honeymoon, Edith moved from her home in Islington Green to 21 Fish Street. She brought her maid, Elizabeth Mee, with her, but there were no other servants at Fish Street. The house was still used for seeing patients, and Holmes hired a young assistant, Rennie Joseph, who lived at the house and helped with the routine patients of the practice. Life as the wife of a busy surgeon would be very different from her previous experiences, but Holmes had an extensive circle of social and professional connections in the city, and Edith was able to keep up her contacts with family and her friends in London society.

Following the publication of his book on Asthma and Consumption, Holmes had built up a reputation for treating chest complaints. His practice was divided between his office in Margaret Street and Fish Street. In addition to his routine professional work, he was also called upon to examine bodies that had been found locally and asked to provide medical evidence at inquests on deaths in the vicinity of his house.

One such case occurred on Monday, December 28th, 1840, when the body of a child was found in the gutter at Old Change, Cheapside. The body of the infant was discovered by a labourer, Mr Horne, who first thought it was the body of a dog or cat as it had been wrapped in brown paper. The body was removed to the vaults of the local church, and John Pocock Holmes was called to perform an examination.

At an inquest, held at the Falcon Inn in Old Fish Street, Holmes told Mr Payne, the coroner, that the body was of a full-grown child of eighteen months to two years, but he was unable to determine the sex of the child. He was of the opinion that the body had been kept in a dry place, given the lack of decomposition. He added that the body was mutilated around the head, but this appeared to have been after death and occasioned by dogs. Such discoveries of bodies of infants or young children were not uncommon and could occur as a result of the abandonment of a newborn baby, in an effort to conceal a pregnancy, or following the death of the child from neglect or violence. Cases of child murder and mutilation of the body were reported quite frequently in the press, and in one inquest held in 1841, with regard to the discovery of the body of a full-grown infant in the Regent's Canal, the foreman of the jury stated that he had no doubt that *'the vast increase in the commission of child murder was attributable to the bastardy clause of the New Poor-Law Act'*. The 'Bastardy Clause' of the Act effectively made it more difficult and more expensive for a mother to make a claim for affiliation against the father of her illegitimate child, and if the mother was unable to support herself and the child, then the only option was to enter a workhouse. Some mothers faced with this prospect were thought to have murdered their child rather than suffer the conditions of a workhouse.

Holmes continued to develop his practice and often travelled to see his patients who could not attend at his consulting rooms. He would of course have charged for his expenses in travelling at a standard rate per mile. On April 20th, 1841, Holmes wrote a letter to the editor of the Morning Advertiser expressing his opinions on the proposals for fees for medical men travelling by rail on professional business. His letter was in response to an article which suggested that the custom of medical men charging one guinea a mile for travel to see patients had been rendered outdated by the advent of the railway. A journey could now be completed in a third of the time previously taken when using horse and carriage. The article proposed that the fee should be based on the time spent travelling, rather than the distance travelled. The article concluded by saying that *'The fees which were adequate remuneration for a distinguished ornament of his profession to journey to Liverpool to conduct a cause when the old system of travelling prevailed, might admit of abatement in proportion to the abridgement of time which railroads create.'*

In response, Holmes wrote: '*Having read in your paper yesterday, the 19th inst., an article respecting the adequate remuneration for medical men when travelling by railway, I beg to say I have been nearly five and thirty years in the profession, fifteen years of which was passed abroad, therefore have had much travelling; and I have no hesitation in stating that £3. 3s. per hour by railway (expenses included) is a sufficient remuneration, Sir, for any distance.*

I have the honour to be, Sir, your obedient servant.

J.P Holmes MD

No 15 Maddox- street, Hannover Square, April 20.'

His address of 15 Maddox Street is one that Holmes had not used in previous correspondence. The Hanover Square area housed a number of private houses, lodging houses, offices, apartments and private clubs. His letter gives no clue as to the nature of number 15, however, the address was being used by at least one other doctor, a German by the name of Gustav Krauss, who specialised in treating orthopaedic deformities, and this may have been an office Holmes was using instead of his previous consulting room at 27 Margaret Street.

Despite the apparent success of Holmes in his professional and personal life, he was about to make a sudden and unexplained change in his plans which would lay the foundations for the extraordinary events which were to fill the remaining years of his life.

Chapter 16

The Adventurer Returns

In 1842, Holmes left England abruptly, and it was rumoured that this was due to dissatisfaction with his professional circumstances. Edith, left alone in London, made no comment publicly on the matter. She made enquiries of his whereabouts in America, having heard from an acquaintance of her family that he had been living in New York after his arrival, but was unable to trace him after that.

There is no available official record of Holmes' arrival in New York as he does not appear in either immigration records or passenger lists. There was, however, a notice in the New York Daily Tribune recording the arrival of the ship George Wilkinson on August 4th, 1842. This ship was a six-hundred-ton sailing vessel carrying merchandise destined for Glover and McMurray Merchants of 100 Pine Street. The George Wilkinson was a wooden built sailing ship constructed in 1828 from black birch and hackmatack wood and was advertised as taking immigrants to America and Canada. A steerage ticket for the voyage from Bristol to New York for an adult cost £4.10s, although a berth in a cabin would cost at least five times that amount. Ships such as the George Wilkinson, which were primarily cargo vessels, would advertise a departure date but would not leave until fully laden with cargo. The voyage in June 1842 had originally been advertised to depart on June

1st, and then June 8th, but finally left ten days later and did not sail direct but called at Le Havre for either more cargo or extra passengers. The ship, having departed from Bristol on June 18th, 1842, sailed via Le Havre, taking forty-six days to make the journey to New York. On board were thirty-seven steerage passengers and three other passengers who had travelled in the passenger cabins. They were named as Miss Gibbs, Mr Cole and Dr Holmes.

Advertisement for The George Wilkinson. *Source: Gloucester Chronicle 1842*

Soon after his arrival in New York, Holmes made acquaintances both in New York and Williamsburg. He is reported to have been known as a man of science in his profession and made particular friends with someone who the Evansville Daily Journal described as *'a gentleman… who appears to have been the first friend the Doctor made in the country'.* In a letter written in May 1858, this person described how Holmes was a constant visitor to his house in Williamsburg, and adds, *'I was contemplating, at that time, coming West, and the Doctor expressed a wish to come with me, and said as he was getting old and feeble, he would like to live and end his days with me'.* Williamsburg, originally a Dutch West India Company town, was situated across the river from New York and became part of the City of Brooklyn in 1855. Holmes soon settled in New York and became involved with committees and organisations in the city. In February 1843, he was one of the vice presidents of the committee which was to organise the celebration of Washington's birthday at the Broadway Tabernacle. The event was to be a spectacular affair, with a platform forty feet square with the president of the committee and the vice presidents sitting on chairs arranged in a crescent around a flag, depicting Washington crossing the Delaware. The committee had also asked for the loan of Washington's sword, which he used at the Battle of Trenton, and the First Company of the Washington Temperance Guards were to perform the ceremony of relieving the guard, which the New York Herald anticipated would have a very imposing effect. The weather on the day was not conducive to the crowds enjoying the outdoor parades which passed through the streets, as there was a storm of wind and sleet. By contrast, the indoor celebrations at the Tabernacle in the evening were well attended and the event was described as *'densely crowded'.* The music, military demonstrations and addresses were all deemed to have been a success.

Despite having settled well into New York Society and having a comfortable life, when his friend from Williamsburg made the definite decision to move with his family to the West, Holmes decided to move as well. It was agreed that Holmes would set off first and find a suitable location for them all. Holmes left New York in 1843 and travelled West in preparation for the arrival of his friend. He would have been able to take advantage of the fact that there was an increasing number of commercial operations providing transport west from New York. A rapidly expanding river boat service was being set up, with boats advertising both cargo and passenger transport, direct from New York down to the Ohio Valley and on to locations such as New Orleans, with the opportunity of alighting anywhere along the route of the Mississippi.

The journey by boat had been made possible by the construction of the Eerie Canal, linking the Hudson River with the Great Lakes in 1820, and the linking of Lake Eerie with the Ohio River following the building of the Cleveland Ohio canal in the 1830s. These two enormous projects provided a direct waterway link from New York through Lake Eerie to the Ohio River, and then on through the frontier states to the Mississippi River and the route to New Orleans. The junction of the Ohio and the Mississippi at Cairo was a staging place for those heading further west. Cairo was a small and unremarkable collection of buildings to which Charles Dickens took a great dislike when he arrived in 1842, having sailed from Pittsburgh in a paddle steamer along the Ohio. He used Cairo as the basis for the fictional city of Eden in his novel Martin Chuzzlewit, describing it in his American Notes as *'at the junction of the two rivers, on ground so flat and low and marshy, that at certain seasons of the year it is inundated to the house-tops, lies a breeding-place of fever, ague, and death; vaunted in England as a mine of Golden Hope, and speculated in, on the faith of monstrous representations, to many people's ruin. A dismal swamp, on which the half-built houses rot away: cleared here and there for the space of a few yards; and teeming, then, with rank unwholesome vegetation, in whose baleful shade the wretched wanderers who are tempted hither, droop, and die, and lay their bones'.* Holmes' direction of travel from Cairo would duplicate Dickens' 1842 travel as he headed north up the Mississippi as far as St. Louis. However, Holmes then headed west along the Missouri River, whereas Dickens travelled east to view the Glass Prairie before setting off on his return journey to Niagara.

By the spring of 1845, Holmes was living near Boonville, Missouri, a small town situated at the start of the Santa Fe trail where, twenty years earlier, the famous frontiersman Kit Carson had lived. Holmes' timely intervention in treating the victim of a serious shooting accident was recorded in the pages of the Boons Lick Times of April 12th, 1845. The accident had occurred near the start of April when General Henry W. Crowther, who commanded a division in the so-called 'Mormon War' in 1838, and his friend William Gibson, were on a duck shooting expedition on the Lamine River. Gibson was pulling a gun into the skiff when it discharged, striking him in his right elbow with a large amount of buckshot. General Crowther applied a makeshift bandage using his cravat and stemmed the bleeding. It took them an hour and a half to travel the nine miles home in the skiff. When they arrived, it was discovered that the arm was so damaged as to be in need of amputation. The operation was described in the Boons Lick Times as being *'a double flap amputation performed by Dr J. P. Holmes of the Royal College of Surgeons of London, the operation was a success and William Gibson was reported as fast recovering.'*

Whilst Holmes was living in Missouri, his friend completed the journey from Williamsburg in 1845 and found a property near Memphis. He had not heard any news from Holmes since his departure from New York, but after three months Holmes arrived in Memphis to join him. The stay in Memphis was not prolonged, as it was decided that the area was *'an unhealthy location'*, so Holmes' friend and family then moved *'to a place... three miles from Nashville, on the Cumberland river, with which the Doctor was very much delighted, and he expressed a desire to end his days on it'*. Nashville, at this time, was an expanding centre of trade and commerce, with the Cumberland River providing a route for the steamboat trade to transport goods all over the south of the country. Holmes lived near Nashville for the next four years and was acquainted with many of the eminent and highly respectable gentlemen in Tennessee, whose friendship and intimacy he enjoyed, and whose esteem for him was expressed in their correspondence to him in very flattering terms.

In the autumn of 1848, Holmes made the acquaintance of Joseph W. Vance of Hernando, Mississippi. Vance recounted his meeting with Holmes in a letter written to the Evansville Journal in May 1858.

'myself and my wife made the acquaintance of Doct. Holmes, by an accident. Our carriage broke down near the house where he was living, a short distance from Nashville nine years ago last fall. We were so captivated with his unaffected frankness, heartiness and general intelligence, that without knowing who he was, I gave him urgent invitation to visit us. I sent for him and he came and staid two or three week, and all of us were delighted with him. He finally concluded to remove to our town, bag and baggage, and he said he would stay with us until I could locate him in some good place in the country'.

Joseph W. Vance was a thirty-five-year-old lawyer from Kentucky who moved to Hernando, Mississippi in the early 1840s. His first wife, Mary Elizabeth, had died some years earlier leaving him with the care of their two children, Mary, born in 1837, and Reinzi, born in 1840. Vance remarried in 1844 to a widow, Eliza Clarke, with whom, by 1848, he had another two children. Together with Eliza's two children from her first marriage, Vance already had six children to support. Holmes' decision to move to Hernando from Nashville, where he had been settled with his friends, seemed to have been made after only a short acquaintance with Vance and his family. Hernando, like many towns, had suffered a major depression in 1837 when a period of national inflation had plunged banks and companies into a financial crisis, and many local people had lost all their money in the collapse of the Hernando Railroad and Banking Company. By the time Vance moved there in 1840, the area was beginning to recover and large areas of farm land were being cleared and developed, and the local economy was beginning to improve. For his age, Vance was relatively prosperous. The Federal Census for 1850 recorded his profession as a Judge of Probate, and his taxation assessment for 1851 gave an indication of his assets. The list in the county tax rolls shows those possessions which attracted a tax from owners. These included luxury items such as pleasure carriages, clocks, watches, duelling pistols, race horses, pianos and ten-pin alleys as well as gold, silver, land, cattle and slaves. Vance, like the majority of landowners in Mississippi, was a slave owner, with twenty-three slaves whose ages ranged from forty-five to two years. His possessions included fifteen cattle as well as a racehorse, a watch and a clock.

Shortly after arriving at Hernando, Holmes, aged fifty-four, was taken seriously ill and was not expected to live. From the descriptions of his illness, he had suffered a major stroke with paralysis of his left side and the loss of sight in his left eye. Vance described the events in his letter in 1858:

'He was paralyzed soon after he came back to our house from Tennessee, and was completely bed ridden for several months. Expecting to die, soon after he was attacked, he made his will, and bequeathed to his physician his instruments — my wife his elegant snuff box — and to me the rest of his property. But he very unexpectedly partially recovered, and expressing a desire to spend the remainder of his days in seclusion — as I knew the Shakers at South Union, Ky. — I advised him to seek their protection; and gave him a letter to the leading men of the communion.'

When Holmes had left Nashville in the autumn of 1848 to move to Hernando, he had between $15,000 and $20,000 in money and securities in his possession, as well as his two gold medals, a very valuable lady's watch and two diamond finger rings. By the Spring of 1849, he was destitute with what he described in a letter as only £5 and a few shillings to his name. It seemed he had been persuaded to invest his money in a venture in Mississippi which had failed, and he had lost it all. By May 1849, Holmes had recovered sufficiently to leave Hernando and made his way back to Nashville, despite the fact that he was still suffering from the effects of the stroke. Having fallen on hard times, apparently through unwise investments, Holmes wrote to The Hudson's Bay Company to solicit help in the form of income, estimating that he needed £30 a year to 'manage'. His pension from the company in 1821 had been £60 a year for seven years, so his request was essentially for a half pension for the remainder of his life, which he suggested would only be another three or four years.

'Nashville State of Tennessee 3rd of May 1849

To the Governor, Deputy Governor and Committee of the Hon'ble Hudsons Bay Company, London

Hon'ble Sirs

I entered your Hon'ble service at the age of 21 in the year 1805 as Surgeon to Churchill Factory and remained in your Hon'ble service till the year 1821 which makes it upwards of 16 years. The first year I past the winter at Churchill and the following summer 1806 I was sent inland with Mr George Charles and remained first in one place and then in another for 15 years acting both as Surgeon and Trader. After the second year I was one of the best Linguists in the country. During the time I was in your hon'ble service I built 19 Big Canoes besides several small ones which I do not count. The year before I returned to England I built 3 big canoes at Cumberland House, one of which hangs in your house, one for the expedition Capt. Franklin and the other for Norway House. I made five pairs of show shoes for Capt. Franklin and party. The year Churchill Factory was burnt down I lost every thing. I had worth upwards of £100. In 1823 I bought the lease of a house at 21 Old Fish Street Drs Commons. London which I paid £300 including repairs, 9 years unexpired. 6 years after it was burnt down all but the Back front by Mr Banks Sugar Bakers. In 1829 I got a lease for 21 years and to repair the house which cost £800. My wife died in 1833 & in 1839 I married again. She turned out a most abandoned wretch and left me about 2 1/2 years after in 1842. I immediately sold all off and went over to New York, North America.

I have been unfortunate all my life and I am sure no man ever strove harder than myself night and day but still it seemed to avail nothing. Mr Smith, your secretary and myself were acquainted upwards of

20 years. I believe he will speak well of me. Since I have been in this country I have had very bad health. Last winter I lost my left eye. The other is very weak. In consequence I am now 65 years of age in a strange land, without friends and nearly blind. I do not expect to live long, perhaps not more than three or four years. Neither do I wish it for I am poor sickly, infirm and destitute. I have but £5 and a few shillings in the world. I can manage to live here upon £30 per annum. I hope Hon'ble Sirs you will take pitty upon a poor old broken down man & any sum you send I shall be satisfied. I do not wish to trouble you any more. This will be the last time. I now close and hope Hon'ble Sirs you will pardon me for the great liberty I have taken in addressing you on such a subject.

Wishing you all Hon'ble Sirs every blessing a kind providence can bestow and believe me to remain your most obd. humble servt. J. P. Holmes

Direct as follows — J.P. Holmes, M.D. Post Office Nashville, State of Tennessee, United States of A.'

In May 1850, Holmes started to insert a series of very long and detailed advertisements in the Nashville newspapers advertising his medication for treating a variety of chest conditions for sale. He prefaces the two full columns of the advertisement for the *'Balm of Life'* with his qualifications:

'Prepared by J.P. Holmes, Member of the Royal College of Surgeons, London. Fellow of the University of Erlangelen, Bavaria. Member of the Society of Arts; Member of the Medical Society, member of the Chirurgical Society and many years Operator at the new London Hospital, Brixton, London.'

His claimed fellowship of the University of *'Erlangelen, Bavaria'* must refer to the University of Erlangen which in 1810, transferred to the state of Bavaria as a result of the French Occupation of Prussia. This qualification is not mentioned in any of his previous publications or letters. The *Physikalisch-medizinischen Sozietät zu Erlangen* was founded in 1808. Other English Doctors in the nineteenth century had used membership of the society in their list of qualifications, in the main using the term 'corresponding member', though there is no evidence available to suggest that a 'Fellowship' existed.

Holmes offers the Balm of Life for $1.25 for a half-pint and $2 for a pint, which was on sale from Ewin, Brown & Co. or Zimerman & Co. druggists of Nashville. It was also stated to be on sale from *'my Office, Deaderick Street'*. The advertisement contains quotations from reviews of his publication on friction and inhalation in consumption and a number of testimonials from patients in London which are not contained in the original publication. The advertisements for the Balm of Life continued in the Nashville newspaper until May 1851. Left with meagre resources and no regular source of income, Holmes left Nashville in 1851 and, on the recommendation of John Vance, travelled north, heading for the sanctuary of a Shaker Community in Kentucky.

Chapter 17

The Shaker Period

In April 1851, Holmes arrived at South Union Shaker Village, having been advised that it was a place where he could seek accommodation and find the seclusion he was said to have desired. The Shaker Village near Bowling Green in Kentucky was established in 1807 by the United Society of Believers in Christ's Second Coming, a group that broke off from the Quakers. They were known as 'Shakers' because of their habit during worship of dancing in extravagant postures and whirling with great rapidity, eventually falling lifeless to the floor. The communities were characterised by their adoption of celibacy, equality of the sexes, pacifism, communal living and simple lifestyles, with a readily identifiable simplicity in their furniture, dress and architecture. The communities kept detailed records of events in the villages, and the arrival of Holmes is recorded, together with two significant occurrences and his final departure for Evansville in 1858.

'*April 2, 1851* — *Dr Holmes* — *late of Miss* — *formerly of England came today to the East House as an enquirer.*'

Holmes was welcomed into the community and, as with any new arrival, he was expected to join in all the daily duties and customs. He was housed in East House with what the Shakers referred to as a 'family', a grouping of men, women and children living as a community. East House was used to house new arrivals and was called the 'gathering order'. New converts were lodged here to live and work with the family, and this was seen as a first step towards membership of the community. The daily routine at South Union would follow the same pattern as in all the Shaker communities across the country. The day would start at five in the morning when all the members of 'the family' would rise to complete their morning chores. The family slept in the family house, East House, with men and women having separate sleeping accommodation. An hour after rising, the breakfast bell would ring and everyone would return to the house for breakfast at a long table with men on one side and women on the other. The meal would be consumed in strict silence, served by family members on a rota basis.

East House South Union. *Source: South Union Shaker Village*

In keeping with the guiding principles of celibacy and renouncing personal property, the sleeping quarters were segregated, with men in rooms on one side of the sleeping area and women on the other. The bedrooms were sparsely furnished, with a bed space and a hook for hanging clothes allocated to each person. Unless there was someone aged or infirm in the room, then only one chair would be present. The rooms were all shared and there would often be four or more brethren or sisters in a room.

Photograph of Male Bedroom South Union. *Source: Author's photograph*

On April 25th, 1851, shortly after his arrival at South Union, and despite his infirmity after the stroke, Holmes assisted two visiting doctors, Dr Patterson, and Dr Holland, to set a fractured femur. Mary Bomer, a young girl who was moving with her family to Missouri, fell from the wagon and fractured her thigh bone. The accident occurred near Lockharts by the East Section farm, so she was brought to the East House. The setting of such a fracture would have required a number of doctors to exert sufficient traction to overcome the strength of the thigh muscles and reposition the bone into a suitable position. Whether any anaesthetic was available is not recorded, but despite the Shakers' great expertise in manufacturing and marketing herbal remedies, they were ready to accept outside assistance and adopt innovations and advances in the treatment of conditions. Ether and chloroform were recognised as effective anaesthetic agents from 1846 onwards and in England, the use of an anaesthetic by Queen Victoria when she gave birth in 1851 led to a widespread acceptance of the use of pain relief in labour. American Physicians and Surgeons began using ether and chloroform in their practices in the late 1840s and 1850s. Without anaesthetic, the procedure for setting a fractured femur would rely on either giving the patient enough alcohol to cause them to lose consciousness, packing the area with ice to dull the pain or accepting that the patient would faint from the pain and proceeding quickly before they recovered. Holmes had brought his surgical instruments with him to South Union so would have been able to assist with minor operations and to treat such injuries. It appears that his possessions were seen as valuable, as the South Union journal records that: *'May 1, 1853 — Horse STOLEN — Last night Joseph McGee stole a horse from the East House, also Dr Holmes' watch and some of his surgical instruments.'* The transcribed version of the regular diary entries of H. L. Eades at South Union Village gives a detailed account:

'Last night Joseph McGee (Alias John Lutin) stole a horse at the East House, also Dr Holmes' watch and some of his Surgical

Instruments and left (as he had been residing there a short time).
He was followed by Eli and Jefferson. The horse found this side of
Bowling Green, the thief caught in Franklin and taken to Russellville
the 5ᵗʰ of May and thrust to jail to await the Action of the law 'made
and provided' for such cases'.

After living in the Shaker Community for nearly seven years,
Holmes made the decision to leave and after some false starts,
finally left on March 28ᵗʰ, 1858. His departure was recorded by
John Eades, the head of the South Union community; *'Departure,*
from the East House, Dr Holmes left today, started North'. Eades
also wrote a detailed letter to the Evansville Journal in 1858
which gives great insight into the time Holmes lived with the
Shakers.

'Dr Holmes came to South Union about seven years since, in a very
helpless and dependent condition — was advised to make his way here,
by his excellent friend, Col. Vance, of Hernando, Miss, with whom he
had been boarding; and to whom of late, he was greatly anxious to
return. We received him kindly, though we viewed him as an uncommon
strange; yet, he gave every assurance, of which he was capable, that he
would comply with every virtuous or religious requirement that would
be demanded of the most humble votary of our faith, although he had
not a full understanding of us as a people, further, than informed by
his friend Vance.

He was at that time paralyzed in one whole side — dead, as it
were in the same, and almost powerless; but from which, by careful
treatment, he finally recovered some and could help himself with more
ability. We however, provided him a comfortable room; and for the past
seven years have attended to his want, and for which, most of that time,
he has manifested much gratitude for kindnesses received; in which
feeling, and in his favours towards particular friends, he was apt to

be unreasonably extreme; and on the other hand as greatly the reverse towards those, for whom he formed a dislike. He continued in this state of feeling till within a year or more before his withdrawal, at times manifesting much restlessness and disquietude. Those best acquainted with his case, conceived the cause to be, the retired condition in which he was necessarily placed, being so contrary to his former habits and inclination; and in addition to this, the increasing inflammation of his eye, seemed to irritate his brain and nervous system, and give a force to his feelings of disquietude, that he was unable to govern.-

About a week previous to his departure, he walked off a mile and a half to a public house on the road, without giving any knowledge to the family of his absence. This was an unexpected circumstance, and a matter of surprise to every one acquainted with it.

Upon being asked why he did do, being so helpless as he was he could make no other reply, but to manifest his unreconciliation. In the course of three or four days he returned; but was still indomitable in his resolution to return again to his friend Vance; and when asked by those who had done the most for him, why he would act so inconsistently in his helpless state? His unfailing reply was about this; ' The d---l has got in me, and I can't get him out'. We therefore, at his request, furnished him with a wagon and horses and took him and his effects 15 miles to Bowling Green, free of charge; neither was any charge made for any services rendered during his stay with us — neither any reduction made in the amount of money received in his name — (a note of some $800 or more, but when shorn of his dues, amounted to $220, and also a small amount of $40. For medicine sold on commission) — amounting in all to $260; most of which he seemed to have at his decease.

We feared some that the result of undertaking so great a journey might be bad; and in conversation with him, after he was seated in the wagon, he seemed almost to predict his own end in saying;- 'Well, I expect I will die in some hole.' In this way he left; and from all appearance judging from the past, we thought he might live years and probably would, had he continued in the careful and regular way he had been living with us. But it would seem, that with all his medical knowledge, the remaining vigor of a naturally powerful constitution, was not sufficient to sustain him in the journey he had undertaken.'

It is clear from Eades' journal that Holmes was not to be dissuaded from leaving South Union. His decision to travel south to meet up with Vance may have been driven by his financial situation. He had none of the considerable funds left that he had brought with him to America, and his attempts to sell his 'remedies' in Nashville had failed. Vance was probably the only friend he knew who was financially well off and might be able to support him.

Holmes had lost all contact with his wife, Edith, since his sudden and unexplained departure from England sixteen years ago and had only had sporadic contact by letter with his sister, Elizabeth, in South Leverton over this time. Even if he wished to return to his family, he certainly would not have been able to afford the passage back to England and given his poor state of health, it would seem unlikely that he would have survived the voyage across the Atlantic. From Eades' account, Holmes was aware of the risks of any journey given his poor health, but despite this, he packed his few remaining treasured possessions and boarded a river boat headed towards Evansville, Indiana, where he hoped to continue down river to Memphis, and then to make the twenty-five-mile journey by road to join his friend Vance in Hernando, Tennessee.

Chapter 18

The End of the Story?

In April 1858, the Evansville Daily Journal carried a long news report recording Holmes' arrival in Evansville and his subsequent fate.

'*Evansville Daily Journal (1858)*

EVANSVILLE, IND

MONDAY MORNING APRIL 19

A Homeless Stranger

'A week ago on Saturday, the steamer Union brought from Green River, an apparently poor and afflicted man, past the age of eighty. One eye had been destroyed by a cancer, and the other by sympathy was so swollen and affected as to be sightless. One leg was paralysed and the poor sufferer seemed utterly helpless, destitute and friendless. No one knew whence he came from, nor whither he was bound, except from the desire he expressed to be taken to Memphis. As the Union was going no further down the river, he was taken from the steamer and placed on Messrs. O'Riley & Co's wharf boat, — on the deck of which he lay unattended and uncared for, from Saturday evening till Sunday afternoon, when his condition became known to Dr A. C. Hallock, our Good Samaritan, who visited him and found him in a most afflicted condition,- helpless, blind, suffering with pain, and a mind wandering in delirium. The doctor, by intercession with old 'Aunt Hannah' the black nurse, induced her to give up her only bed and take him in, and attend upon him. He was bathed — clean clothes were procured for

him, and his cancer dressed. He refused medicine — appearing to have a perfect professional knowledge of the nature of his disease and condition; — said there was no medicine that would help him, and that he only wanted care and quiet. He remained with his faithful nurse, who was unremitting in her attentions day and night by him, and was visited daily by Doctors Hallock and Casselberry, who ministered to his necessities. The progress of his disease was rapid and he sunk fast under its effects, and on Thursday night he expired alone in the house of the good negro woman, who had given him shelter, with no friend or clergy to soothe his spirit in his last mortal agony.

He was respectably buried by the Sons of Temperance in the Oak Hill Cemetery.

On examining his effects after his death, papers were found which proved him to have been DOCTOR JOHN POCOCK HOLMES, a member of the College of Surgeons of London. Among them was an original certificate of Sir Astley Cooper, testifying to his qualifications as a Surgeon, with numerous testimonials from other eminent Surgeons of his ability and faithfulness as a member of their profession. It appeared from other original papers that he had been, previous to 1827, sixteen years in the employ of the Hudson Bay Company, at various posts on this continent.-

In 1827 he was a practising Surgeon in London, holding intercourse with the most eminent men. Among the papers he appears to have preserved with care, is a card of invitation from the Lord mayor and Mayoress of London to dine at the Mansion House on the 12th May, the year omitted. But the papers which he seems to have deemed the most precious, are the package of letters from CAPT PARRY, the great Arctic explorer, with whom he seems to have enjoyed a free and cordial intimacy. It appears that the deceased had rendered some useful service — as a chemist and from the knowledge he had gained in the Hudson Bay Company's service, in the manufacture of Pemmican for the exploring expedition — for which Capt. Parry gives him much praise, and the Admiralty vote him an acknowledgement of £150.- Capt. Parry invites him in free and familiar terms to call at his house in London, and at another time to visit him on board the Hecla at the Nore, before sailing. The notes and letters of the celebrated explorer are interesting and valuable as autographs.

Among his effects, found since his death, were two large and beautiful gold medals awarded to 'Doctor John Pocock Holmes by medical societies for his valuable inventions of obstetrical and surgical instruments.' There are also a large number of letters from eminent professional men- from the nobility, and medical and scientific societies, acknowledging the receipt of 'Doctor John P. Holmes' very valuable and able treatise on consumption and asthma.' There are two cards of invitation to Doctor J.P. Holmes and lady to dine at Guildhall, on the occasion when Queen Victoria honoured the Mayor and Common Council with her presence.

There are letters from eminent and highly respectable gentlemen in Tennessee and Mississippi, whose friendship and intimacy he has enjoyed, and whose esteem for him is expressed in their correspondence in very flattering terms.-

He appears at one time to have resided near Nashville, in Tennessee; and from other papers, we are led to suppose he has been residing recently with the community of Shakers at West Union, not far from Bowling Green in Kentucky.

Whether he had just withdrawn from them when he arrived here, or why he should have left them in the afflicted and helpless condition in which he was found, is not explained by his papers, nor did he give those who took care of him any explanation before his death —neither did he give them any account of himself, nor tell of the strange *vicissitudes by which he in his old age had been cast among strangers a homeless and friendless wanderer. In his last moments he spoke of a sister, but gave no clue to her name or residence. Before his death he committed his funds, which he had kept concealed about his person, amounting to about $250, to Dr Hallock, but left no instructions in regard to the disposal of them. His other effects were of little or no value. His estate will be duly administered upon, and after the expenses are paid, the balance will be sent to his friends. He was evidently a man of correct habits and great intelligence. By what misfortunes he who had enjoyed high professional reputation, and had been the associate and friend of eminent men, was left homeless and poor and died at last alone in the shanty of a poor negro nurse, is unknown. It is a painful lesson of the sad vicissitudes of life.'*

This report from the Evansville Daily Journal was reprinted over the next months across newspapers and journals both in America and England. Professional Journals such as The Lancet and the Medical Gazette published obituaries based on the Evansville report. The article resulted in a number of letters being sent to the Journal providing information on Holmes' previous experiences.

John Eades, in his letter to the Evansville Journal in 1858, concluded his account of Dr Holmes' time with the Shakers by a description of what they had learned from Holmes about his previous life. *'During our acquaintance with Dr Holmes he gave but a limited account of his origin and ancestry. He has spoken of his father as an Episcopalian clergyman, and of his brother Charles, as occupying the same position and calling. Other members of the family, he did not incline to say much about; nor did he say much concerning his own, though it would appear he had been twice married. By the first wife he had two children, a girl and a boy; and during her life, lived in affluence and splendor, after the order of the aristocracy of London. The daughter died young. The son, when grown up, made a choice of going to sea, and was never heard of afterwards. By the second wife he had no children; and for some cause, the union between them was dissolved; and in this (if he had explained it), we suppose, lay the cause of his separation finally from the higher classes of society he once enjoyed. After this, if we understand him, his time was spent in the various hospitals of London and Paris, and in the service of the Hudson's Bay Company, procuring furs from the Indians; and was, for a term of years, Governor in that Territory. He then came to the Unites States, visited various points, located for a season in New York city, in Nashville, Tennessee, at some point in Arkansas, and near Hernando, Miss, from which place he came to South Union.*

This silence in regard to himself, still leaves his separation from the refined society of London, a mystery, and which, we are inclined to believe, was a fixed purpose in his own mind; and will perhaps so remain, except revealed by some of his own class, many of whom must still survive, as he could not, from anything we could learn of him, exceed seventy years of age at his decease.

With due regard to all, and on behalf of our communion.

John R Eades.'

John Vance in his letter to the journal explained how he had introduced Holmes to the Shaker Community. *'They received him kindly, and he wrote to us afterwards, that he was well pleased with his new home. Knowing that the rules of the communion forbids its members to hold correspondence with people in the world, I did not write to him, and our correspondence ceased. But the Shakers were in the habit of paying us annual visits in the distribution of their seeds, and changed messages, congratulations and good wishes. The Shakers who came to us always spoke in the highest terms of the Doctor, and their relations, as far as I could learn, were mutually pleasant. I knew members of the society well — had every confidence in their goodness, and was sure they would treat him kindly.*

I believe he regarded me as his warmest friend, and was probably trying to make his way to our house when he died. We heard from Mr O'Riley that he was in Evansville, and we had resolved to take care of him if he arrived, as long as he lived. We thank, in the name of God, the kind gentlemen who ministered to him in his sickness, and paid a decent respect to his memory when dead. He was much loved by us. He gave us but little information in regard to his family. He received letters from a sister in England, while with us, but her name and residence I do not recollect. He grieved much over the loss of his half breed son George. Scarcely a day passed but he would utter some words of sorrow over his fate. He was a great blessing to our family, and an instrument, in the hands of God, in restoring the health of our son, now a healthy boy. He fully compensated us for all we did for him in his helplessness. We are glad to know his end was peaceful, though the manner of his death is sad, and painful to his friends to hear.'

On May 13th, 1858, the Evansville Daily Journal continued with its reports on the death of Doctor Holmes, stating that *'the death of Doctor Holmes has brought us several letters from persons who knew him in London and this country — they disclose a fate so remarkable that we think the letters of sufficient interest to present to our readers.'*

One of the letters was from Doctor Peckover, a dental surgeon, with a practice in Paris, Kentucky, who in 1860 was president of the Kentucky State Dental Association, described in the article as *'a highly respected physician of Paris, Bourbon county, Ky., who received his medical education under Doct. Holmes, in London'*.

Peckover Advertisement 1859. *Source: The Cynthiana News*

His letter dated May 5th, 1858 was published in full as follows:

'I feel much gratified and obliged by your kind attention to my inquiries, respecting Doct J. P. Holmes. I quite approve of the plan of the gentlemen, who have his effects in charge, to erect a monument to one who was beloved by all who knew him. My acquaintance with him commenced in the Spring of 1827, after his return from the service of the Hudson Bay Co., and continued till 1832, when I left England for this country; for two years of that time, I lived principally in his family. There were two other students beside myself, Mr Bird and a Mr Holman, one of whom, at least was studying at Dr Holmes' expense. The Doctor married late in life, a very beautiful and accomplished young lady. They never had any children. He had a half breed son, by an Indian wife, while in the Hudson Bay Company's territories, whom he was educating in England. What became of him I do not know. He had no other family that I ever heard of. His wife had one sister, whose name I have forgotten. The Doctor was a member of the Royal College of Surgeons, and also of the 'Medical Society of Bolt Court' He was also a member of the common council, of London, from the Ward in which he lived, which was, I think, Dowgate.

The last time I saw him was in 1839, while I was visiting London. He was still living in his old home in Great Fish Street, and had an office somewhere in the West End of London, where he treated consumptive patients on a plan of inhalation. — He had published a work on consumption, which gave him high repute, and was known to the profession by the title of 'Holmes on consumption and asthma'. The medals mentioned as found among his effects, I have seen many times. He was the inventor of a craniotomy forceps, with separate blades. When a boy, I assisted him in making the models.

He was very intimate with Abernathy and Aston Key, but was not on friendly terms with Astley Cooper nor any of the surgeons of Guy's Hospital. His practice was very large, but not as remunerative as he might have made it, as he invariably attended the calls of the poor as well as the rich, and always refused money from those whom he considered not able to pay. He was generous to a fault. I have known him when visiting a poor family, destitute of means- having no money in his pocket to bestow on them — to pull off his overcoat and give it to them, that they might pawn or sell it to relieve their necessities. Whenever asked for charity he would generally give all the money he had in his pocket; and many times have I heard his beautiful wife chide and scold him for his indiscriminate charities, and inattention to his own interests.

His wife was the daughter of a surgeon, and herself a good Surgeon and Anatomist, and many an hour has she spent demonstrating on a subject for my instruction when I was a lad taking my first lessons in the surgical art. I suppose she is dead, or the Doctor would never have been here in such a condition as you have described him. It is difficult to realise that the poor, old, friendless man, dying as an outcast, was the same, noble, generous friend, respected and beloved by a large circle — both high and low — as I knew him in London twenty years ago. I myself owe him a heavy debt of gratitude.

But I am trying your patience with recollections, which, perhaps are only interesting to myself, for to me he was ever like a father.

I have reason to believe that the Doctor was a Royal Arch Mason, though I cannot vouch for the fact. If his effects are sold, I should like to purchase something as a memento of one I loved so well. I should like one or both of the medals. I don't know I can manage it except through your kindness. I will remit any amount needed for the purpose. Your letter and enclosure I have sent to my brother in London, who will make the unhappy fate of the Doctor known to his friends.

R.P.'

In September 1858, the Evansville Daily Journal published sections of a letter written by Edith Bothilda Holmes to Dr Hallock. The Journal records that in the letter *'she expresses the deepest sadness at the account of his unhappy fate and the highest respect for his memory. She is sincerely grateful to those benevolent men who attended and cared for him in his last extremity and prepared his obsequies. She desires that all the mementoes that he left may be preserved for her, and if it be necessary, she will repurchase them from those who may possess them...*

...I understand that those who have been benefitted by his death, refused to spare a small portion of his funds to erect a monumental stone to his memory. That, therefore will devolve on me, though my means are but limited...

...His age was 74 not 80, as stated by the paper — Will you tell me, without reserve, whether my unhappy husband was sufficiently aware of his state to look forward and prepare for the awful change that awaited him? In the zenith of health and prosperity, during my union with him, he used to resist all serious thoughts; and I will cordially own, I had not at that time, those deep convictions, and abiding faith,

which I trust, will never depart from me. I do hope that he was able to extract from his mind that which alone had occupied it, namely worldly prosperity…

…I am his widow by a second marriage, and for various reasons did not hold any communication with the relatives of his former wife; nor did he till after our separation, to which step I was advised, and, I may say, was compelled to resort. I sued for alimony, and during the legal proceedings he managed to get possession of my property — which my legal advisers at the time assured me was perfectly secure — and therewith left England for New York. He never wrote after his departure, even to his sister Mrs Mickle, to whom he owed many obligations…

…Though the goodness of your motives and inestimable service, as known only to our Heavenly father, can be rewarded but by Him, still I hope in duty to yourself and relatives, you have made a pecuniary claim and that it has been allowed.'

The Journal continues, *'The writer is evidently a lady of cultivation and refined sensibilities, and it is hoped that the medals, instrument, watch and other articles left by the Doctor, which will be precious mementoes to her, may be given up to her and funds allowed by the court to erect a suitable monumental stone over his grave.'*

The Evansville Journal also received a letter from someone they did not identify but described as *'a gentleman in the vicinity of Nashville'* who wrote:

'I have been personally acquainted with Doctor Holmes since his first arrival in the country in 1831(sic). *I was at that time living in Williamsburg, opposite New York. He became a constant visitor at my house, He was known in New York and Williamsburg as a man of science in his profession. I was contemplating at that time, coming West, and the Doctor expressed a wish to come with me, and said as*

he was getting old and feeble, he would like to live and end his days with me. Owing to the unsettled conditions of my affairs, I could not quit the East so soon as the Doctor desired, and he left and came West alone, with a view of selecting a location for us. I followed soon after, and came to Memphis. I had heard nothing from the Doctor, after his departure from New York, but about three months after my arrival in Memphis, he joined us —

Finding Memphis an unhealthy location for my family, we concluded, with the assent of the Doctor, to remove to a place which I had purchased, three miles from Nashville, on the Cumberland river, with which the Doctor was very much delighted, and he expressed a desire to end his days on it. He lived with us four years. At the end of that time, he made the acquaintance of a person from Mississippi, who induced him to go with him into that state, where he became inveigled in some schemes of speculation, by which he lost, I suppose, nearly all his money. When he left me, he had between $15,000 and $20,000 in money and securities. He had I recollect, two gold medals and a very valuable lady's watch and two diamond finger rings, which he preserved with great care. He never spoke to me of any relation, but a sister. After his misfortunes in Mississippi, he wandered mortified and broken hearted to the settlement of Shakers at West Union, where he buried himself from the knowledge and intercourse of his friends.

It appears from other information, that his half breed son, George, went to sea, and was lost.'

Chapter 19

Probate

Believing that Dr Holmes had not left a Will, Allen Hallock proceeded to act as administrator of the money and personal effects which had been found upon his person. At a hearing in Evansville on Friday, March 16th, 1858, Dr Hallock declared that, on his death, John Holmes had $318.90 and several items of personal property. Hallock presented the Court with a bill accompanied by receipts for his expenses as administrator, and for the costs of the care and attention he gave to Holmes during the last days of his life. The bill came to $205.70, leaving a balance of $113.20. The County Judge approved the expenses and directed that the balance should be paid into the Court. In considering the matter of the personal property remaining unsold, the Judge charged the administrator with delivering *'the said personal property of said deceased yet remaining in his hands to the devisees of the said deceased or their legal representatives upon demand.'*

However, reports of the death of John P. Holmes had reached the Shaker Village at South Union soon after his death, prompting the letter to the Evansville Journal from John Eades. The Shaker Village had retained a Will, made by John Holmes on April 18th, 1851, some two weeks after he had arrived at South Union. The act of bequeathing all his possessions to the Shakers would have been part of the Shaker way of life, governed by a number of basic rules. One of these was that, on joining the community, members had to give all their land, possessions, material goods and wealth to the community.

The Will was quite clear in expressing his wishes.

'I John P Holmes of the County of Logan and state of KY being feeble of body but sound in mind do make and ordain this my last will and testament on the following manner viz:

Whatever property I may die possessed of or notes, bonds or any other description. I will and bequeath unto John M Lean & [???] Trustees of the united Society of Shakers at South Union Ky of which I am a member for the sole use and benefits of said society and no other. I do hereby appoint and ordain the said John M Lean and [Raultin?] My lawful Executors to fulfil the intent and purpose of the above will.

In witness whereof I have hereto set my hand and seal the 18th day of April AD 1851.

John P Holmes MD'

This Will, dated April 18th, 1851, would have replaced the one which Col. Vance claimed Holmes had written prior to moving to South Union. That Will, according to Vance, bequeathed to his physician his instruments — to Mrs Vance his elegant snuff box — and to Col. Vance the rest of his property. Vance does not appear to have challenged the Shaker Will and as he was an attorney and probate lawyer, he would have been aware that the second Will was properly constructed and in line with Shaker Community normal practice. The authenticity of the Will needed to be proved, so, through attorneys Baker and Foster, the Shakers applied to the County Court of Logan Kentucky at the county seat, Russellville, for a Court Judgment to allow the Will to be accepted as the true Last Will and Testament of

Holmes. Baker and Foster were attorneys at Law with offices at Third Street, East of Main in Evansville.

On May 24th, 1858, the hearing began, with William J. Morton as the presiding Judge. The Court records show that a document described as *'A writing purporting to be the last will and testament of John P Holmes deceased bearing the date of 18th day of April 1851'* was submitted to the Court. The document was affirmed to be the original Will by John R. Eades and Patterson Johns, surety in addition to the executor was provided by John R. Malone and the Court, having accepted the Will as valid, granted probate to John M. Lean and John M. Malone charging them to *'well and truly pay and deliver all the legacies specified in said will as far as the goods chattels and credits and effects will extend.'* The certified copies of the Will and probate were presented to the Court of the Common Pleas of Vanderburgh County on June 7th, 1858. The Court of Common Pleas had replaced the Probate Court in 1852 and had exclusive jurisdiction over estates, guardianships and matters that did not come under the jurisdiction of the Justices Courts. The Court, with Judge Isa Igleheart presiding, accepted that the documents were valid, and copies of them were entered into the records of the Court. The Clerk to the Court, J.W.B. Moore, transcribed all the documents and the details of the Will into the Court Records. The judgment of the Court was that the documents should be allowed as the Last Will and Testament of *'the said John P Holmes deceased and the said motion is now here granted and it is ordained by the Court that the said instruments be and the same is hereby allowed as the last will of the said John P Holmes deceased and the Clerk is ordered and directed to file and record the same according to the requirements of the Statute of such case made and provided.'* This Court Judgment accepted the appointment of John M. Lean as the executor of the Will and, by the previous judgement, instructed Dr Hallock to make over to John Lean all the remaining unsold personal items and, through the court, the balance of $113.20.

The items of expenditure that Dr Hallock had claimed as the administrator would have legitimately included any burial costs, however, the report in the Evansville Newspaper stated that he was *'respectably buried by the Sons of Temperance in the Oak Hill Cemetery'*. The Sons of Temperance was a closed movement with branches called Chapters all across the USA. The organisation had many of the features of Free Masonry, with rituals, secret handshakes and initiation ceremonies, and the fraternity was dedicated to abstinence and temperance. Each member paid an initiation fee and a regular membership fee which acted as an insurance policy for ill health or death. The Sons of Temperance were required to pay $30 to cover the costs of the burial of a member. Although John Holmes is not recorded as a member, he was a member of the Arch Masons, and the payment of his burial costs would have been a charitable act by the local Chapter. The provision of a headstone for the grave appeared to be a separate issue. A letter published on May 8th, 1858, from Dr Peckover expressed approval for *'the plan of the gentlemen who have his effects in charge, to erect a monument to one who was beloved by all who knew him'*. However, later in the year a letter from Holmes' widow, Edith, to Dr Hallock, thanking those who had looked after him in his last days also stated: *'I understand that those who have benefitted by his death, refused to spare a small portion of his funds to erect a monumental stone to his memory. That, therefore will devolve on me, though my means are but limited'*.

When this letter was published, the probate had been

granted to John Lean. Allen Hallock's role as administrator had been relinquished and the fate of the various possessions which Holmes had on his death seems unclear. Edith had requested that they should be returned to her and offered to buy back any that had been sold. Dr Peckover offered to buy one of the gold medals as a memento of his friendship with John Holmes, but no record exists of any sales of the possessions. Allen Hallock retained the menu and invitation to the Guild Hall banquet from when Queen Victoria attended the Guild Hall. These items were inherited by Allen Hallock's daughter, Kate, and displayed in Evansville in 1923.

Whether the cost of a memorial stone was met by the executors, the Sons of Temperance or Edith Holmes, remains unclear. Allen Hallock was an officer of the Sons of Temperance Temple of Honor Divison 54, so he may have organised the gravestone. Nevertheless, a memorial stone was purchased and still stands in the Oak Hill Cemetery in Evansville.

Location map of Holmes' grave. *Source: Oak Hill Cemetery Records*

Photograph of Holmes' gravestone. *Source: Oak Hill Cemetery Records*

Chapter 20

A Final Twist

The Evansville Journal of June 4th, 1858, continued its reporting on the death of Dr Holmes with the publication of a letter from a '*highly respectable*' lady. The letter writer was Dr Hannah Mary Tracy Cutler (H.M.T.C.), a noted campaigner for female rights and the abolition of slavery. She recounted her meeting with Holmes' wife Edith during her visit to London in 1851 when she was an American delegate to the Peace Conference. During the visit, she gained some notoriety for introducing the female fashion of 'Bloomers' to a rather shocked British public. As a campaigner for women's rights, she attended several meetings and made a number of connections with women who were also pursuing women's rights.

She wrote:

'*Dear Sir:- Your favour came duly to hand, for which allow me to tender my thanks, on behalf of my friend. Mrs Esther (sic) Holmes. — It is well to think kindly of our fellow beings; and it is also sometimes well to know that the Good Father does not punish the innocent and good, by rendering them solitary outcasts.*

My knowledge of the poor fallen man, commenced in the winter of 1851 and '52. — At the house of the mother of the present Countess of Harrington, I frequently met among other agreeable guests, a Mrs Holmes, whose intelligence and liberality of sentiment, soon won my high esteem. Our acquaintance soon ripened into intimacy. I supposed she was a widow, as I heard no mention made of her husband. But one evening when at her house, I noticed a very fine bust, and on inquiry, learned that it was her husband's, Dr John Pocock Holmes. She inquired if I had ever met any one in America, who resembled it, and then went on to inform me that, if living, he was in America. In confidence, she related to me a history of her life, and especially of her connection with Dr Holmes. She could not bear to tarnish his reputation, for he had stood so high with the public, and she had suffered much in silence, rather than expose him to the just rigor of the law.

His open handed generosity, and possibly, profligate habits not so well known, had embarrassed him to a considerable extent, and his wife had freely given him two thousand pounds to relieve, as he said, a temporary pressure, in his affairs. She had four thousand more in bank, so secured that he could not draw it without her signature. He wished her to give him this, but told him, if he was really so much embarrassed, he had better let his creditors settle his affairs (as he was notorious for not collecting for himself), and she had better retain the small sum she had, for any future emergency.

He was angry, and in the hearing of a servant of her mother's, made some threats which were afterwards remembered. She was taken with a sick headache, and he administered a portion (sic) which he said would soon relieve her, and went out. She noticed the phial from which he took it, and observed that it tasted strangely. She begged him to send her maid to her, but instead of doing so, he went down and ordered her not to go into her mistress' room till she had slept an hour or two. She became deathly sick and vomited freely. The maid, a woman of a good deal of experience, came into the room, perceived an odor, and inquired what she had taken. She told her she did not know, but pointed to the phial. She put it in her bosom, and soon as she could leave *her mistress, went to a chemists shop and learned that it was a poison. Mrs Holmes was naturally a good deal alarmed, and as soon as she was able to ride, went to her mother's. The Doctor did not return till after she had left. She felt afraid to return, and her friends thought it not best that she should do so, until he should make some explanations. I think her brother saw him, but I do not recall all the particulars. She was ill for some time, and when able to go out, went to the bank to draw some money. To her utter astonishment, she learned that the Doctor has been there with a lady, personating herself, and had drawn the whole amount. This money was a property left her by a deceased friend, and the Doctor had never any claim to it. He had promised her a marriage settlement of £20,000, which he had never arranged. When she made inquiry for him he had left, and was not to be found; subsequently she traced him to America through the aid of, I think, a brother-in-law of the distinguished Chevalier Bunsen, whose family treated her with great kindness. So the $20,000 he brought with him was stolen from his wife, and who could wonder that his speculations did not prosper. Beyond the State of New York she was not able to trace him distinctly, though she believed he was in the West. His motives she could never fathom. His position was so high, his pride of character so great, it was to her unaccountable. I should have before stated that she was his second wife, and the daughter of a Danish gentleman, who had married an English lady. In his youth he had been an intimate friend of the Crown Prince of Denmark.*

Such is a brief outline of the tragic tale that I heard, and I promised if I ever heard of him, to communicate the same to her. I have done so, and given her your address, so that she may communicate with you, if desired.

Yours truly H.M.T.C.'

The letter from Hannah Mary Tracy Cutler was re-published

by many of the newspapers which had reprinted the original story of Holmes' death from the report in the Evansville press. The new information changed the nature of the reports with headlines such as:

'A Mystery Unfolded — WHY DR. J.P. HOLMES LEFT ENGLAND — HIS ROBBERY OF AND AN ATTEMPT TO POISON HIS WIFE — A VERY SAD STORY'.

Chapter 21

The sad vicissitudes of life?

The Evansville Journal article of April 1858 ended with a question:

'By what misfortunes he who had enjoyed high professional reputation, and had been the associate and friend of eminent men, was left homeless and poor and died at last alone in the shanty of a poor negro nurse, is unknown. It is a painful lesson of the sad vicissitudes of life'.

We are left with a number of possible answers to the question, and a number of views of John Pocock Holmes' character, his life and his career. We have the John Holmes who is a noble and generous man. The sort of man who, when visiting a poor family, would pull off his overcoat and give it to them so that they could pawn or sell it to relieve their poverty, a man whose wife would chide and scold him for his indiscriminate charities and inattention to his own interests. Was his generosity and sense of responsibility for caring for those less well off than himself a fault, as implied in the letter from Hannah Mary Tracy Cutler: *'his open handed generosity, and possibly, profligate habits not so well known, had embarrassed him to a considerable extent'*, or was one of Holmes' strengths that he was generous to a fault, as Dr Richard Peckover described him? *'He invariably attended the calls of the poor as well as the rich, and always refused money from those whom he considered not able to pay.'*

Holmes had of course seen the effects of the extremes of poverty and starvation in his time with The Hudson's Bay Company. He had witnessed the death of his Indian hunters from starvation, and the story that The Split recounted of his cannibalism of his wife and children clearly shocked him, as did the plight of Mrs Donald and her four children when he had to send them away nearly naked and at risk of starving. When he recorded his suspicion that The Knife had also been driven to kill and eat his family, his emotions were evident in the words he used in his journal to describe the event. The journals record many instances of him giving much-needed supplies to those who were in need and occasions when he gave practical help, such as supplying snowshoes or the materials for making them, to Indians who would otherwise have been at risk of death because they were not able to hunt during the severe winters.

During his time with the Shakers at South Union, his generosity towards those who helped and supported him was described as being at times excessive: *'he has manifested much gratitude for kindnesses received; in which feeling, and in his favours towards particular friends, he was apt to be unreasonably extreme'.*

We also encounter the John Pocock Holmes whose strength of generosity was matched by the force of his animosity towards anyone who he believed had slighted him in any way: *'... and on the other hand as greatly the reverse towards those, for whom he formed a dislike'.* This was a trait he had shown many times in his dealings with the North West Traders, both in his letters to them and in his willingness to defend himself with physical violence when his position was threatened. His resort to physical demonstrations of his anger persisting even when he was a respected member of the London medical community, as he described to the court in 1828 when he gave the hapless William Garstang *'a good shaking'* in the street for attempting to cheat him out of the proceeds of the debt collection. In his professional life, he also showed similar extremes of behaviour. On the one hand, his eager support of Ryan during the trials for libel, and on the other hand his abrasive comments in his letter titled *'Ignorance or Forgetfullness, or something worse'*, which he wrote about Ramsbotham, who he felt had neglected to give him sufficient credit for his design of obstetric instruments.

There is the Holmes who was very active in developing and promoting his career in London. His books, letters to the press and membership of medical and civic societies, all placed him in a good position to publicise his practice and gain more patients and therefore more income. His desire to increase his wealth was described by Edith Holmes as being his main preoccupation: *'I do hope that he was able to extract from his mind that which alone had occupied it, namely worldly prosperity'*. Yet this seems in direct contrast to the descriptions of his generosity and his failure to collect debts from his patients, which his student Richard Peckover described in his letter to the Evansville Daily Journal.. There were many steps that Holmes could have taken to increase his income. There was a great public appetite for the use of medications advertised in the press as being able to cure any number of afflictions. Holmes did lend his name to supporting one particular remedy, 'Woodhouse's Aetherial Essence of Jamaica Ginger', which was widely advertised in 1835 for treatment of cholera and other disorders of the bowel, and presumably, he received some financial reward for allowing the use of his name as a patron of the substance. He refrained for many years from advertising and selling his own 'secret remedy', relying more on sales of his book to attract patients. It was only when he became unwell and without any source of income in 1850 that he began to advertise his 'Balm of Life' for sale through chemists in Nashville. His involvement in the trade of corpses for dissection and his connection with the Webb Street Anatomy School in 1831 may well have been another source of income. Although he strenuously denied any active involvement, the letter from Richard Grainger with regard to the bodies taken from Hanley Castle suggests otherwise.

However successful Holmes' practice was, he appears to have run into severe financial difficulties after his marriage to Edith. Both Hannah Tracy Cutler and Edith, in their letters to the Evansville Journal, refer to this. By the time he arrived in New York, it appears that he was in possession of between $15,000 and $20,000, together with several items of expensive jewellery. The value of his dollars in 1840 would have been equivalent to £4,500 to £5,500 at that time, which in today's current value is in the region of £250,000. Hannah Tracy Cutler's account of the events when Holmes left England states that he took £4,000 of Edith's money. This would seem to lend substance to the suggestion that he had fraudulently obtained access to Edith's bank account, and that this is the source of the $20,000 which he had when he arrived in America. Edith in her letter is more circumspect in her description of how he got access to the funds, stating only that *I sued for alimony, and during the legal proceedings he managed to get possession of my property*. Holmes' version of the events, which he outlined in his letter to The Hudson's Bay Company in 1851 described Edith as *a most abandoned wretch*, claiming that she left him in 1842 and that he then sold off all his property and possessions and went to New York.

If the account of Holmes attempting to poison Edith and then withdrawing all her money from the bank by persuading a woman to impersonate her was true, then he would have needed to make a rapid departure from the country to avoid being arrested when the fraud was discovered. It would certainly explain why he would be reluctant to contact anyone in England and reveal where he was living. However, his sister, Elizabeth Mickle, must have been aware that he was living in Mississippi, as Col. Vance mentions that Holmes received letters from her during his time in Hernando.

There were many voices joining in the discussion that arose through the pages of the Evansville Journal in 1858, all with their own perspective on the character of Holmes and the reasons for his descent into poverty and distress. It was suggested that the reason he came to lose his wealth and be in such a state of destitution that he sought refuge at South Union was because he had been induced by *'a person from Mississippi'* to move from Nashville, and during his time there had been *'inveigled in some form of speculation'*, through which he lost all his money. The identity of this person was not revealed in the correspondence from *'the gentleman in the vicinity of Nashville'*, but Col. Vance in his letter to the Evansville Journal acknowledges that it was he who invited Holmes to move from Tennessee to Hernando, Mississippi. Eades, in his letter to the Journal, described Holmes' connection with Vance and described him as Holmes' *'excellent friend'*, explaining the departure from South Union as being driven by an overwhelming desire on the part of Holmes to see Vance again. It is clear from the reports from Evansville that the route Holmes planned to take on his last journey would have taken him on from Evansville and south towards Mississippi and Vance's home in Hernando.

There are, as may be expected, a number of contradictions between the various descriptions of Holmes and his departure from England. Edith claimed that Holmes did not contact his sister after he went to America, yet Vance recalls letters arriving from her. Hannah Tracy Cutler, in her description of her conversation with Edith, states that Edith had *'suffered in silence, rather than expose him to the just rigor of the law'*. Yet Edith, in her letter to the Evansville Journal, describes *'suing him for alimony'* prior to him getting access to her bank account.

On a superficial level, the narrative of Holmes' life appears to move from a Boys' Own adventure story set in the wilds of Canada, through a Dickensian tale of poverty, power and society, and culminating in a Victorian melodrama of poison and stolen fortunes with the moralistic downfall of the antihero. The day-to-day documentation of the reality of his struggles to survive in the wide expanses of Manitoba often deals with hard decisions and the need to persevere, whatever setbacks may occur. His single-minded pursuit of his career in London showed more evidence of his stamina and perseverance, as he used his intellectual skills to promote his practice through writing and skilful use of his social and professional connections. He would not, it seems, have thought of himself as a man without a conscience. His writings, both in his journals and in his books, show evidence of someone who did have a sense that taking the correct action was more important than achieving a result through unprofessional or un-gentlemanly means. He showed compassion for the native hunters that he traded with and operated in his professional life with a care for the needs of the poor. The loss of his son, George, appears to have played particularly on his mind, with both Vance and Eades recalling his frequent expressions of sorrow at George's early death.

It is difficult to reconcile these images of his life with the reported attempt to poison Edith and defraud her of all her savings. The fact that he was so possessive of his personal and professional reputation may at some level have allowed him to rationalise his actions as justified, given her refusal to provide him with a loan to make the finances of his medical practice secure. The question does arise as to whether his rather sudden marriage to Edith, a woman of some substance, only six months after Charlotte's death, was part of a rather cynical plan to access her wealth. A married woman, prior to the 1882 Marriage Act, had few rights with regard to her property and possessions. Money or property settled on her through a Trust before marriage was protected, but any other of her possessions were automatically transferred to her husband. Edith, in her letter, talks of separation from her husband, suing for alimony and legal proceedings. She places the time of Holmes' departure from England and his gaining possession of her property as being during the process of these legal proceedings. There were only a limited number of routes available in 1842 for a married woman to pursue a claim for alimony, and the process for obtaining a legal separation was complex and expensive. After Holmes' departure to New York, Edith gained support from her family and friends. Her attempts to trace her husband were assisted by the brother-in-law of the Chevalier Bunsen, but she was unable to locate his whereabouts once he left New York. Whilst Holmes appears to have abandoned his wife and left her to manage without support, there may have been some residue of his estate which finally reverted to Edith. In 1851, when Hannah Cutler Tracy was visiting England, Edith lived for a period of time in Upper Dorchester Street, Paddington. Whilst there had been no provision in Holmes' Will for Edith, a notice appeared in the London newspapers in April 1864 some six years after his death. The advertisement requested Mrs Edith Holmes, widow of the late John Pocock Holmes, to contact a firm of solicitors by the name of Messrs. Frere and Co. of 28 Lincolns Inn Fields, where she would hear something to her advantage. Whether this was related to John Holmes' estate or that of a relative of his is not known, but Edith described herself as an 'annuitant' on census returns. She appears to have lived either in rented accommodation or with relatives for the last period of her life. In 1871, she was a boarder at the house of a musician, Paul Calligrand, at 124 Charlotte Street, St. Pancras. Ten years later in 1881, she was living with her widowed sister, Axelina, at Lambeth, where she died on November 23rd, 1882. Her estate was valued at £1,183 15s 7d and her sole executor was her banker, Edward Stainton. In her Will, written in 1881 when she was living at 11 Granville Road, Lewisham, she left £500 to her sister Axelina and a number of smaller bequests to nephews and nieces in New Zealand. The residue of the estate, including her possessions, was left to Axelina.

Holmes had, of course, married three times and he had made provisions for his wife Betsy and her children before he left Hudson Bay. Betsy died in 1853, their daughter Charlotte had died in 1833 and their son George was lost at sea sometime after his arrival in England in 1823. Their daughter Elizabeth married one of the Red River settlers, James Murray in 1838, but he died a year later having shot himself in a hunting accident. Elizabeth was left with their son Alexander to care for, and in

1844 remarried to William Sinclair Stevenson, with whom she had eight children. The family settled in Headingley, Manitoba in 1852 where Elizabeth died at the age of eighty-nine in 1898.

Elizabeth Holmes. *Source: Marshall Bowman*

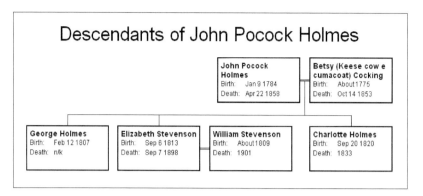

Descendants of John Pocock Holmes

John Pocock Holmes	Betsy (Keese cow e cumacoat) Cocking
Birth: Jan 9 1784	Birth: About 1775
Death: Apr 22 1858	Death: Oct 14 1853

George Holmes	Elizabeth Stevenson	William Stevenson	Charlotte Holmes
Birth: Feb 12 1807	Birth: Sep 6 1813	Birth: About 1809	Birth: Sep 20 1820
Death: n/k	Death: Sep 7 1898	Death: 1901	Death: 1833

J.P. Holmes Descendants

Holmes was, as the Evansville Journal had written, a man who had enjoyed a high professional reputation and been the friend and associate of many eminent persons. The truth of his abandonment of Edith and his escape to America appear to be explained in the testimony of Hannah Tracy Cutler and the letter from Edith to Dr Hallock. Holmes, however, remains an enigmatic and fascinating character whose story is indeed *'a painful lesson of the sad vicissitudes of life'*.

Notes on Chapters

The chapters have made use of many original sources, these are acknowledged in the notes on specific quotations which follow. Those chapters which refer to Holmes' time spent in the service of The Hudson's Bay Company (HBC) contain direct quotations from the author's transcripts of microfilm copies of the following documents held in the Archives of the Company and accessed either at the National Archives at Kew or at Keele University.

Quotation sources from the HBC archives include the following documents:

B42/d/86, B42/a/130-149, B141/a/2, B179/a/4, B42/d/90, B61/a/1, B61/a/2, B141/a/5, B141/a/6, B141/a/7, B207/a/1, B81/a/3-4, B239/d/188, B158/a/5-12, B49/a/35-36, D1/3/fo25d, A32/17/fo122, BH1/390/a32/17, C1/100/fo3d.

Details of Births, Marriages and Deaths are sourced from online databases. Biographical details are sourced from Electoral Register and Parish Records unless otherwise indicated.

Newspaper sources include:

Albany Evening Journal, Boons Lick Times, Bristol Mercury, Caledonian Mercury, Evansville Daily Journal, Evening Mail, Gentleman's Magazine, The Times, The Evansville Courier, Leicester Journal, London Courier and Evening Gazette, Morning Advertiser, Morning Chronicle, Morning Post, Morning Telegram, Nottinghamshire Guardian, Public Ledger and Daily Advertiser, London Medical and Surgical Journal, The Era, The Lancet., The Legal Examiner, The London Gazette, The Monthly Review or Literary Journal, The New York Herald., The Religious Tract Society, The Sunday Times.

Quotations from UK newspapers are transcribed by the author with kind permission from British Newspaper Archives, British Library Board. Other newspaper quotations are from original sources.

Notes on Preface

11 *Children from 'mixed blood' marriages were referred to as 'half-breed'...* Brown, J., *Strangers in Blood*, (Oklahoma: UBC Press 1980).

Notes to Chapter 1

15 *The article in the Evansville Journal of April 19th, 1858...* 'A Homeless Stranger' *Evansville Daily Journal*, 19 April 1858.

Notes to Chapter 2

16 *The roads in this part of the country in winter are intolerably bad...* Thoroton. R., *Thoroton's History of Nottinghamshire: Volume 3, Republished With Large Additions By John Throsby*, (Nottingham: J Throsby, 1796): British History Online,<http://www.britishhistory.ac.uk/thorotonnotts/vol3/> [accessed 23 January 2018]

16 *the heavy sulphurous fogs* ... Michnowicz, S., *The Laki Fissure Eruption and UK mortality crises of 1783–1784* (Aberystwyth:Aberystwyth University, 2011).

16 *the Great Meteor which passed over the country from North to South illuminating the sky with an eerie glow...* 'Particular Defcription of the late uncommon Meteor' *The Gentleman's Magazine*, (August 1783), 712.

16 *In the village, some of a superstitious nature would talk of emanations from the decomposing bodies...* Gheorghe, A., Watson, R. and McBeath, A. 'Meteor Beliefs Project: Birth and death superstitions associated with meteors in Romanian and British

folklore', *WGN, the Journal of the IMO* 34(5) (2006), 146–7.

18 *John senior entered the details of the birth in the parish record book...* 'South Leverton Parish Records', *South Leverton Parish Records* (1737–1812).

18 *The Reverend John Holmes' career commenced at the age of twenty-two...* The Clergy of the Church of England Database 1540–1835 <http://theclergydatabase.org.uk/> [accessed 18 January 2015].

20 *a sum which would allow a comfortable existence...* Copeland, E. and McMaster, J., *The Cambridge Companion to Jane Austen* (Cambridge: Cambridge University Press, 1997).

20 *The living was under the gift of a Lady Lucas...* 'Obituary with Anecdotes, of remarkable Perfons', *The Gentleman's Magazine*, (May 1806).

20 *John Cleaver who replaced Simon Lawry on his death in 1806, is recorded as having read a service once in 1807...* Southwell and Nottingham Church History Project. South Leverton (2016). <http :/southwellchurches.nottingham.ac.uk/ southleverton/hincumb.php-jcleaver> [accessed 8 June 2016].

22 *Sarah, who died at the age of two and was buried on January 31st,1788, at South Leverton...* 'Parish Record Book of South Leverton', *Salterwell Diocesan Record Office*, 1737–1812.

22 *The greatest risk period for the death of children around the age of two was in the first three months of a year ...* Heberden, W., 'Observations on the Increase and Decrease of different Diseases and particularly of the Plague', *The Critical Review* 38 (1803), 371.

22 *one in three of the deaths would be expected to be in those aged two or below...* Virgoe, J., 'Causes of death in a rural South-West Lancashire community in the late eighteenth century', *Local Population Studies* 75 (2005), 34–55.

26 *Elizabeth, married the Reverend J. Mickle on June 28th, 1819...* 'Lincoln, July 8. Married', *Stamford Mercury*, 9 July 1819.

26 *then in 1834 became the vicar at South Leverton…* Train, K.S.S., *Lists of the Clergy of North Nottinghamshire* (Nottingham: Thoroton Society, 1961).

26 *Tragically, Mickle shot himself in the head,…* 'The suicide of the Rev. John Mickle', *Nottinghamshire Guardian*, 9 November 1866.

26 *The ruling passion of the deceased through life seemed to be the accumulation of money…* 'Suicide of an aged clergyman', *Morning Advertiser*, 6 November 1866.

26 *Elizabeth continued to live in South Leverton…* 1871 Census, Class: RG10; Piece: 3537; Folio: 35; Page: 12; GSU roll: 839756.

27 *Elizabeth Fletcher was recorded as the only next of kin…* Principal Probate Registry, *Calendar of the Grants of Probate and Letters of Administration made in the Probate Registries of the High Court of Justice in England* (London: Crown Copyright, 1874).

27 *Charles, had followed his father into the Church of England…* 'Clergy Deceased', *The Gentleman's Magazine*, July to December 1838.

27 *John was set on a path that would see him travel many thousands of miles away…* 'Hudson's Bay Company Advertisement c. 1800', *National Archives of Canada*, Negative C-125856.

Notes to Chapter 3

28 *Every candidate for ferving a medical apprenticeship…* Lucas, J., *A Candid Inquiry into the Education Qualifications, and Offices of a Surgeon-Apothecary* (London: Hazard, 1800).

29 *He did, however, talk to acquaintances about having worked in hospitals in Paris…* Eades, J., 'Letter to Editor', *Evansville Daily Journal*, May 14th, 1858.

30 *unless they were 'connected with the staff by family or other ties, or had a large command of capital…* Clarke, J.F., *Autobiographical Recollections of the Medical Profession* (London: Churchill, 1874).

Notes to Chapter 4

31 *The Governor and Company of Merchants-Adventurers trading into Hudson's Bay'...* Wilson, B., *The Great Company*, (London: Smith, Elder & Co 1900).

35 *The dinner was 'as good and substantial as a lavish expenditure of cash could make it'...* Ballantyne, R.M., *Hudson Bay* (London: Nelson,1879).

36 *This 'northabout' route offered a safer passage and easier navigation than the western route through the English Channel...* Hall, N., 'Ocean Crossings: Hudson's Bay Company Seafaring in a Northern North Atlantic World', *Manitoba History*, 71, (2013).

38 *The increased changes in the variation of the compass were thought by some officers to be due to the presence of a 'magnetic...* Chappell, E., *Voyage to Hudson's Bay in her Majesty's Ship Rosamund* (London: J. Mawman, 1817).

Notes to Chapter 5

The events in this chapter relate to entries in the following Hudson Bay Archive documents unless otherwise indicated:

Churchill Factory Record. 1808, B.42a 131, B.42/4/90, Reel IM34

Nelson House Journal 1808–1809, B.141/a/2, Reel IM97

Holmes, J.P. Bedford House (Egg Lake Journal). 1809, B.61/a/1, Reel 1M51

Holmes, J.P. Bedford House (Egg Lake Journal). 1810, B.61/a/2, Reel 1M51.

40 *Like all other servants, surgeons signed formal contracts...* Toman, C., 'George Spence: Surgeon and Servant of the Hudson's Bay Company, 1738–41', *Canadian Bulletin of Medical History* 18 (2001), 17–42.

41 *She was one of the daughters of Matthew Cocking, who had served with the company from 1765 to...* Spry, I.M., 'Mathew Cocking', *Dictionary of Canadian Biography* (University of Toronto) <http://www.biographi.ca/en/bio/cocking_matthew_4E.html> [accessed 23 August 2015].

42 *whilst there married Sarah Elizabeth Bayliss in London on January 5th, 1798 ...* 'Marriages of remarkable persons', *The Gentleman's Magazine*, (1798), 83.

42 the Council of York asked that part of the annuity was given as; *'Ginger Bread, Nuts, etc. as they have no other means of obtaining these little luxuries, with which the paternal fondness of a father formally provided...* York Factory Correspondence 1749–1809. B.239/b/79,fo.28d. In: IM258.

43 *and it was not uncommon for women to have two or more husbands during their life...* Van Kirk S., *Many Tender Ties – Women in Fur-Trade Society 1670–1870* (Oklahoma: University of Oklahoma, 1983).

44 *The Company had, by the time of Holmes' marriage, reluctantly accepted that the families of employees might be provisioned at the Company's expense...* Ibid.

44 *Charles had invited Duplein over to his house for breakfast and when he confessed to the theft, put him in irons and sent him back to Churchill Factory to await trial...* Tyrrell, J.B., 'Early exploration of the Churchill River', *Geographical Review*, 3(5) (1917), 375–381.

45 *Mr Charles became unwell, with what was described as 'Palsy and Putrid Fever'...* 'Biographical Sheets', *Hudson's Bay Company Archives*, E.3/3, fo. 35.

46 *It was reported that the men had to 'stomach affronts varying from actual imprisonment, robbery of Indians, brutal ill-treatment and assaults in their own houses, to allegations that their whiskey*

was bad and to swearing and blaspheming without either manners or discretion... Rich, E.E., *Colin Robertson's Correspondence Book, September 1817 to September 1822* (London: The Champlain Society, 1939).

46 *'The most miserable hovel that imagination can conceive. Surely such abominably disgraceful styes must affect the Natives...* Ibid.

46 *Campbell waged a war of intimidation and robbery towards Spence and his men, and there were regular confrontations between the two...* Wilson, B., *The Great Company, 1667–1871* (London: Smith, Elder and Co, 1900).

47 *Mr Jamison was anxious and the men were able to return within a few days... 'Nelson House Journal 1808–1809', Hudson's Bay Company" to leave Nelson House on a journey to Weir Lake, so the goods requested were packed overnight, and the men were able to return within a few days...* 'Nelson House Journal 1808–1809', *Hudson's Bay Company Archives*, B141/a/2.

49 *Against his wages, he drew bills of payment to the amount of £7 5s...* 'Fort Churchill Account Book 1807–1808', *Hudson Bay Archives*, B42/d/88 (1808).

49 *The Weir River, which flows east into Nelson River, was also known as 'Old Fish-dam River', a translation of the Cree name Kesamachiskun, meaning 'dam of poles or twigs' for catching fish....* Geographical Names of Manitoba, (Winnipeg: Manitoba Conservation, 2001)

49 *Later payments show the recipient as Miss Elizabeth Birkett Holmes...* 'Churchill Factory' *Hudson Bay Archives*, B42/4/90 (1808).

50 *as the Indians viewed him as a mean man who was reluctant to dispense brandy to them...* Nicks, J., 'Tomison, William', *Dictionary of Canadian Biography*, (University of Toronto) <http://www.biographi.ca/en/bio/tomison_william_6E.html> [accessed 24 January 2018].

50 *he and Jamison were having to send two of their own men to*

live with their traders to prevent the Canadians from stealing their furs... 'Nelson House Journal', *Hudson Bay Archives*, B141/a/2 (1809)

51 *He was hired as a surgeon by the Hudson's Bay Company in 1790, but like many surgeons, his career with the HBC was more to do with the fur trade than surgery...* Foster, J.E., 'Willian Auld', *Dictionary of Canadian Biography*, (University of Toronto) <http://www.biographi.ca/en/bio/auld_william_6E.html> [accessed 23 January 2018].

51 *'Mr Holmes I have appointed to proceed with three men to establish a post to the S.E. of the Frog Portage where the Indians mean to winter most year. He has goods sufficient until he will get more of a large complement of men in the Fall.'...* Auld, W. B., 'Nelson House Journal', *Hudson Bay Archives*, 141/a/2, (1809).

52 *This day arrived at Egg Lake after a... of 16 days... of foul winds & rain...* Holmes J.P., 'Bedford House (Egg Lake Journal 1809–1811)', *Hudson Bay Archives* .

55 *'This Day an Indian arrived at the Canadian Tent he came over to my House & informed me he had 3 Beaver skins for me upon an Island about a mile from the house sent 1 of the men to fetch them immediately traded them for a debt belonging to Mr Charles.'...* Holmes, J.P., 'Bedford House (Egg Lake Journal 1809–1810)'. *Hudson Bay Archives.*

Notes to Chapter 6

The events in this chapter relate to entries in the following Hudson Bay Archive documents unless otherwise indicated:

Holmes, J.P. Bedford House (Egg Lake Journal). 1810, B.61/a/2, Reel 1M51

Nelson House Journal 1811–1812. B.141/a/5, Reel 1M97

Nelson House Journal, 1812–1813, B141/a/6, Reel 1M97.

62 *'What to do I cannot tell. If the Indians do not kill some Moose soon we shall surely die'...* 'Mr Holmes Journal 1810–1811', *Hudson Bay Archives*, B.61/a/2.

72 *The trout, however, could weigh up to twenty pounds in some rivers and were considered a tasty dish,* Fisher V., *Pemmican.* (London: Robert Hale, 1956).

75 *Holmes set off from Nelson House at the start of July in the 21ft canoe he had built at Egg Lake...* 'Nelson House Journal' *Hudson Bay Archives,* B.141/a/5, Reel 1M97, (1811–1812).

Notes to Chapter 7

The events in this chapter relate to entries in the following Hudson Bay Archive documents unless otherwise indicated:

Nelson House Journal, 1812–1813, B141/a/6, Reel 1M97.

Nelson House Journal, 1813–1814, B141/a7, Reel 1M97.

87 *On the first day, the expedition was beset by fog...* Holmes, J.P., 'Nelson House Journal', *Hudson Bay Archives,* B141/a/6, (1812–1813).

91 *In 1810, Andrew and his wife Margaret were at the Hudson's Bay Post at Ile la Crosse, and in July they had an argument which resulted in her leaving the post and going to the North West Company post on her own...* MacDougall, B., *One of the Family: Métis Culture in Nineteenth Century Northwestern Saskatchewan* (Vancouver: UBC Press, 2011).

92 *Three days after this threat, Andrew left the Canadians and returned to Ile la Crosse but without his wife...* 'Andrew Kirkness', *RedRiver Ancestry* <https://www.redriverancestry.ca/KIRKNESSANDREW1770>* [accessed 27 October 2016].

99 *Holmes' suspicions of cannibalism would have been heightened*

by the events of three years previous at James Bay... Chabot, C., 'Witiko possession and starvation cannibalism among the James Bay Cree: monstrosity or madness?', *Creating Humanity, Discovering Monstrosity: Myths and Metaphors of Enduring Evil*, Nelson, E., Burcar, J. and Priest, H. (eds) (Oxford: Inter Disciplinary Press, 2010), 3–15.

103 *Holmes was to remain in charge at Nelson House for the next season of 1813-14, and on June 1st he opened a new journal book...* Holmes, J.P., 'Nelson House Journal', *Hudson Bay Archives*, B141/a7, (1813–1814).

108 *On September 6th, 1813, Holmes and Betsy's second child Elizabeth was born...* 'Obituary', *Morning Telegram*, 12 September 1898.

108 *Peter Fidler, for instance, kept a separate private notebook in which he recorded the details of the births of his fourteen children...* Van Kirk, S., *Many Tender Ties: Women in Fur-Trade Society, 1670–1870* (Norman, OK: University of Oklahoma, 1983).

111 *As ill health is the reason of Mr H. wishing to return we hope the Honble Co. will consent to his recall. Allowed'...* 'Biographical sheets', *Hudson's Bay Company Archives*, A30/1, (1814).

Notes to Chapter 8

The events in this chapter relate to entries in the following Hudson Bay Archive documents unless otherwise indicated:

Fort Churchill Journal 1814, B42/a/140-142, Reel 1M34

Split Lake House Journal, 1815–1816, B.207/a/1, Reel 1M144.

Gordon House Post Journal1816–1817, B81/a/4. Reel 1M59

Pelican Lake Journal 1818–1819, B.158/a/1, Reel 1M116

Cumberland House Journal 1818–1819, B.49/a/35–6, Reel 1M40.

113 *'Late in the evening Messrs. Sutherland, Holmes & Costello arrived from Inland with 19 men in 3 boats'...* 'Churchill House Journal', *Archives of Hudson Bay Company*, BH1/566, (1814).

120 *In September 1815, Holmes was appointed to take charge of the Nelson River District...* 'Split Lake House Journal', *Archives of Hudson Bay Company*, B.207/a/1, (1815 – 16)

126 *The master of Rock Depot was Robert Logan, who had originally been an employee of the North West Company ...* Rea JE., 'Robert Logan', *Dictionary of Canadian Biography* (University of Toronto, 1976) <www.biographi.ca/en/bio/logan_robert_9E.html> [accessed 28 February 2018].

126 *'Came up with Mr Holmes who gave the Indians a dram, and I was obliged to promise them an Extraordinary dram at night with a weeks...* 'Gordon House Post Journal', *Archives of Hudson Bay Company*, B81/a/4. IM 59, (1816–1817).

127 *Holmes' purchases were in the main of clothing and material such as:..* 'Pelican Narrows men's debt book', *Archives of Hudson Bay Company*, B158/d/1, Reel 1M570, (1817–1818).

128 *as the high waves on the lake carried the risk of a capsize...* Houston, C.S. (ed.) *To the Arctic by Canoe 1819–1821: The Journal and Paintings of Robert Hood* (Quebec: McGill-Queens, 1974).

143 *they had been obliged to set up a house at Pelican Lake in opposition to Holmes...* Auld, W., 'Cumberland District Report', *Archives of Hudson Bay Company*, B49/e/2 IM777, (1819).

144 *Holmes had his wife and family living with him at Cumberland House, and his daughter Elizabeth...* 'Obituary', *Morning Telegram*, 12 September 1898.

145 *The letter from Governor Williams, written at Rock House*

Depot, appeared to cast doubt on Holmes' ability to continue in charge of Cumberland House ... 'Governor Williams, Correspondence Book – outwards 1820', *Archives of Hudson Bay Company,* D.1/3, Reel 3M1.

146 *Holmes' sudden departure from Cumberland House at the orders of the Governor is surprising...* Rich EE., Colin Robertson's Correspondence Book, September 1817 to September 1822 (London: The Champlain Society; 1939).

147 *The cause was laid before Mr Gary, who after taking a proper view of the thing decided in favour of Dr Holmes...* Ibid.

147 *From Norway House, Holmes and his family...* 'Norway House Account Book', *Archives of the Hudson Bay Company,* B154/d.29 fo 51d, (1827–1828).

Notes to Chapter 9

149 *Can any thing be conceived more dreary and disheartening, than the prospect before a young London physician, who without friends or fortune, yet with high aspirations after professional eminence, is striving to weave around him what is technically called 'a connection' ?...* Warren, S., *Passages from the Diary of a Late Physician* (London: The Standard Library Company, 1837).

149 *The ships continued through the straits without further incident, and the layover at York Factory gave time for the more permanent repairs to be made...* 'The Prince of Wales Ships Log', *Archives of the Hudson's Bay Company* (1821).

150 *The return voyage from York Factory to England was uneventful, and the ship arrived at Stromness at the end of October. A letter to the Caledonian Mercury reporting the ship's arrival, stated that there were a hundred and fifty Hudson's Bay 'servants' on board...* 'Extract of a letter from Kirkwall', *The Caledonian Mercury,* 8 November 1821.

152 *The term 'idiot' was a well-recognised term that differentiated those with a 'defect in mind from birth'…* Crotty, H.D., 'History of insanity as a defence to crime in English Criminal Law', *California Law Review* 12(2) (1924),105–23.

152 *to be dealt with as directed by the coroner at Elizabeth Martin's inquest, who had said that if the jury returned a verdict that he was insane, he should be removed to Bedlam to be confined during His Majesty's pleasure …* 'Death occasioned by a Lunatic', *Morning Post*, 8 July 1822.

152 *He spent the rest of his life in that hospital, dying of erysipelas…* 'Bethlem Hospital. Register for 1836', *Patient Admission Registers and Case Books, 1683–1932* (London).

153 *Mr Sturtevant's death at the age of seventy-five was reported as 'an awful instance of sudden death…* 'An awful instance of sudden death', *Morning Post*, 19 October 1822.

156 *Charlotte was christened by her father…* England, Select Births and Christenings, 'England Births and Christenings, 1538-1975', *Genealogical Society of Utah, Salt Lake City.*

156 *In May 1818 his Trustee, Lancelott Dowbiggin…* 'Notice to Creditors', *Hereford Journal*, 6 May 1818.

158 *Richard Bowen's case was posted in the London Gazette…* 'By order of the Court of Relief', *London Gazette,* 15 May 1819.

158 *Meanwhile, the badgered debtor struggles…* 'The Law Courts of London', The Leisure Hour, 3 March , 1850. p157

158 *The wedding took place on September 15th, 1823, at St. Nicholas Cole Abbey…* 'London Marriages and Bans', *London Metropolitan Archives*, <www.cityoflondon.gov.uk/thingstodo/londonmetropolitanarchives> [accessed 15 June 2014].

159 *Charlotte was under the age of twenty-one, having been born*

in October 1802 and baptised on October 7th, 1802, in Mainstone... 'England Births and Christenings, 1538-1975', *Genealogical Society of Utah, Salt Lake City.*

Utah Family Search, Salt Lake City, 1538–1975.

159 *As she was a minor, she needed her parents' permission to get married, and the declaration of her mother that she was a widow...* 'London and Surrey, England, Marriage Bonds and Allegations, 1597–1921- Record of 1823', *London Metropolitan Archives,* www.cityoflondon.gov.uk/things-to-do/london-metropolitan-archives.

162 *George, then aged sixteen, was due to set sail on the Prince of Wales in September 1823...* 'The Prince of Wales Ships Log', *Archives of the Hudson's Bay Company* (1823).

164 *but he was unable to say whether this was from gunpowder, or a scald, or a burn, but was very possibly the scorch from gunpowder...* 'Admiralty Sessions', *Public Ledger and Daily Advertiser,* 20 December 1823.

164 *Smith was now a free man, and the next year published his account of his experiences...* Smith, A., *The Atrocities of the Pirates* (London: G & W B Whittaker; 1824).

164 *He returned to the sea and eventually became a sea captain, but in 1826 was, bizarrely, again on trial for alleged piracy committed in 1822. Once again, he was acquitted...* 'Admiralty Sessions', *London Courier and Evening Gazette,* 14 July 1829.

165 *Mr Boast, a surgeon who was described as having knowledge of the effects of gunpowder in wounds...* 'Admiralty Sessions', *Public Ledger and Daily Advertiser,* 20 December 1823.

165 *it was only where particles of gunpowder had entered the skin that an indelible bluish tinge could be...* Bird, J., 'Lectures on military medicine and surgery', *The Lancet* 2 (1855), 487.

165 'Serjeant of Marines', remarked that he had often seen wounds produced by the explosion of gunpowder... 'Admiralty Session', Morning Advertiser, 20 December 1823.

165 Holmes became a Member of the Royal College of Surgeons,... Royal College of Surgeons of England. Members of the Royal College (London: Royal College of Surgeons of England, 1977).

165 The Royal College of Surgeons examinations in 1824 consisted of a one-hour oral examination comprising four fifteen-minute discussions with examiners... Moxon, W., 'A review of the present system of medical education in London', The Lancet 127 (1886), 945–6.

167 The admission papers dated June 24th 1824 show that he was accepted as suitable for admission into the Company of Wax Chandlers as a Freeman by redemption... Freedom admissions papers, 1681 – 1930 (London: London Metropolitan Archives).

169 The oath that he took had remained unchanged since 1664... Dummelow, J., The Wax Chandlers of London (London: Phillimore, 1973).

171 The three appeared in court at the Old Bailey, the central criminal court, on June 30th and Holmes was called as a witness... Hitchcock, T., Shoemaker, R., Emsley, C., Howard, S. and McLaughlin, J., 'Proceedings of the Old Bailey of 1825', The Old Bailey Proceedings, 1674–1913 [accessed 29 July 2016].

172 The court reports in the Morning Advertiser of July 4th noted that 'Upon hearing the judgment, the latter prisoner appeared dreadfully affected... 'Old Bailey Report', Morning Advertiser, 4 July 1825.

172 In 1826, Dr Holmes was awarded 'The Gold Vulcan Medal of the Society of Arts' for the design of craniotomy forceps... Society for the Encouragement of Arts & Manufactures. Transactions of

the *Society of Arts* (London: Society of Arts, 1826).

173 *James Blundell, a pioneer of blood transfusion and midwifery who undertook the first human-to-human blood transfusion…* Welck, M., Borg, P., and Ellis, H., 'James Blundell MD Edin FRCP (1790–1877): Pioneer of Blood Transfusion' *Journal of Medical Biography*18 (2010), 194–7.

173 *His commendation of Dr Holmes' instruments was repeated in his lectures and published in his collected lectures…* Castle, T. (ed.), *The Principles and Practice of Obstetricy as at Present Taught by James Blundell MD* (London: Cox, 1834).

174 *The audience were subscribers and friends of the Society for the Encouragement of Arts Manufactures and Commerce, and a number of distinguished guests…* 'Society for the Encouragement of Arts & Manufactures', *Morning Advertiser*, 29 May 1826.

176 *In 1827 Holmes made another submission to the Society for the Encouragement of Arts and was awarded the large gold medal for his improved obstetrical…* Society for the Encouragement of Arts & Manufactures. *Transactions of the Society* (London: Society for the Encouragement of Arts, 1828).

176 *On entering the hallway of the Company House, visitors were greeted with 'a vast pair of horns of the Moose deer, weighing 56 pounds and various canoes'…* Thomas, H., *The Wards of London* (London: Gifford, 1828).

176 *while over the door a larger canoe made of bark, in which one of the directors of the company, in days gone by, ventured on many an arduous…* The Religious Tract Society, *The Visitor* (London: William Jones, 1849).

176 *The contribution of John Holmes to the Parry expedition of 1827 is noted in the 'Narrative of an attempt to reach the North Pole' published in 1828…* Parry.W. *Narrative of an attempt to reach*

the North Pole in boats fitted for the purpose, and attached to His Majesty's ship Hecla, in the Year MDCCCXXVII, under the command of Captain William Edward Parry (London: John Murray, 1828).

178 *the various constituents of ergot were identified and standard preparations of the active components became available...* Lee, M.R., 'The history of ergot of rye (Claviceps purpurea) I: from antiquity to 1900', *Journal of the Royal College of Physicians, Edinburgh* 39 (2009) 179–84.

179 *The author had suggested that the powder of birth be renamed pulvis ad mortum...* Hosack, D., 'Observations on ergot', *The New York Medical and Physical Journal 1* (1822).

179 *'the use of ergot is appropriate when it is desired to produce a premature labour but that cases do exist where this potent remedy may be useless and its action injurious unless the unyielding membranes be perforated...* Holmes, J.P., 'Ergot of Rye', *The Lancet 2* (1828) 794–5.

181 *Garstang had received eight shillings from 'a poor man under threat of commencing legal proceedings in Mr Holmes's name' nine days after the authority was removed...* 'Police Report', *The Times*, 14 July 1828.

182 *there were two other students with Holmes at the same time, a Mr Bird and a Mr Holman...* 'Dr Holmes', *Evansville Daily Journal,* 12 May 1858.

183 *Doctors' Commons which was the Ecclesiastical Inn of Court located near St. Paul's Cathedral, where issues regarding opening graves or re-siting graves would be...* Jones, P., *Ecclesiastical Law* (London: Wordpress, 2012). <https://ecclesiasticallaw. wordpress.com/2012/05/17/doctors-commons/> [accessed 23 July 2015].

184 *John Connolly, a hairdresser of Hendon, told the court;...* 'Middlesex Sessions', *Morning Chronicle,* 7 November 1828.

186 *John Pocock Holmes was moved to write a letter to the Times which was published on January 22nd,...* Holmes, J.P., 'To the Editor of the Times', *The Times*, 2 January 1829.

189 *He was brought before Mr Alderman Winchester...* 'Police report', *The Times*, 1 February 1830.

190 *the Metropolitan force established by Robert Peel was gradually replacing the older ward based force...* Leigh, S., *Leigh's New Picture of London* (London:Hodgdon & Biggs, 1842).

191 *The area surrounding Newgate Street and the Old Bailey has been described as 'the hub of London resurrection culture' north of the Thames...* Wise, S., *The Italian Boy* (London: Pimlico, 2005).

191 *St Bartholomew's was one of the many sources of income for ..* Bailey, J.B. *The Diary of a Resurrectionist* (London: Swan Sonnenschein & Co, 1896).

192 *the body of the female was that of Mary Colston aged 22 of Newbridge Green who had been buried on January 11ᵗʰ...* Wilkinson, S., 'Mr Cale and the Resurrectionists' <http ://www.upton. uk.net/history/doctors/bodysnatchers.html>{accessed 20 April 2015]

194 *Richard Grainger dealt fairly with the suppliers of the bodies... Ibid.*

Notes on Chapter 10

This chapter is based on Holmes, J.P., *Popular Observations on diseases incident to Females* (London: Jones & Son 1831)

Notes on Chapter 11

210 *He gave his qualifications as MRSL and MRAS,...* Anon. *A defence of John St. John Long in the case of the late Miss Catherine Cashin; founded upon the evidence against him. By a graduate of*

Trinity College, Cambridge, and member of the Middle Temple. (London: C. Chapple, 1831).

211 *he would give a hundred guineas if he could produce similar favourable signs in some other of his patients,…* 'John St John Long', *The Newgate Calendar*, Part III (1830).

211 *At this appearance he was however found not guilty and the charges were dismissed…* 'Old Bailey', *Morning Advertiser*, 21 February 1831.

212 *Holmes was to recall in his evidence to the Ramadge v Ryan trial in the following year…'* Ramadge v Ryan', *The Legal Examiner*, (1832) 351–54.

212 *Holmes was moved to reply…* The Sunday Times, 19 June 1831.

213 *Ryan developed an editorial around the text of the letter which focussed very clearly on Ramadge's support of St John Long…* 'Ramadge v Ryan', *The Legal Examiner*, 14 July 1832.

214 *Ramadge initially brought a libel action against Wakely…* 'Ramadge v Wakley', *The Evening Mail*, 26 June 1832.

215 *In reply to the question Holmes stated…* 'Ramadge v Ryan – Evidence of Mr Holmes, Mr Field &c,. *The London Medical and Surgical Journal* (7 July 1832) 722.

216 *A final motion was proposed by Holmes to the effect that…* 'Ramadge v Ryan', *Morning Chronicle*, 30 July 1832.

216 *the total raised from 40 subscribers was 149 pounds eight shillings and ten pence…* 'Subscription for Dr Ryan', *The Lancet*, (1832) 351–2.

219 *There was a long history of such celebrations being accompanied by bonfires, sporadic rowdiness and window smashing of houses that did not illuminate…* Stevenson, R., *Popular Disturbances in England 1700–1832* (London: Routledge; 1991).

220 *John Holmes was one of the voices within the Bread Street Ward giving support for this idea which proposed an alternative to Illuminations...* Low, S., *The Charities of London* (London: Sampson Low, 1850).

221 *The organisers of this plan hoped 'to induce the people in general to subscribe the money which they would have wasted in the glittering follies of a night...* Institution of the London Almshouses, *The Institution of the London. Almshouses, in Lieu of an Illumination, to Commemorate Reform in Parliament:* (London: Lake 1834).

221 *On November 16ᵗʰ 1832 a meeting of the householders of the Bread Street Ward was held at the White Horse Tavern to discuss the Alms House proposal,...* 'Bread Street Ward', *The Morning Advertiser*, 26 November 1832.

221 *Holmes continued to be a supporter of the Institution and was one of the members of the Institution who sold tickets for the ceremony...* 'London Almshouses', *The Morning Advertiser*, 31 May 1834.

221 *The ceremony was performed by Lord John Russell MP...* Scherer, P., *Lord John Russell A Biography.* (London: Selinsgrove, 1993).

222 *... we are induced to lay before our readers the following statement...* Ryan, M., 'Ramadge v Ryan Damages and Costs £647', *London Medical and Surgical Journal* 2 (1832), 542.

222 *John Minter Hart was later tried for another case of fraud in 1833...* Ryan M., 'Beauties of Administration of Justice – St John Long', *London Medical and Surgical Journal* (1833).

223 *in repairing gas pipes at the bottom of Lambeth Hill when there was an escape of gas from the pipe...* 'Dreadful Accident', *The Morning Post*, 15 November 1833.

224 *respectable men are now retiring because the Common Councils of the present day were becoming inundated with men of a different character.* 'City Elections', *The Morning Post*, 23 December 1833.

Notes on Chapter 12

225 *In a long letter to The Lancet headed 'Ignorance or Forgetfullness, or something worse, of F.H.Ramsbotham.'* Holmes J.P., 'MR. HOLMES'S CRANIOTOMY FORCEPS', *The Lancet*, 26 July 1834, 636–7.

226 *The committee decided to appoint two or three surgeons as assistants to 'help' the physicians...* Seligman, S.A., 'The Royal Maternity Charity: the first hundred years', *Medical History* 24 (1980), 403–18.

226 *'I cannot coincide with their views in wishing to be placed upon an equal footing858." of rank and remuneration with the physicians... responsibility should rest with the physicians, the surgeons being only required to attend urgent cases in the unavoidable absence of the... Ibid.*

228 *There was great competition for patients within the City of London area and a successful practitioner would rely on word of mouth and success in treatment in a specialised area to ensure that patients would consult him even if they were in the territory of a rival doctor...* Digby, A., *Making a Medical Living*, (Cambridge: Cambridge University Press, 1994).

231 *Mr John Pocock Holmes does not seem to be aware that his doctrine would go to the length of preventing all medical publications which do not embrace the whole science*, 'Letter to the Editor', *Morning Advertiser*, 24 August 1836.

231 *He had previously written on the subject in his book on female diseases.* Holmes J.P., *Popular Observations on diseases incident to Females* (London: Jones & Son, 1831).

231 *'Then again as to tight lacing, which has received so much animadversion, I cannot believe it produces the serious effects which have been attributed to it.'.* Ibid.

233 *Benjamin Franklin had written of his experiences working in a printing shop...* 'Ben Franklin's Letter on Lead Poisoning', *NEW SOLUTIONS: A Journal of Environmental and Occupational Health Policy* 7 (1998), 80–1.

233 *Chronic poisoning from lead is an insidious disease...* American Public Health Association, *Lead Poisoning*, (New York: A.P.H.A, 1930).

235 *The Gerard's Hall located on the south side of Basing Lane and Bread Street had a coffee room, a ball-room, good wines, beds for 78 guests and an ancient Norman Crypt.* Cunningham, P., *Dirty Old London* (Yale University Press, 2014).

235 *After what was described as a most sumptuous dinner the evening proceeded with great hilarity up until a late hour.* 'The Tradesmen of Bread Street', *Public Ledger and Daily Advertiser*, 25 May 1837.

242 *Holmes challenged the view that the disease was incurable.* Daniel, T.M., 'The history of tuberculosis', *Respiratory Medicine*, 100 (2006), 1862–70.

245 *Holmes' ideas on the key factors of causation, which were at variance with the more general view in Northern Europe of the disease being a heritable condition...* Ibid.

Notes on Chapter 13

246 *The details of the day were recorded in the newspapers and in a report produced for the Court of Mayor and Aldermen from the various committees which had been charged with organisation of the event...* The Court of Mayor and Aldermen of the City of

London, *Reports relating to the entertainment of her Majesty the Queen in the Guildhall of the City of London on Lord Mayor's day 1837,* (London: The Court of Mayor and Aldermen, 1837).

246 *the members of the Guild had the honour of attending the Mayor in the procession to Westminster.* Burgess, B., 'To the Editor of the Morning Chronicle', *Morning Chronicle,* 13 November 1837.

247 *A contemporary account was recorded by one of the guests, William S. Samuel, in a letter to his brother-in-law written the week after the event…* Samuel, W., *Lord Meyor's Show 1837* (London: The Jewish Museum, 1950).

248 *A full description of both the menu and invitation are given in an article in the Evansville Courier of February 4th 1923,* Hunt, T.J., 'The Pocket Periscope' *The Evansville Courier,* 4 February 1923.

250 *The Common Council of the City of London is the lower chamber of the Corporation…* City of London Corporation, 'History of the government of the City of London' <http ://www.cityoflondon.gov.uk/aboutthecity/aboutus/Pages/ historyofthegovernment-of-the-city-of-london.aspx>

251 *As a member of the Common Council of the City of London, Holmes and his lady were amongst the group of dignitaries…* The Court of Mayor and Aldermen of the City of London. *Reports relating to the entertainment of her Majesty the Queen in the Guildhall of the City of London on Lord Mayor's day 1837* (London: The Court of Mayor and Aldermen, 1837).

251 *Seating plans for the banquet showing the various tables allocated by Ward to the members of Common Council were contained within the report on the event to the Court and Aldermen,…* Ibid.

257 *the London Courier on 22nd December carried the following*

tribute to Holmes who retired as a member of the Court,... 'Bread Street Ward', *London Courier and Evening Gazette*, 22 December 1837.

257 *Mary Stewart, who appeared in court gaudily attired and conducted herself with much effrontery...* Ryan M., *Prostitution in London, with a comparative view of that of Paris and New York, with an account of the nature and treatment of the various diseases, caused by the abuse of the reproductive system* (London: H. Bailliere, 1839.

259 '*It has never been my duty since I had the honour of occupying this chair...* 'Court Proceedings', *National Archives London.*

263 *there is not the slightest doubt that she is a most abandoned profligate wretch...* Ryan M., *Prostitution in London, with a comparative view of that of Paris and New York, with an account of the nature and treatment of the various diseases, caused by the abuse of the reproductive system* (London: H. Bailliere, 1839).

Notes on Chapter 14

264 *Dr Henry Clutterbuck MRCP had come to the attention of the medical profession following the publication of a treatise on fever in 1807.* Clutterbuck H., *Inquiry into the Seat and Nature of Fever,* (London: Boosey, Murray, Callow and Cox, 1807).

264 *a second publication on the prevention and treatment of typhus fever in 1819.* Clutterbuck H., *Observations on the Prevention and Treatment of the Epidemic fever prevailing in the Metropolis and most parts of the United Kingdom* (London: Longman and Co, 1819).

265 *we are not sure that Dr C. has not sometimes been led to the use of venesection when it was far from beneficial.* 'Clutterbuck's Observations on Fever', *The Monthly Review or Literary Journal,*

September to December (1822), 46

266 *The use of bleeding in a case of haemorrhage was advocated by Clutterbuck.* Clutterbuck H., 'Theory and Practice of Physic', *Lancet* 10, (1826), 97–102.

267 *Common causes of death in adults were typhus, consumption, dysentery and cholera epidemics...* McCulloch J.R., *A dictionary geographical, statistical, historical of the various countries, places and principal objects in the world,* (London: Longman, 1854).

267 *in addition to the recent loss from this malady, of many valuable members of society, there have been in London no less than five distinguished members of the medical profession who have fallen victim to Typhus.* Shipman G., 'Typhus Fever', *Morning Advertiser,* 13 April 1838.

Notes on Chapter 15

268 *Henry Frederick Horneman had his appointment as Danish Consul-General to London approved by the Prince Regent on July 23rd 1814...* The London Gazette, (London: Foreign Office, 1814).

269 *This tour would have been their honeymoon which by the 1830's, had become a standard part of the marriage ritual, with a continental tour being popular with those from wealthy professional backgrounds.* Phegley J., *Courtship and Marriage in Victorian England* (Phaeger: 2012).

270 *the body was mutilated around the head, but this appeared to have been after death and occasioned by dogs* 'Suspicion of child murder', *The Era,* 3 January 1841.

271 *the vast increase in the commission of child murder was attributable to the bastardy clause of the New Poor-Law Act.* 'The Poor Law Act', *The Era,* 29 August 1841.

271 *if the mother was unable to support herself and the child then*

the only option was to enter a workhouse.

Higginbotham P., 'The Workhouse'<http://www.workhouses.org.uk/poorlaws/newpoorlaw.shtml> [accessed 2 May 2017].

271 *Holmes wrote a letter to the editor of the Morning Advertiser expressing his opinions on the proposals for fees for medical men travelling by rail on professional business.* 'Medical Remuneration for Travelling', *Morning Advertiser,* 22 April 1841.

272 *The fees which were adequate remuneration for a distinguished ornament of his profession to journey to Liverpool to conduct a cause when the old system of travelling prevailed, might admit of abatement in proportion to the abridgement of time which railroads create...* 'The effect of railroads upon the fees of medical men', *Morning Advertiser,* 19 April 1841.

Notes on Chapter 16

273 *the ship 'George Wilkinson' on August 4th 1842. This ship was a 600 ton sailing vessel carrying merchandise destined for Glover and McMurray Merchants of 100 Pine Street.* 'New York', *Lloyd's List,* 23 August 1842.

273 *The voyage in June 1842 had originally been advertised to depart on June 1st and then June 8th but finally left 10 days later and did not sail direct but called at Le Havre for either more cargo or extra passengers.* 'Emigration from Bristol to New York', *Gloucester Chronicle,* 7 May 1842.

274 *On board were thirty-seven steerage passengers and three other passengers who had travelled in the passenger cabins, they were named as Miss Gibbs, Mr Cole and Dr Holmes* 'Passengers Arrived', *New York Daily Tribune,* 5 August 1842.

275 *'I was contemplating, at that time, coming West, and the*

Doctor expressed a wish to come with me, and said as he was getting old and feeble, he would like to live and end his days with me. 'Dr Holmes', *Evansville Daily Journal.* 12 May 1858.

275 *The committee had also asked for the loan of Washington's sword which he used at the Battle of Trenton, and the First Company of the Washington Temperance Guards were to perform the ceremony of relieving the guard, which the New York Herald anticipated would have a very imposing effect.* 'Celebration of Washington's Birthday', *The New York Herald,* 9 February 1843.

275 *the music, military demonstrations and addresses were all deemed to have been a success.* 'The Birthday of Washington', *New York Daily Tribune,* 23 February 1843.

276 *He used Cairo as the basis for the fictional city of Eden in his novel Martin Chuzzlewit.* Dickens C., *American Notes for General Circulation.* (London: Chapman & Hall,1913).

277 *General Henry W. Crowther, who commanded a division in the so-called 'Mormon War' in 1838.* Missouri General Assembly, *Document Containing the Correspondence, Orders, &c. In Relation to the Disturbances with the Mormons* (Fayette: Democrat Office, 1841).

277 *The operation was described in the Boons Lick Times as being 'a double flap amputation performed by Dr J. P. Holmes of the Royal College of Surgeons of London* 'Extract of a letter' *Boons Lick Times,* 12 April 1845.

278 *Nashville at this time was an expanding centre of trade and commerce with the Cumberland River providing a route for the steamboat trade to transport goods all over the south of the country.* McDonough J.L., *Nashville The Western Confederacy's Final Gamble* (Knoxville: University of Tennessee, 2004).

278 *Vance recounted his meeting with Holmes in a letter written to the Evansville Journal in May 1858.*Vance C., Letter to Editor,

Evansville Daily Journal, 14 May 1858.

279 *By the time Vance moved there in 1840 the area was beginning to recover and large areas of farm land were being cleared.* DeSoto County Geneological Society, 'A Brief History of DeSoto County Mississippi' <http ://www.desotocountyms. gov/DocumentCenter/View/56>.[accessed 11 February 2017]

279 *These included luxury items such as pleasure carriages, clocks, watches, duelling pistols, race horses, pianos and ten-pin alleys as well as gold, silver, land, cattle and slaves…* County Tax Rolls County of De Soto, *Department of Archives and History* (1851).

280 *Holmes wrote to The Hudson's Bay Company to solicit help in the form of income, estimating that he needed £30 a year to 'manage'.* Holmes J.P., Letter to The Governor of The Hudson's Bay Company, *Manitoba Archives: on microfilm* (1849).

282 *In May 1850 Holmes started to insert a series of very long and detailed advertisements in the Nashville newspapers advertising his medication for treating a variety of chest conditions for sale.* Holmes JP., 'Consumption Curable' *Republican Banner Nashville,* 8 May 1850.

282 *His claimed fellowship of the University of 'Erlangelen, Bavaria'.* List of 18th Century German Universities, *University of Manchester* [accessed 20 September 2015].

283 *The Physikalisch-medizinischen Sozietät zu Erlangen was founded in 1808…* Physikalisch-medizinischen Sozietät zu Erlangen, *Festschrift der Physikalisch-medizinischen Sozietät zu Erlangen zur Feier ihres 100 jährigen Bestehens am 27. Juni 1908* (Erlangen: 1908).

Notes on Chapter 17

284 *April 2, 1851 – Dr Holmes – late of Miss – formerly of England came today to the East House as an enquirer.* Eades, H.L., *South Union Shaker Village Library* (1851).

285 *The daily routine at South Union would follow the same pattern as in all the Shaker communities across the country.* Evans F., *Autobiography of A Shaker, and Revelation of the Apocalypse* (New York: American News Co, 1888).

287 *The accident occurred near Lockharts by the East Section farm so she was brought to the East House* Eades, HL., *South Union Shaker Village Library* (1851).

287 *Last night Joseph McGee stole a horse from the East House, also Dr Holmes' watch and some of his surgical instruments.* Eades, H.L., 'Record Book' *South Union Shaker Village Library* (1853).

287 *The transcribed version of the regular diary entries of H. L. Eades at South Union Village give a detailed account.* Reynolds R.C., Reynolds H.R., *Record B 1851–1855 from pages 181-255 of Record Book kept by H.L. Eades 1836–1864 Shakers, South Union, Kentucky* (Briar Hill Press: 1997).

288 *March 28, 1858 – Departure, from the East House, Dr Holmes left today, started North...* Eades, H.L., 'Record Book C', *South Union Shaker Village Library* (1858).

288 *Eades also wrote a detailed letter to the Evansville Journal in 1858 which gives great insight into the time Holmes lived with the Shakers.,* Eades J., 'Letter to Editor', *Evansville Daily Journal,* 14 May 1858.

Notes on Chapter 18

291 *In April 1858 The Evansville Daily Journal...* 'A Homeless Stranger', *Evansville Daily Journal,* 19 April 1858.

294 *John Eades, in his letter to the Evansville Journal...* Eades J., 'Letter to Editor', *Evansville Daily Journal,* 14 May 1858.

295 *John Vance in his letter to the journal explained how he had introduced Holmes to the Shaker Community.* Vance C., 'Letter to Editor', *Evansville Daily Journal,* 14 May 1858.

Notes to Chapter 19

304 *Baker and Foster were attorneys at Law with offices at Third Street, East of Main in Evansville.* Hawes GW., *Indiana State Gazetteer and Business Directory* (Indianapolis: G. W Hawes, 1858).

304 *The Court of Common Pleas had replaced the probate Court in 1852 and had exclusive jurisdiction over estates and guardianships.* Elliott J.P. *A History of Evansville and Vanderburgh County* (Indiana: Keller Printing Company, 1897).

304 *The court, with Judge Isa Igleheart presiding, accepted that the documents were valid and copies of them were entered into the records of the court,* 'Court of Common Pleas of Vanderburgh County Probate hearings 1858.' Willard Library Evansville .

305 *Each member paid an initiation fee and a regular membership fee which acted as an insurance policy for ill health or death.* Ivy J.D. *Alcohol and Temperance in Modern History*, ed.by Blocker J.S., Fahey D.M., Tyrell I.R., (Santa Barbara: ABC Clio, 2003).

306 *Allen Hallock was an officer of the Sons of Temperance Temple of Honor Divison 54* 'Evansville City Directory 1858' *Evansville Vanderburgh Public Library Digital Archive.*

Notes to Chapter 20

308 *The Evansville Journal of June 4ᵗʰ 1858 continued its reporting of the death of Dr Holmes with the publication of a letter from a 'highly respectable' lady* 'The mystery unfolded', *Evansville Daily Journal*, 4 June 1858.

311 *A Mystery Unfolded – WHY DR. J.P. HOLMES LEFT ENGLAND –* 'A mystery unfolded', *Albany Evening Journal.* 10 June 1858.

Notes to Chapter 21

312 *The Evansville Journal article of April 1858 ended with a question.* 'A Homeless Stranger', *Evansville Daily Journal,* 19 April 1858.

Selected Bibliography

American Public Health Association, *Lead Poisoning* (New York: A.P.H.A., 1930)

Anon, *A Defence of John St John Long in the Case of the Late Miss Catherine Cashin; Founded Upon the Evidence against Him. By a Graduate of Trinity College, Cambridge, and Member of the Middle Temple.* (London: C Chapple, 1831)

Bailey, James Blake, *The Diary of a Resurrectionist* (London: Swan Sonnenschein & Co, 1896)

Ballantyne, Robert Michael, *Hudson Bay* (London: Nelson 1879)

Bethlem Hospital, 'Patient Admission Registers and Case Books 1683–1932'

Bird, James, 'Lectures on Military Medicine and Surgery', *The Lancet,* 2 (1855), 487

Brightman, Robert, *Grateful Prey – Rock Cree Human-Animal Relationships* (Berkeley: University of California Press, 1993)

Brown, Jennifer, S.H., *Strangers in Blood,* (Oklahoma: UBC Press 1980)

Castle, Thomas, *The Principles and Practice of Obstetricy as at Present Taught by James Blundell MD* (London: Cox, 1834)

Chabot, Cecil, 'Witiko Possession & Starvation Cannibalism among the James Bay Cree: Monstrosity or Madness?', in *Creating Humanity, Discovering Monstrosity: Myths & Metaphors of Enduring Evil,* ed. by Elizabeth Nelson, Jillian Burcar and Hannah Priest (Inter Disciplinary Press, 2010), 3–15

Chappell, Edward, *Voyage to Hudson's Bay in Her Majesty's Ship Rosamund* (London: Mawman, J., 1817).

City of London Corporation, 'History of the Government of the City of London', (2012)

Clarke, James Fernandez, *Autobiographical Recollections of the Medical Profession* (London: Churchill, 1874)

Clutterbuck, Henry, *Inquiry into the Seat and Nature of Fever* (London: Boosey, Murray, Callow and Cox, 1807)

Clutterbuck, Henry, *Observations on the Prevention and Treatment of the Epidemic Fever Prevailing in the Metropolis and Most Parts of the United Kingdom* (London: Longman and Co., 1819)

Copeland, Edward, and Juliet McMaster, *The Cambridge Companion to Jane Austen* (Cambridge: Cambridge University Press, 1997)

Crotty, Homer, D., 'History of Insanity as a Defence to Crime in History of Insanity as a Defence to Crime in English Criminal Law', *California Law Review*, 12 (1924), 105–123.

Daniel, Thomas M., 'The History of Tuberculosis', *Respiratory Medicine*, 100 (2006), 1862–1870

DeSoto County Geneological Society, 'A Brief History of Desoto County Mississippi' <http://www.desotocountyms.gov/DocumentCenter/View/56> [Accessed 11th February 2017]

Dickens, Charles, *American Notes for General Circulation*. Cheap Edition edn (London: Chapman & Hall, 1850)

Digby, Anne, *Making a Medical Living* (Cambridge: Cambridge University Press, 1994)

Dummelow, John, *The Wax Chandlers of London* (London: Phillimore, 1973)

Eades, Elder Harvey, 'South Union Shaker Village Library', Record C (1858)

Elliott, Joseph Peter, *A History of Evansville and Vanderburgh*

County Indiana (Keller Printing Company, 1897)

Evans, Frederick William, *Autobiography of a Shaker, and Revelation of the Apocalypse* (New York: American News Co, 1888)

Fisher, Vardis, *Pemmican* (London: Robert Hale, 1956).

Franklin, Benjamin, 'Ben Franklin's Letter on Lead Poisoning', *NEW SOLUTIONS: A Journal of Environmental and Occupational Health Policy,* 7 (1786), 80–81

Freedom of City Admission papers 1681–1925, 'April–October', (1824)

Gheorghe, Andrei Dorian, Roy Watson and Alastair McBeath, 'Meteor Beliefs Project: Birth and Death Superstitions Associated with Meteors in Romanian and British Folklore', *WGN, the Journal of the IMO,* 34:5 (2006), 146–47

Hart, Arthur Tindal., *A Curates Lot* (London: John Baker 1970).

Hawes, George W, *Indiana State Gazetteer and Business Directory*. Vol. 1 (Indianapolis: G. W Hawes, 1858)

Hearne, Samuel., *A Journey from Prince of Wales's Fort, in Hudson's Bay, to the Northern Ocean Undertaken by Order of the Hudson's Bay Company. For the Discovery of Copper Mines, a North West Passage, &C. In the Years 1769, 1770, 1771, & 1772.*

(London: A. Strahan and T. Cadell:, 1795)

Heberden, William, 'Observations on the Increase and Decrease of Different Diseases and Particularly of the Plague', *The Critical Review,* 38 (1803), 371

Higginbotham, Peter, 'The Workhouse' <http://www.workhouses.org.uk/poorlaws/newpoorlaw.shtml> [Accessed 2 May 2017].

Hitchcock, Tim, Robert Shoemaker, Clive Emsley, Sharon Howard and Jamie McLaughlin, 'The Old Bailey Proceedings

Online, 1674–1913') [Accessed 29 July 2016]

Holmes, John Pocock, *A Treatise on the employment of certain methods of friction and inhalation in Consumption, Asthma and other Maladies* (London: Samuel Holdsworth, 1837)

Holmes, John Pocock, *Popular observations on diseases incident to females* (London: Jones and Son., 1831).

Hosack, David, 'Observations on Ergot', *The New York Medical And Physical Journal,* 1 (1822)

House of Commons Papers, 'Courts of Requests.', in *Document type: HOUSE OF COMMONS PAPERS; ACCOUNTS AND PAPERS* (1833)

Houston C. Stuart, ed., *To the Arctic by Canoe 1819–1821 the Journal and Paintings of Robert Hood* (Quebec: McGill – Queens, 1974)

Hunt, Thomas James, 'The Pocket Periscope', *The Evansville Courier,* 4th February 1923

Ivy, James D, *Alcohol and Temperance in Modern History.* ed. by Jack S. Blocker, David Fahey and Ian R. Tyrell, (Santa Barbara: ABC Clio, 2003)

Jackson, Lee, *Dirty Old London* (Yale University Press, 2014).

Jones, Philip, 'Ecclesiastical Law' (2012) <https://ecclesiasticallaw.wordpress.com/2012/05/17/doctors-commons/> [Accessed 23 July 2015]

The Institution of the London Almshouses , *The Institution of the London Almshouses, in Lieu of an Illumination, to Commemorate Reform in Parliament:* (Lake, London 1834).

Lee, Michael Radcliffe, 'The History of Ergot of Rye (Claviceps Purpurea) I: From Antiquity to 1900', *J R Coll Physicians Edinb,* 39 (2009), 179–184

Leigh, Samuel, *Leigh's New Picture of London* (London: Hodgson & Biggs, 1842)

London and Surrey, 'England, Marriage Bonds and

Allegations, 1597-1921'

---, 'London Marriages and Bans 1754-1921'.

Low, Sampson, *The Charities of London* (London: Sampson Low, 1850)

Lucas, James, *A Candid Inquiry into the Education Qualifications, and Offices of a Surgeon-Apothecary;* (London: Hazard, 1800)

MacDougall, Brenda, *One of the Family: Métis Culture in Nineteenth Century Northwestern Saskatchewan* (UBC press, 2011)

McCulloch, John Ramsay, *A Dictionary Geographical, Statistical, Historical of the Various Countries, Places and Principal Objects in the World.* 2 vols. Vol. 2 (London: Longman, Brown, Gren and Longman, 1854)

McDonough, James Lee, *Nashville the Western Confederacy's Final Gamble* (Knoxville: University of Tennessee, 2004)

Michnowicz, Sabina, *The Laki Fissure Eruption and UK Mortality Crises of 1783-1784* (Aberystwyth, 2011)

Moxon, W., 'A Review of the Present System of Medical Education in London', *The Lancet,* 127 (1886), 945-46

Naragon, Steve, 'List of 18th Century German Universities', <http://www.manchester.edu/kant/universities/UnivBriefHistories.htm> [accessed 20th December 2017].

Nicks, John, 'Tomison, William', in *Dictionary of Canadian Biography,* (Toronto: University of Toronto/Université Laval, 2003)

Parish Record Book of South Leverton, 'Salterwell Diocesan Record Office', (1737-1812)

Parry, William Edward, *Narrative of an Attempt to Reach the North Pole in Boats Fitted for the Purpose, and Attached to His Majesty's Ship Hecla, in the Year MDCCCXXVII, under the Command of Captain William Edward Parry.* (London: John

Murray, 1828)

Phegley, Jennifer, *Courtship and Marriage in Victorian England* (Phaeger, 2012)

Physikalisch-Medizinischen Sozietät Zu Erlangen, *Festschrift Der Physikalisch-Medizinischen Sozietät Zu Erlangen Zur Feier Ihres 100 jährigen Bestehens Am 27. Juni 1908* (Erlangen: 1908)

Principal Probate Registry, 'Calendar of the Grants of Probate and Letters of Administration Made in the Probate Registries of the High Court of Justice in England.' , (London: Crown Copyright, 1874)

Reynolds, Richard C. and Elizabeth H. Reynolds, *Record B 1851–1855 from Pages 181–255 of Record Book Kept by H.L Eades 1836–1864 Shakers, South Union, Kentucky* (Briar Hill Press, 1997)

Rich, Edward Ernest, *Colin Robertson's Correspondence Book, September 1817 to September 1822* (London: The Champlain Society, 1939)

Royal College of Surgeons of England, 'Members of the Royal College', (London: 1977)

Ryan, Michael, *Prostitution in London, with a Comparative View of That of Paris and New York, with an Account of the Nature and Treatment of the Various Diseases, Caused by the Abuse of the Reproductive System.* (London: 1839)

Samuel, Wilfred, *Lord Meyor's Show*. Vol. 3, *Jewish Museum Publications* (London: The Jewish Museum, 1837)

Scherer, Paul, *Lord John Russell a Biography* (London: Selinsgrove, 1993)

Seligman, Stanley Albert, 'The Royal Maternity Charity: The First Hundred Years', *Medical History*, 24 (1980), 403–18.

Smith, Aaron, *The Atrocities of the Pirates* (London: G & W B Whittaker, 1824)

Society for the Encouragement of Arts & Manufactures,

Transactions of the Society. Vol. 46 (London: Society for the Encouragement of Arts, 1828)

———, *Transactions of the Society of Arts*. Vol. 44 (London: Society of Arts, 1826)

South Leverton Parish Records, 'South Leverton Parish Records', Salterwell Diocesan (Nottingham: 1737–1812)

Southwell and Nottingham Church History Project, 'South Leverton' 2016) <http://southwellchurches.nottingham.ac.uk/south-leverton/hincumb.php#jcleaver> [Accessed 8 June 2016]

Stevenson, John, *Popular Disturbances in England 1700 –1832*. 2nd Edition edn (London: Routledge, 1991)

The Court of Mayor and Aldermen of the City of London, 'Reports Relating to the Entrtainement of Her Majesty the Queen in The Guildhall of the City of London on Lord Mayor's Day 1837', (London: The Court of Mayor and Aldermen, 1837)

The Religious Tract Society, *The Visitor* (London: William Jones, 1849)

Thomas, Henry, *The Wards of London* (London: Gifford, 1828)

Thoroton, Robert, *Thoroton's History of Nottinghamshire: Volume 3, Republished with Large Additions by John Throsby*, . (Nottingham: J Throsby, 1796): British History Online, <http://www.britishhistory.ac.uk/thorotonnotts/vol3/> [accessed 23 January 2018]

Toman, Cynthia, 'George Spence: Surgeon and Servant of the Hudson's Bay Company, 1738–41', *Canadian Bulletin of Medical History*, 18 (2001), 17–42

Train, Keith, *Lists of the Clergy of North Nottinghamshire*. Vol. XX (Nottingham: Thoroton Society, 1961)

Tyrrell, Joseph Burr, 'Early Exploration of the Churchill River', *Geographical Review*, 3 (1917), 375–81

Van Kirk, S., *Many Tender Ties – Women in Fur-Trade*

Society 1670 – 1870 (Oklahoma: University of Oklahoma, 1983)

Virgoe, John, 'Causes of Death in a Rural South-West Lancashire Community in the Late Eighteenth Century', *Local Population Studies* 75 (2005), 34 –55

Wade, John., *The Extraordinary Black Book: An Exposition of Abuses in Church and State, Courts of Law, Representation, Municipal and Corporate Bodies* (London: Effingham Wilson, 1832)

Warren, Samuel, *Passages from the Diary of a Late Physician* (London: The Standard Libary Company, 1837)

Welck, Matthew, Philip Borg and Harold Ellis, 'James Blundell MD Edin FRCP (1790–1877): Pioneer of Blood Transfusion', *Journal of Medical Biography*, 18 (2010), 194–197

West, John, *The Substance of a Journal During a Residence at the Red River Colony* (London: Seeley, 1824)

Wilkinson, Simon, 'Mr Cale and the Resurrectionists' 2015)<http://www.upton.uk.net/history/doctors/bodysnatchers.html> [accessed 20 April 2015]

Wilson, Beckles, *The Great Company 1667–1871*. Vol. 1 & 2 (London: Smith, Elder and Co, 1900)

Wise, Sarah, *The Italian Boy* (London: Pimlico, 2005)

Glossary

Alteratives — herbs to restore the proper function of the body and increase health.

Annuitant — a person who receives an annuity or pension.

Aperients — a drug used to relieve constipation.

Buffalo Robes — the hide of an American buffalo dressed with the hair on, commonly trimmed to a rectangular shape and used as a cloak or bed covering.

Castoreum — the product of the oil glands of the beaver and had been used since the time of Hippocrates in the preparation of a number of medicines.

Erysipelas — is a form of cellulitis, a bacterial infection affecting the skin, also known as St. Anthony's fire.

Factor — this is an agent or deputy of the company.

Fomentations — the application of hot moist substances to the body to ease pain.

Green Meat — fresh meat.

Hackmatack wood — a species of larch native to Canada.

In debt — an advance paid to a hunter often in kind which established a claim on any future furs traded and left them in debt to the trader.

Métis — are people of mixed European and Indigenous ancestry, and one of the three recognized aboriginal people in Canada. The term métis (mixed) and brulé (burnt) was originally used by the French Canadians.

Pemmican — a pressed cake of pounded dried meat mixed

to a paste with melted fat and other ingredients.

Portage — a portage is the carrying of goods or boats across land between navigable waters and around obstructions in streams.

Servants — Hudson's Bay Company servants were labourers, tradespeople, accountants, clerks and surgeons.

Solatium — a thing given to someone as compensation or consolation.